MANY VOICES

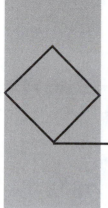

MANY VOICES

A Multicultural Reader

Linda Watkins-Goffman
Eugenio Maria de Hostos College
of the City University of New York

Richard W. Goffman

Prentice
Hall

Upper Saddle River, New Jersey 07458

Library of Congress Cataloging-in-Publication Data

Watkins-Goffman, Linda.
    Many voices : a multicultural reader / Linda Watkins-Goffman, Richard W. Goffman.
        p.   cm.
    Includes index.
    ISBN 0-13-975624-8
        1. College readers.   2. Pluralism (Social sciences)—Problems, exercises, etc.   3. English
language—Rhetoric—Problems, exercises, etc.   4. Report writing —Problems, exercises,
etc.   5. Readers—Pluralism (Social sciences)   6. Culture—Problems, exercises, etc.   7.
Readers—Culture.   I. Goffman, Richard W.   II. Title.

PE1417.W28 2001
808'.0427—dc21   99-056714

Editorial Director: Charlyce Jones Owen
Editor in Chief: Leah Jewell
Acquisitions Editor: Craig Campanella
Editorial Assistant: Joan Polk
AVP, Director of Manufacturing
    and Production: Barbara Kittle
Managing Editor: Mary Rottino
Production Liaison: Fran Russello
Project Manager: Linda B. Pawelchak
Manufacturing Manager: Nick Sklitsis
Prepress and Manufacturing Buyer: Benjamin Smith
Cover Director: Jayne Conte
Cover Design: Bruce Kenselaar
Cover Art: The Lowe Art Museum, The University of Miami /Super Stock
Marketing Manager: Brandy Dawson
Proofreading: Maine Proofreading Services

Acknowledgments begin on page 224, which constitutes
a continuation of this copyright page.

This book was set in 10/12 Palatino by Pub-Set, Inc.
and was printed and bound by Courier Companies, Inc.
The cover was printed by Phoenix Color Corp.

© 2001 by Prentice-Hall, Inc.
A Division of Pearson Education
Upper Saddle River, New Jersey 07458

Printed in the United States of America
10 9 8 7 6 5 4 3 2 1

ISBN 0-13-975624-8

Prentice-Hall International (UK) Limited, *London*
Prentice-Hall of Australia Pty. Limited, *Sydney*
Prentice-Hall Canada Inc., *Toronto*
Prentice-Hall Hispanoamericana, S.A., *Mexico*
Prentice-Hall of India Private Limited, *New Delhi*
Prentice-Hall of Japan, Inc., *Tokyo*
Pearson Education Asia Pte. Ltd., *Singapore*
Editora Prentice-Hall do Brasil, Ltda., *Rio de Janeiro*

CONTENTS

CHAPTER 3   Voices from the Family   **38**

Glossary of Writing and Cultural Terms   222

Acknowledgments   224

Index   227

Preface

◆ WRITING ABOUT READING

This book was designed to encourage critical thinking about the ideas contained in the reading selections. We believe that students will get the most benefit from this text if they begin with Chapter One. Although the readings are in the first person singular, the assignments and writing prompts for the most part encourage academic, text-driven writing in which both the authors' and the readers' ideas can connect in a coherent essay. Using the Revising and Editing Checklists should help refine and correct students' drafts. These checklists can be used both to facilitate group activity and to help individuals refine and edit their drafts.

◆ PREREADING

The prereading questions are designed to provoke thoughts and feelings about the ideas contained in the readings. They may be used to evoke discussion and writings, or they may be assigned as a prereading assignment or a group activity. Their purpose is to guide the reader in making his or her own connection with the text. With this mind set, the reading will be more meaningful.

◆ WORKING WITH WORDS

The "Working with Words" section is designed to encourage thinking about vocabulary in context as well as to develop word skills. Students should feel free to add similar words and expressions to the list.

◆ EXAMINING CONTENT

The "Examining Content" questions encourage students to recall key ideas in the selection they have just read. These questions could also be used to help students summarize the main ideas of the excerpts and stories. They are focused on the important ideas in the content with the intention of helping students prepare for the more difficult questions and writing prompts that follow.

◆ RESPONDING TO IDEAS

Designed to elicit discussion and more abstract thinking and writing, the "Responding to Ideas" questions can be answered either individually or in groups. The ideas could also be used as writing prompts for reader-response essays. In addition, students should feel free to add their own questions to this list. Chapter One discusses the writing of the reader-response draft.

◆ MORE WRITING TOPICS

In addition to Reader Response Topics, other abstract writing prompts in this section give readers more practice with academic, expository writing. Students may choose to write as many drafts as time permits. In addition, students should use the Revising and Editing Checklists to prepare the final copy.

◆ MAKING THE FINAL COPY

Additional writing prompts and revising and editing exercises and checklists are provided in order to prepare the draft for its final evaluation. Students are encouraged to add to the Revising and Editing Checklists as needed.

◆ ACKNOWLEDGEMENTS

We would like to thank every writer whose poem, story, article, or excerpt appears in this book.

We would also like to acknowledge the ideas and feedback from the students of Hostos Community College, The Bronx, New York. A special thank you to Virginia DeLeon, whose draft appears in Chapter One.

We thank former Acquisitions Editor Maggie Barbieri, Acquisitions Editor Craig Campanella, Editorial Assistant Joan Polk, and Production Editor Linda Pawelchak. The following reviewers made invaluable suggestions at an earlier stage of the writing: Keith Coplin, Colby Community College; Margo L. Eden-Camann, Georgia Perimeter College-Clarkston; Kathryn Gleason, New York City Technical College; Mary Helen Halloran, University of Wisconsin-Milwaukee; Harvey Rubinstein, Hudson County Community College; Karen Standridge, Pikes Peak Community College; and Charles Wukasch, Austin Community College.

We hope that a deeper appreciation of the many voices of these writers from diverse corners of the world will be one of the results of reading this book, and that this will, in some small way, promote world communication and understanding.

Linda Watkins-Goffman
Richard Goffman

MANY VOICES

1 Introduction

◆ INTRODUCTION TO INTERACTIVE READING

How, when, and why do you read? Some people read only for information. Others like to read for pleasure. Some people take a book to bed and fall asleep reading, while others read on the train or bus, so they don't have to look around them. This text asks you to read differently from the way to which you have become accustomed. It wants you to read *interactively*.

This means you will read with a pen or pencil in your hand and possibly a highlighter nearby. You will *read as if you are having a conversation with the writer.* You will ask questions in the margin, writing down key words that strike you as important. You will underline and highlight as well, but the most important thing is that you are *actively seeking to connect with the words* in the text, rather than letting the words simply wash through your mind.

Here are some questions with which you might approach something you are reading in this interactive fashion. You can think of them as questions to ask yourself, *or you can direct the questions or comments at the writer and the text.*

1. What is the writer's purpose?
   OR, *To the writer: What's your purpose? Why did you write this?*

2. What is this paragraph or text about? What is it really saying?
   OR, *To the writer: What are you really saying?*

3. When was it written? And where?
   OR, *To the writer: When and where did you write this?*

4. What strikes me as the most interesting? Why? (What part is boring? Why?)
   OR, *To the writer: This part is most/least interesting to me.*

5. What am I learning that I didn't already know?
   OR, *To the writer: This part is news to me!*

6. Does the writer have a hidden message, aside from his or her main purpose?
   OR, *To the writer: Okay, what are you* really *getting at?*

7. What particular passages or words strike me as especially interesting or effective? Why?
   OR, *To the writer: How did you ever think of putting it just this way? And choosing exactly those words?*

8. If you could ask a question of the writer right now, what would you say?
   OR, *To the writer: Here's what I would like you to tell me.*

Here is a copy of a text that has been marked up by an interactive reader. It is a poem, written in 1986, by Aurora Levin Morales (1954–   ).

Child of the Americas

I am a child of the Americas,
a light-skinned mestiza of the Caribbean,
a child of many diaspora, born into this
    continent at a crossroads.

You mean "crossroads" as metaphor?

5   I am a U.S. Puerto Rican Jew,
a product of the ghettos of New York I have
    never known.
An immigrant and the daughter
and granddaughter of immigrants.
10 I speak English with passion: its the tongue
    of my consciousness,
a flashing knife blade of crystal, my tool,
    my craft.

Why do you speak English with passion? Why is English like a knife blade?

I am Caribeña, island grown. Spanish is in my
15   flesh,
ripples from my tongue, lodges in my hips:
the language of garlic and mangoes,
the singing in my poetry, the flying gestures
    of my hands.

I like this imagery "Spanish is in my flesh"

20   I am of Latinoamerica, rooted in the history
  of my continent.

I speak from that body.
I am not african. Africa is in me, but I cannot
  return.   *Do you mean you are*
25   I am not taina. Taino is in me, but there is no   *part African and*
  way back.   *part Taino?*
I am not european. Europe lives in me, but I
  have no home there.

I am new. History made me. My first language   *What about your*
30   was spanglish.   *Jewish heritage?*
I was born at the crossroads
and I am whole.

  Now just for practice, try writing a four- or five-paragraph response to the preceding poem. You may use the following section to help you do so.

◆ THE READER-RESPONSE JOURNAL

Throughout this book you will be asked to keep a "reader-response" journal. In it you will write your reaction to the texts that you read. You will be asked to think of one of the most important questions that *you asked the text* while you were reading, and write a response statement around it. Remember: the response statement is *not a summary*. It is *not a restatement* of what you just read. It is instead *your own ideas,* your own opinion. It is *your* reaction to the text. (Of course, you may have more than one reaction to any given text. For the purpose of your reader-responses, stick to one idea or one reaction. You can, if you want, always come back and write another one on the same material later on.) Some readers like to picture themselves talking to the writer of the text. Once you decide what your main point or thesis will be, you can then develop your ideas in the following ways:

1. Refer to specific passages of the text.
2. Refer to your own experience or observation of real life, as it relates to the topic.
3. Refer to other texts you have read, or even material from music, movies, theater or television.
4. Once you have written a main idea based on the preceding three suggestions, you may use the following techniques of development in subsequent paragraphs:
   ◆ explaining

◆ giving reasons why
◆ cause and effect
◆ examples
◆ compare and contrast

Read the following student draft of a reader-response. Notice that the first sentence is the response statement, and that it contains the main idea. What development techniques mentioned in the preceding list are used in this example?

Multiculturalism is a constant reality in our society. Modern interaction allows people from different backgrounds and heritages to live in harmony learning from one another. Author Morales clearly shows how being a mestiza gives her a chance to be part of many worlds, even those she has not known physically.

"I am new," states Morales. "History made me." With these statements she tried to express how her identity was the way history developed and also affects the individual, the "new American," she is. She is part of a cultural fusion that has made her a better person who understands she does not have to be categorized like a "one-size-fits-all person."

Morales is very proud of her Latino heritage; nevertheless, she believes that with the English language, she can express her thoughts better. She can fight to achieve what she desires and also prepare for future enrichment. I identify very much with these ideas because as a young Latino woman, I have had to learn how to use my heritage only at the right moments. I have had to accept that even if I know as much of both the American and Latino cultures, only the American culture can get me where I want to go.

Sometimes my people see me as a "sell-out" even though I will never put my Latino identity down. I am a proud Latino Queen. And then when I'm out there in the world, it's like I don't entirely fit in because I'm different. I speak English, but because my family is Puerto Rican, I know Spanish also. I also know how to write, but sometimes it is not enough. If America gives me more paths to follow, I can make it in either world.

Compare your own draft with this student's draft. Then, refer to the revising checklist that appears on page 7. Could the author of this student draft have improved her draft by revising it? Could you improve your draft by applying these revising suggestions?

◆ THE EXPOSITORY ESSAY

In addition to writing a response essay, which is a more general response to text, you will be asked to write an expository essay on a specific topic. This is a composition in which you are asked to take a position or state an opinion and then "defend" or argue in favor of your position. If you feel like you need help getting started, the following exercises will help you. A sample expository essay exercise is the following: Write an essay explaining how being bilingual can be an advantage in today's society.

◆ GETTING STARTED: PREWRITING EXERCISES

1. Brainstorming

You can get into a group with two or more people and ask each other for the first opinion that comes to mind. Do not be concerned whether any idea is "silly" or irrelevant. Brainstorming allows everyone to spill out whatever ideas pop into their heads. When you examine all those ideas, you will often find that some of them prove useful for writing or provoke other ideas that you will later use. Remember that any idea may eventually lead to something, and those that don't lead anywhere didn't do us any harm.

2. Freewriting

Freewriting is like brainstorming, but you do it on your own. Write down anything that comes to your mind, and don't worry about errors in spelling, grammar, or punctuation. We will deal with these issues later on in revising and editing. Just write anything that comes to mind while thinking about the text onto the paper, without making any value judgments. Don't worry—no one is reading over your shoulder.

3. Clustering

Make a diagram like the one following in which the topic or main idea is in the center and the little circles around them are supporting ideas. Write down *any words* that relate to the idea in the circle. They can be thoughts, ideas, feelings, actions, objects, events, anything that your brain relates with the idea in the center. After you write each word outside the circle, always return back to the main word inside the circle, so that all your ideas relate directly to the original word and don't become a continuing train of word associations. You will soon have dozens of things that you associate with that one idea, and possibly an idea about how to begin writing your response.

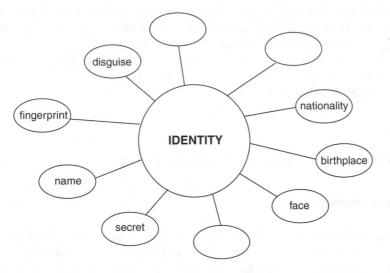

Sample Cluster Diagram

4. Processing

Sometimes, an unpleasant association may keep you from writing. Write a quick letter to yourself about this, like a diary entry. You need not show it to anyone. Read it over and see if your fears and negative notions have been dispelled. If they have, you can try one of the preceding techniques or move directly to response statements.

For example, here is a diary entry:

> I am having problems with the fact that this is a poem. The last time I studied poetry, it was with a teacher that didn't like me. Whenever I raised my hand, he seemed to ignore it, and went to the next person. But the writer of this poem seems to be an interesting person, with so much to say about identity.

Both a response entry and an expository essay will have a similar structure. Most often they will look something like this:

◆ Introduction Paragraph
   Usually contains the response statement
◆ First Developmental Paragraph

Contains anecdotes,[1] *explanations, reasons, comparisons, examples from text, observation of life, or your own experience*

◆ Second Developmental Paragraph

Continues and expands the previous paragraph's ideas, with additional supportive material (More than two developmental paragraphs may be appropriate.)

◆ Conclusion Paragraph

Should reflect on your position statement or response statement. Should let the reader know that the composition is ending.

We suggest that you write more than one draft. The following questions will help you improve your first draft. You may prefer to do this with another classmate, checking each other's draft. You can gain objectivity and see problems as well as strengths when you invite someone to read your writing with you.

◆ REVISING CHECKLIST

Read over the draft you have completed for the purpose of revising it—that is, improving the content. Use the following questions as a starting point for revision.

◆ Does the composition have an introduction? Does the introductory paragraph of the composition make the main idea of the composition clear? Remember, there is more than one way to write an introduction. It must include the most important point, however.

◆ Is the development clear and specific? Remember to avoid generality. Be specific. For instance, if you are telling an anecdote remember to include the answers to *Where? When? Who? Why?* Be sure it is clear *how* the anecdote is related to the topic.

◆ Is the choice of language appropriate? Be wary of street language, slang, and trendy expressions. Academic writing is usually more formal. (Of course, if you are writing dialogue, you have some flexibility in terms of writing in the way your characters would realistically speak.)

◆ Are any ideas repeated? Sometimes writers repeat and are not aware of it.

---

[1]Anecdote: a short description of an event that illustrates your point

◆ Are any ideas irrelevant? If so, these need to be deleted. Sometimes writers digress from the topic. Ask yourself after each sentence, "How does this relate to the ideas preceding and following it?"

◆ Is the conclusion appropriate? Does it reflect the main idea and let the reader know that the essay is ending?

◆ SAMPLE EXPOSITORY ESSAY

The Advantages of Being Bilingual in the United States

Being bilingual in the United States is very advantageous, particularly for immigrants. If they know English and another language, doors will open for them. They will obtain good jobs and will have a better life. A person who is bilingual has an important skill—being able to use two languages.

My friend Eva speaks Polish and English. She was able to become a bilingual architect. She has a degree in architecture from a college in the New York area. She can handle clients who are Polish-speaking as well that those who speak English. I watched her switch from talking on the phone in English to a client standing in her office in Polish. It was amazing!

Another friend speaks Spanish and English. She is a nurse at Columbia Presbyterian Hospital. Her ease in the two languages makes her able to respond to patients' needs readily and easily. She does not need to call an interpreter. An English or Spanish patient in her care can be relaxed and know that she will be able to understand patient charts and information in either language.

I speak French and English. I have found that I can enjoy literature in the original source. This is definitely a good quality for a teacher and researcher to have. Another side benefit is that I have so many friends in both languages. Also, what a pleasure to view a film in French and one in English! I feel that I have a richer life.

Definitely, it is an advantage to know two languages in today's world in this country. I would advise anyone starting school to study at least two languages, and I would encourage immigrants to keep their own language while learning English.

Questions: What ways were used to develop the preceding essay: example, cause and effect, explanation, comparison, or anecdote? What other ways could you suggest to discuss the topic? Refer to the preceding Revising Checklist.

✔ *A TIP:* Whenever time permits, it is always a good idea to wait a day or so after finishing your first draft before revising it. In this way, when you look it over, you can be more objective. Of course, your schedule may not always permit this. If it does not, try to *pretend* you are *unfa*miliar with the material when you read it over—try to be someone who doesn't already know what you "meant to say." Would someone picking up your paper for the first time get the point without any explanation that is not there on the page?

Now that you have written and revised your draft, it is time to edit it. Read it over once more, checking for mechanical errors. Use the following questions as a starting point for editing.

◆ EDITING CHECKLIST

- ◆ Is each sentence complete? Avoid fragments. Does each sentence have a subject and a verb and make complete sense?
- ◆ How long are your sentences? Are they too long and contain too many commas? Remember, a comma may not connect two complete sentences. If necessary, refer to an English usage guide.
- ◆ Did you indent each paragraph? Are the paragraphs an appropriate length?
- ◆ Is your verb tense consistent? If you are telling an anecdote in the past, stay in the past. Do not switch to the present or another tense unless you have a very good reason.
- ◆ Does agreement exist between the subject and verb, especially when the present tense is being used? (Example: Steve, one of the tallest boys on the basketball team, almost always wears [NOT *wear*] blue shorts.) Remember that verbs may consist of more than one word. Make sure the auxiliary verbs are also correct.
- ◆ Are proper nouns capitalized? Does every sentence begin with a capital?

Now read the draft over again one last time. When you are satisfied that all corrections have been made, and that the essay says what you wanted it to say, then you are finished.

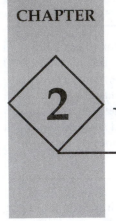

CHAPTER

2 Voices from School

◆ **PREREADING**

Discuss and then write the answers to the following questions:

1. Have you, or has anyone you know, ever had to change schools? Explain.
2. What can you report about someone you know who has come to a new school in the United States?
3. Why do children sometimes feel intimidated by adults? Why are they afraid to express themselves?
4. Do adults always listen carefully to children? Why or why not?
5. How can children be encouraged to develop their own point of view?

◆ **VOCABULARY**

The following words may be unfamiliar. While you read, underline any other words that you need to look up. Keep a dictionary handy.

droopy (para. 1)—tired-looking, sagging
mouthiness (para. 8)—bold or aggressive verbalization
pushy (para. 18)—aggressive
equivalent (para. 18)—something of equal value
pointedly (para. 22)—on purpose, clearly
churning (para. 22)—moving around
outcasts (para. 24)—those excluded from a group

When I Was Puerto Rican
Esmeralda Santiago

Carefully read the following excerpt from When I Was Puerto Rican *by Esmeralda Santiago, who came to this country from a poor village in Puerto Rico as an adolescent, one of eleven children. She won a scholarship to the High School of Performing Arts in New York City, then to Harvard. In this segment, she describes her first day at a Brooklyn elementary school.*

⇒ NOTE: As with many of the reading excerpts in this book, you will notice some unusual words and some foreign words. Aside from the more challenging vocabulary words, such as those listed in the Vocabulary section, these unusual or foreign words will be italicized and explained in footnotes near the text. Most if not all of these would be difficult or impossible to find in a standard English dictionary.

The first day of school Mami walked me to a stone building 1
that loomed over Graham Avenue, its concrete yard enclosed by an
iron fence with spikes at the top. The front steps were wide but shallow and led up to a set of heavy double doors that slammed shut behind us as we walked down the shiny corridor. I clutched my
eighth-grade report card filled with A's and B's, and Mami had my
birth certificate. At the front office we were met by Mr. Grant, a
droopy gentleman with thick glasses and a kind smile who spoke
no Spanish. He gave Mami a form to fill out. I knew most of the
words in the squares we were to fill in: NAME, ADDRESS (CITY, STATE),
and OCCUPATION. We gave it to Mr. Grant, who reviewed it, looked at
my birth certificate, studied my report card, then wrote on the top of
the form "7–18."

Don Julio had told me that if students didn't speak English, the   2
schools in Brooklyn would keep them back one grade until they
learned it.

"Seven gray?" I asked Mr. Grant, pointing at his big numbers,   3
and he nodded.

"Ino guan seven gray. I eight gray. I teeneyer."   4

"You don't speak English," he said. "You have to go to the sev-   5
enth grade while you're learning."

"I have A's in school Puerto Rico. I lern good. I no seven gray   6
girl."

Mami stared at me, not understanding but knowing I was being   7
rude to an adult.

"What's going on?" she asked me in Spanish. I told her they   8
wanted to send me back one grade and I would not have it. This was
probably the first rebellious act she had seen from me outside my
usual mouthiness within the family.

"Negi, leave it alone. Those are the rules," she said, a warning   9
in her voice.

"I don't care what their rules say," I answered. "I'm not going   10
back to seventh grade. I can do the work. I'm not stupid."

Mami looked at Mr. Grant, who stared at her as if expecting her   11
to do something about me. She smiled and shrugged her shoulders.

"Meester Grant," I said, seizing the moment, "I go eight gray   12
six mons. Eef I no lern inglish, I go seven gray. Okay?"

"That's not the way we do things here," he said hesitating.   13

"I good studen. I lern queek. You see notes." I pointed to the A's   14
on my report card. "I pass seven gray."

So we made a deal.   15

"You have until Christmas," he said. "I'll be checking on your   16
progress." He scratched out "7–18" and wrote in "8–23." He wrote
something on a piece of paper, sealed it inside an envelope, and gave
it to me. "Your teacher is Miss Brown. Take this note upstairs to her.
Your mother can go," he said and disappeared into his office.

"Wow!" Mami said, "You can speak English!"   17

I was so proud of myself, I almost burst. In Puerto Rico, if I'd   18
been that pushy, I would have been called *mal educada* by the Mr.
Grant equivalent and sent home with a note to my mother. But here
it was my teacher who was getting the note, I got what I wanted and
my mother was sent home.

"I can find my way after school," I said to Mami. "You don't   19
have to come get me."

"Are you sure?"   20

"Don't worry," I said. "I'll be all right."   21

I walked down the black-tiled hallway, past many doors that   22
were half glass, each one labeled with a room number in neat black
lettering. Other students stared at me, tried to get my attention, or
pointedly ignored me. I kept walking as if I knew where I was going,
heading for the sign that said STAIRS with an arrow pointing up. When
I reached the end of the hall and looked back, Mami was still standing at the front door watching me, a worried expression on her face.
I waved and she waved back. I started up the stairs, my stomach
churning into tight knots. All of a sudden, I was afraid that I was
about to make a fool of myself and end up in seventh grade in the
middle of the school year. Having to fall back would be worse that just
accepting my fate now and hopping forward if I proved to be as good
a student as I had convinced Mr. Grant I was. "What have I done?" I
kicked myself with the back of my right shoe, much to the surprise of
the fellow walking behind me, who laughed uproariously, as if I had
meant it as a joke.

Miss Brown's was the learning disabled class, where the ad-   23
ministration sent kids with all sort of problems, none of which, from
what I could see, had anything to do with their ability to learn but
more with their willingness to do so. They were an unruly group.
Those who came to class, anyway. Half of them never showed up, or,
when they did, they slept through the lesson or nodded off in the
middle of Miss Brown's carefully parsed sentences.

We were outcasts in a school where the smartest eighth graders   24
were in the 8–1 homeroom, each subsequent drop in number indi-
cating one notch less smarts. If your class was in the low double dig-
its (8–10 for instance), you were smart, but not a pinhead. Once you
got into the teens, your intelligence was in question, especially as the
numbers rose to the high teens. And then there were the twenties. I
was in 8–23, where the dumbest most undesirable people were placed.
My class was, in some ways, the equivalent of seventh grade, perhaps even sixth or fifth.

Miss Brown, the homeroom teacher, who also taught English   25
composition, was a young black woman who wore sweat pads under
her arms. The strings holding them in place sometimes slipped outside

the short sleeves of her well-pressed white shirts, and she had to turn her back to us in order to adjust them. She was very pretty, with almond eyes and a hairdo that was flat and straight at the top of her head then dipped into tight curls at the ends. Her fingers were well manicured, the nails painted pale pink with white tips. She taught English composition as if everyone cared about it, which I found appealing.

After the first week she moved me from the back of the room to   26
the front seat by her desk, and after that, it felt as if she were teaching me alone. We never spoke except when I went up to the blackboard.

◆ WORKING WITH WORDS

In the first two sentences of this selection, Santiago describes, in strong, highly descriptive language, her impressions on the first day at a new school. Starting school can be an intimidating experience for any child. But the first day at a new school in a new country, which is what this excerpt describes, can be terrifying. The language she uses in this description is very effective.

Read the following version of those first two sentences, with the descriptive language taken out:

> The first day of school Mami walked me to a building on Graham Avenue, with a playground and a fence. The front steps led up to a set of double doors through which we entered a shiny corridor.

Compare this altered version of the first two sentences of the excerpt with the actual sentences themselves (para. 1). They tell the same basic information, but with less feeling. Now, list the words and phrases that have been deleted, and, next to each one, tell how that word or phrase contributed to the feeling that the author intended.

◆ EXAMINING CONTENT

Refering to the preceding excerpt, answer the following questions:

1. What was wrong with the way Esmeralda was classified by the principal?
2. How had she performed in school before this?

3. What was her impression of Miss Brown?
4. Who was more fluent in English, Esmeralda or her mother?
5. What lesson did she learn when she talked the principal into putting her into the eighth grade?

◆ RESPONDING TO IDEAS

The following questions are intended to stimulate discussion and writing about ideas found in the excerpt. Answering them may help you write a response.

1. How do you think Esmeralda felt when she found out the principal was going to send her back to the seventh grade? Why did she feel that way?
2. Why do you think her mother was worried?
3. What do you think Miss Brown's opinion of Esmeralda was?
4. What do you think eventually happened?
5. Do you think Esmeralda would have been better off or worse off in a bilingual classroom? Why?
6. What do you think being in the "dumbest" class did to Esmeralda's self-esteem?
7. How could Esmeralda's placement been handled differently?
8. Write a response essay, a rough draft that answers a question in "Responding to Ideas," using ideas from the preceding questions, or examples from the text, and connecting them with your own experience and observation of life to support your response. Refer to Chapter One if you have questions as to how to write a response essay.

◆ OPTIONAL: WRITING A LETTER

If you prefer, instead of a standard reader-response as described in Chapter One, you can choose one of the following options:

1. Write a letter to the principal telling him how you feel about the way he handled placement of Esmeralda in 8–23.
2. Write a letter to Miss Brown helping her understand the best way to teach English to Esmeralda.
3. Write a letter to Esmeralda's mother, explaining how schools function in the United States.

4. Write a letter to Esmeralda from the point of view of Miss Brown, Mr. Grant, or her mother.

◆ MORE WRITING TOPICS

Should parents be involved with their children's education? Write a rough draft answering this question. Then, share in groups what each of you has written. Reread the revising and editing suggestions in Chapter One. Using these, share feedback with one another on your drafts and revise, considering the suggestions from your classmates.

◆ PREREADING

Answer the following questions with one other student or in a group:

1. Actors, artists, and writers sometimes change their names. Can you think of reasons why?
2. Imagine, just for a moment, that you have a totally different name than the one you have always had. Pick one. Think of yourself as the person with that name. How does it feel? What if someone else, say, your English teacher, *gave* you a new name?
3. Have you ever felt that the people around you don't know who you really are? What, if anything, did you do about it?

◆ VOCABULARY

Review the following words; then look for them when you read. Underline them when you find them.

pummeling (para. 1)—hitting with fists

dervishes (para. 1)—priests in a Muslim sect known for spinning and dancing

crinolines (para. 1)—stiff petticoats

seismic (para. 2)—having a strong impact

abstraction (para. 2)—an idea (as opposed to a physical thing)

hobgoblin (para. 2)—ghost

Lost in Translation
Eva Hoffman

Carefully read the following excerpt from Eva Hoffman's Lost in Translation, *telling about her first day at school in Vancouver, British Columbia. Eva Hoffman's family emigrated from Poland to Canada in 1959 because of religious persecution of the Jewish population in her home country. She won a scholarship to Rice University, then went to Harvard, and she became one of the editors of the* New York Times Book Review.

"Shut up, shuddup," the children around us are shouting, and it's   1
the first word in English that I understand from its dramatic context.

My sister and I stand in the schoolyard clutching each other, while kids all around us are running about, pummeling each other, and screaming like whirling dervishes. Both the boys and the girls look sharp and aggressive to me, the girls all have bright lipstick on, their hair sticks up and out like witches' fury, and their skirts are held up and out by stiff, wiry crinolines. I can't imagine wanting to talk their harsh-sounding language.

We've been brought to this school by Mr. Rosenberg, who, two days after our arrival, tells us he'll take us to classes that are provided by the government to teach English to newcomers. This morning, in the rinky-dink wooden barracks where the classes are held, we've acquired new names. All it takes is a brief conference between Mr. Rosenberg and the teacher, a kindly looking woman who tries to give us reassuring glances, but who has seen too many people come and go to get sentimental about a name. Mine—"Ewa"—is easy to change into its near equivalent in English, "Eva." My sister's name—"Alina"—poses more of a problem, but after a moment's thought, Mr. Rosenberg and the teacher decide that "Elaine" is close enough. My sister and I hang our heads wordlessly under this careless baptism. The teacher then introduces us to the class, mispronouncing our last name—"Wydra"—in a way we've never heard before. We make our way to a bench at the back of the room; nothing much has happened, except a small, seismic mental shift. The twist in our names takes them a tiny distance from us—but it's a gap into which the infinite hobgoblin of abstraction enters. Our Polish names didn't refer to us; they were as surely us as our eyes or hands. These new appellations, which we ourselves can't yet pronounce, are not us. They are identification tags, disembodied signs pointing to objects that happen to be my sister and myself. We walk to our seats, into a roomful of unknown faces, with names that make us strangers to ourselves.

When the school day is over, the teacher hands us a file card on which she has written, "I'm a newcomer. I'm lost. I live at 1785 Granville Street. Will you kindly show me how to get there? Thank you." We wander the streets for several hours, zigzagging back and forth through seemingly identical suburban avenues, showing this deaf-mute sign to the few people we see, until we eventually recognize the Rosenberg's house. We're greeted by our quietly hysterical mother and Mrs. Rosenberg, who, in a ritual she has probably learned from television, puts out two glasses of milk on her red

2

3

Formica counter. The milk, homogenized and too cold from the fridge, bears little resemblance to the liquid we used to drink called by the same name.

◆ WORKING WITH WORDS

There is a powerful contrast at work in this excerpt. Hoffman's piece is about the confusion she and her sister felt surrounded by people speaking English, a language new to them; yet the piece is written in that "new" language, and the way in which she uses it indicates that she has obviously mastered it, and even enjoys using it well. Using the context, and, if necessary, a dictionary, explain in your own words the meaning of the following words, as the author uses them in the excerpt:

1. appellations (para. 2)
2. disembodied (para. 2)
3. baptism (para. 2)
4. rinky-dink (para. 2)
5. hysterical (para. 3)
6. ritual (para. 3)

◆ EXAMINING CONTENT

Answer the following questions in complete sentences. Remember a complete sentence must have a subject and a verb and correct punctuation and must contain a complete unit of logical thought on its own.

1. Why did the teacher change Eva Hoffman's name?
2. How did it make her feel? Did the new name affect her self-image? How?
3. Why does Eva call the sign the teacher gave them a "deaf-mute sign"?
4. Why was Eva's mother "hysterical"? Compare Eva's mother to Esmeralda's mother in the preceding excerpt.
5. Why didn't Eva like the milk Mrs. Rosenberg gave her?

◆ RESPONDING TO IDEAS

In complete paragraphs, write answers to the following questions. Be prepared to read your answers aloud to the class.

1. Children have a particularly difficult time when they emigrate to another country. Can you think of reasons why?
2. Do you think a teacher should be able to communicate with a child in his or her native language? Give examples to explain your response.

◆ WRITING TOPICS

From your own experience, or the experience of someone you know, or your reading, you may know something about how an immigrant feels on arriving in the United States. Using this knowledge, write a response to one of the following statements. (Remember, Chapter One contains suggestions to help you get started.)

1. Our names affect how we think about ourselves.
2. We should not translate an immigrant's name.
3. Teachers could do more to make a newcomer feel at home.

◆ **PREREADING**

Discuss the following:

1. Have you ever been placed in the wrong class in school? In other words, were you ever assigned to a class that was doing work below or above your level of ability? Was your ability level ever misjudged? Describe the situation.
2. How can being placed in the wrong class affect a person's life? Give an example to explain.

◆ **VOCABULARY**

vocational (para. 1)—work or job related

hypotheses (para. 1)—ideas or theories

scuttling (para. 1)—crawling

mediocre (para. 2)—unexceptional

wherewithal (para. 2)—ability

somnambulant (para. 2)—sleepwalking

deliverance (para. 3)—escape

dissecting (para. 4)—cutting open for examination or study, as a biology specimen

cytoplasm (para. 4)—part of a cell

Lives on the Boundary
Mike Rose

The following excerpt is from a book called Lives on the Boundary, *by Mike Rose. The son of Italian immigrants, Rose was incorrectly placed in a vocational education track when his parents moved to California. Later, the mistake was rectified, and Rose eventually became a writer and professor at UCLA, where he has dedicated himself to helping students unlock their potential.*

In this excerpt, Rose remembers that school experience.

Students will float to the mark you set. I and the others in the vo-   1
cational classes were bobbing in pretty shallow water. Vocational education has aimed at increasing the economic opportunities of students

who do not do well in our schools. Some serious programs succeed in doing that, and through exceptional teachers—like Mr. Gross in *Horace's Compromise*—students learn to develop hypotheses and troubleshoot, reason through a problem, and communicate effectively—the true job skills. The vocational track, however, is most often a place for those who are just not making it, a dumping ground for the disaffected. There were a few teachers who worked hard at education; young Brother Slattery, for example, combined a stern voice with weekly quizzes to try to pass along to us a skeletal outline of world history. But mostly the teachers had no idea of how to engage the imagination of us kids who were scuttling along at the bottom of the pond.

And the teachers would have needed some inventiveness, for none of us was groomed for the classroom. It wasn't just that I didn't know things—didn't know how to simplify algebraic factions, couldn't identify different kinds of clauses, bungled Spanish translations—but that I had developed various faulty and inadequate ways of doing algebra and making sense of Spanish. Worse yet, the years of defensive tuning out in elementary school had given me a way to escape quickly while seeming at least half alert. During my time in Voc. Ed., I developed further into a mediocre student and a somnambulant problem solver, and that affected the subjects I did have the wherewithal to handle; I detested Shakespeare; I got bored with history. My attention flitted here and there. I fooled around in class and read my books indifferently—the intellectual equivalent of playing with your food. I did what I had to do to get by, and I did it with half a mind. . . . 2

My own deliverance from the Voc. Ed. world began with sophomore biology. Every student, college prep to vocational, had to take biology, and unlike the other courses, the same person taught all sections. When teaching the vocational group, Brother Clint probably slowed down a bit or omitted a little of the fundamental biochemistry, but he used the same book and more or less the same syllabus across the board. If one class got tough, he could get tougher. He was young and powerful and very handsome, and looks and physical strength were high currency. No one gave him any trouble. 3

I was pretty bad at the dissecting table but the lectures and the textbook were interesting; plastic overlays, that, with each turned page, peeled away skin, then veins and muscle, then organs down to the very bones that Brother Clint, pointer in hand, would tap out on 4 our hanging skeleton. Dave Snyder was in big trouble for the study of life—versus the living of it—was sticking in his craw. He worked out a code for our multiple-choice exams. He'd poke me in the back, once for the answer under A, twice for B, and so on; and when he'd hit the right one, I'd look up to the ceiling as though I were lost in thought. Poke: cytoplasm. Poke, poke: methane. Poke, poke, poke: William Harvey. Poke, poke, poke, poke: islets of Langerhans. This didn't work out perfectly, but Dave passed the course, and I mastered the dreamy look of a guy on a record jacket. And something else happened. Brother Clint puzzled over this Voc. Ed. kid who was racking up 80s and 90s on his tests. He checked the school's records and discovered the error. He recommended that I begin my junior year in the College Prep program. According to all I've read since, such a shift, as one report put it, is virtually impossible. Kids of that level rarely cross tracks. The telling thing is how chancy both my placement into and exit from Voc. Ed. was; neither I nor my parents had anything to do with it. I lived in one world during spring semester, and when I came back to school in the fall, I was living in another. . . .

Switching to College Prep was a mixed blessing. I was an erratic student. I was undisciplined. And I hadn't caught on to the rules of the game: why work hard in a class that didn't grab my fancy? I was also hopelessly behind in math. Chemistry was hard; toying with my chemistry set years before hadn't prepared me for the chemist's equations. Fortunately, the priest who taught both chemistry and second-year algebra was also the school's athletic director. Membership in the track team covered me; I knew I wouldn't get lower than a C. U.S. history was taught pretty well, and I did okay. But civics was taken over by a football coach who had trouble reading the textbook aloud— and reading aloud was certainly an improvement over the vocational program—at least it carried some status—but the social science curriculum was weak, and the mathematics and physical sciences were simply beyond me. I had a miserable quantitative background and ended up copying some assignments and finessing the rest as best I could.

Let me try to explain how it feels to see again and again material you should once have learned but didn't.

You are given a problem. It requires you to simplify algebraic factions or to multiply expressions containing square roots. You know this is pretty basic material because you've seen it for years. Once a teacher took some time with you, and you learned how to carry out these operations. Simple versions, anyway. But that was a year or two or more in the past; and these are more complex versions, and now you're not sure. And this, you keep telling yourself, is ninth- or even eighth-grade stuff.

Next it's a word problem. This is also old hat. The basic elements are as familiar as story characters; trains speeding so many miles per hour or shadows of buildings angling so many degrees. Maybe you know enough, have sat through enough explanations, to be able to begin setting up the problem: "If one train is going this fast . . ." or "This shadow is really one line of a triangle. . . ." Then: "Let's see . . ." "How did Jones do this?" "Hmmmm." "No." "No, that won't work." Your attention wavers. You wonder about other things: a football game, a dance, that cute new checker at the market. You try to focus on the problem again. You scribble on paper for a while, but the tension wins out and your attention flits elsewhere. You crumple the paper and begin daydreaming to ease the frustration.

◆ WORKING WITH WORDS

Fill in the blanks with the appropriate word from the Vocabulary list.

1. Mike Rose was incorrectly placed into a _____ program in his school.
2. Teachers soon found that Rose was a superior, not a _____ student.
3. The professor prepared a _____ for his course.
4. The scientist designed an experiment so she could test her _____ .
5. Next week, the class will be _____ a frog.
6. For many, a college degree will represent _____ into a better lifestyle.

◆ EXAMINING CONTENT

Look for the answers to the following questions in the preceding excerpt. Write the answers in complete sentences.

1. How did Mike Rose feel in the vocational education program?
2. How did the teacher discover that Mike was incorrectly placed in the vocational education program?

3. What happened when he was placed in the correct classes?

4. How did Mike feel about the material he should have learned but didn't?

5. Describe the process in which students lose focus and their attention wanders.

◆ RESPONDING TO IDEAS

Consider the following writing prompts carefully. Be certain that your responses include examples from the text to develop your main ideas, in addition to any information from your own experience or observation.

1. Write a letter to the math teacher Mike encountered when he was taken out of vocational education. Explain what long-term effects his incorrect class placement might have on him.

2. Write a letter to the principal of the school Mike attended. Include suggestions for preventing the same mistake from happening again.

3. Write about a time you were frustrated by a task or assignment, and how you resolved the situation.

◆ MORE WRITING TOPICS

Select one of the following suggestions and develop an essay in response to it. You may use information from the Mike Rose reading, or you may use other facts, but be sure to support your position with facts.

1. Education varies from culture to culture (or from city to city).

2. How would it feel to be misunderstood and underestimated by your teachers?

◆ **PREREADING**

Answer the following in a class discussion. Or, choose one and write a quick draft answering it.

1. Who was your favorite teacher?
2. Do you think a teacher can make a difference in a person's life?
3. If you had a son or daughter who was going to become a teacher, what advice would you give?
4. How do people perceive teachers as a class of people?

◆ **VOCABULARY**

illustrations (para. 2)—pictures in a book or article
atrophy (para. 3)—wither away from lack of use
instinctive (para. 6)—coming from the unconscious; not requiring thought
expansion (para. 6)—growth
formative (para. 6)—developmental
dun (para. 8)—a dull, neutral color
nucleus (para. 22)—center or core

Teacher
Sylvia Ashton-Warner

An educator from New Zealand, Sylvia Ashton-Warner developed a creative method of teaching Maori children that has been admired and imitated worldwide. In the following excerpt from her book Teacher, *she explains part of her method, which she calls "Key Vocabulary."*

Children have two visions, the inner and the outer. Of the two   1
the inner vision is brighter.

I hear that in other infant rooms widespread illustration is used   2
to introduce the reading vocabulary to a five-year-old, a vocabulary
chosen by adult educationists. I use pictures, too, to introduce the reading vocabulary, but they are pictures of the inner vision and the captions are chosen by the children themselves. True, the picture of the

outer, adult-chosen pictures can be meaningful and delightful to children; but it is the captions of the mind pictures that have the power and the light. For whereas the illustrations perceived by the outer eye cannot be other than interesting, the illustrations seen by the inner eye are organic, and it is the captioning of these that I call the "Key Vocabulary."

I see the mind of a five-year-old as a volcano with two vents: 3 destructiveness and creativeness. And I see that to the extent that we widen the creative channel, we atrophy the destructive one. And it seems to me that since these words of the key vocabulary are no less than the captions of the dynamic life itself, they course out through the creative channel, making their contribution to the drying up of the destructive vent. From all of which I am constrained to see it as creative reading and to count it among the arts.

First words must mean something to a child.   4

First words must have intense meaning for a child. They must 5 be part of his being.

How much hangs on the love of reading, the instinctive incli- 6 nation to hold a book! *Instinctive.* That's what it must be. The reaching out for a book needs to become an organic action, which can happen at this yet formative age. Pleasant words won't do. Respectable words won't do. They must be words organically tied up, organically born from the dynamic life itself. They must be words that are already part of the child's being. "A child," reads a recent publication on the approach of the American books, "can be led to feel that Janet and John are friends." *Can be led to feel.* Why lead him to feel or try to lead him to feel that these strangers are friends? What about the passionate feeling he has already for his own friends? To me it is inorganic to overlook this step. To me it is an offence against art. I see it as an interruption in the natural expansion of life of which Erich Fromm speaks. How would New Zealand children get on if all their reading material were built from the life of African blacks? It's little enough to ask that a Maori child should begin his reading from a book of his own colour and culture. This is the formative age where habits are born and established. An aversion to the written word is a habit I have seen born under my own eyes in my own infant room on occasion.

It's not beauty to abruptly halt the growth of a young mind and 7 to overlay it with the frame of an imposed culture. There are ways of training and grafting young growth. The true conception of beauty is the shape of organic life and that is the very thing at stake in the transition from one culture to another. If this transition took place at a later age when the security of a person was already established there would not be the same need for care. But in this country it happens that the transition takes place at a tender and vulnerable age, which is the reason why we all try to work delicately.

Back to these first words. To these first books. They must be   8
made out of the stuff of the child itself. I reach a hand into the mind of the child, bring out a handful of the stuff I find there, and use that as our first working material. Whether it is good or bad stuff, violent or placid stuff, coloured or dun. To effect an unbroken beginning. And in this dynamic material, within the familiarity and security of it, the Maori finds that words have intense meaning to him, from which cannot help but arise a love of reading. For it's here, right in this first word, that the love of reading is born, and the longer his reading is organic the stronger it becomes, until by the time he arrives at the books of the new culture, he receives them as another joy rather than as a labour. I know all this because I've done it.

> First words must have an intense meaning.   9
>
> First words must be already part of the dynamic life.
>
> First books must be made of the stuff of the child himself, whatever and wherever the child.

The words, which I write on large tough cards and give to the   10
children to read, prove to be one-look words if they are accurately enough chosen. And they are plain enough in conversation. It's the conversation that has to be got. However, if it can't be, I find that whatever a child chooses to make in the creative period may quite likely be such a word. But if the vocabulary of a child is still inaccessible, one can always begin him on the general Key Vocabulary, common to any child in any race, a set of words bound up with security that experiments, and later on their creative writing, show to be inorganically associated with the inner world: "Mummy," "Daddy," "kiss," "frightened," "ghost."

"Mohi," I ask a new five, an undisciplined Maori, "what word   11
do you want?"

"Jet!"   12

I smile and write it on a strong little card and give it to him.   13
"What is it again?"

"Jet!"   14

"You can bring it back in the morning. What do you want, Gay?   15

Gay is the classic overdisciplined, bullied victim of the respectable mother.   16

"House," she whispers. So I write that, too, and give it into her eager hand.   17

"What do you want, Seven?" Seven is a violent Maori.   18

"Bomb! Bomb! I want bomb!"   19

So Seven gets his word "bomb" and challenges anyone to take it from him.   20

And so on through the rest of them. They ask for a new word each morning and never have I to repeat to them what it is. And if you saw the condition of these tough little cards the next morning you'd know why they need to be of tough cardboard or heavy drawing paper rather than thin paper.   21

When each has the nucleus of a reading vocabulary and I know they are at peace with me I show them the word "frightened" and at once all together they burst out with what they are frightened of. Nearly all the Maoris say "the ghost!" a matter which has racial and cultural origin, while the Europeans name some animal they have never seen, "tiger" or "alligator," using it symbolically for the unnameable fear that we all have.   22

"I not frightened of anysing!" shouts my future murderer, Seven.   23

"Aren't you?"   24

"No, I stick my knife into it all!"   25

"What will you stick your knife into?"   26

"I stick my knife into the tigers!"   27

"Tigers" is usually a word from the European children but here is a Maori with it. So I give him "tigers" and never have I to repeat this word to him, and in the morning the little card shows the dirt and disrepair of passionate usage.   28

"Come in," cry the children to a knock at the door, but as no one does come in we all go out. And here we find in the porch, humble with natural dignity, a barefooted, tattooed Maori woman.   29

"I see my little Seven?" she says.   30

"Is Seven your little boy?"   31

"I bring him up. Now he five. I bring him home to his real family for school eh. I see my little boy?"   32

The children willingly produce Seven, and here we have in the porch, within a ring of sympathetic brown and blue eyes, a reunion.   33

"Where did you bring him up?" I ask over the many heads.   34

"Way back on those hill. All by heeself. You remember your ol'   35
Mummy?" she begs Seven.

I see.   36

Later, standing watching Seven grinding his chalk to dust on   37
his blackboard as usual, I do see. "Whom do you want, Seven? Your
old Mummy or your new Mummy?"

"My old Mummy."   38

"What do your brothers do?"   39

"They all hits me."   40

"Old Mummy" and "new Mummy" and "hit" and "brothers"   41
are all one-look words added to his vocabulary, and now and again I
see some shape breaking through the chalk-ravage. And I wish I could
make a good story of it and say he is no longer violent. . . .

"Who's that crying!" I accuse, lifting my nose like an old war   42
horse.

"Seven he breaking Gay's neck."   43

So the good story, I say to my junior, must stand by for a while.   44
But I can say he is picking up his words now. Fast.

Dennis is a victim of a respectable, money-making, well-dressed   45
mother who thrashes him, and at five he has already had his first nervous breakdown. "I'm not frightened of anything!" he cries.

"Is Dennis afraid of anything?" I asked his young pretty mother   46
in her big car.

"Dennis? He won't even let the chickens come near him."   47

"Did you have a dream?" I asked Dennis after his afternoon rest.   48

"Yes I did."   49

"Well then . . . where's some chalk and a blackboard?"   50

Later when I walked that way there was a dreadful brown ghost   51
with purple eyes facing a red alligator on a roadway. I know I have
failed with Dennis. I've never had his fear words. His mother has de-
feated me. During the morning output period—when everyone else
is painting, claying, dancing, quarrelling, singing, drawing, talking,
writing or building—Dennis is picking up my things from the floor
and straightening the mats, and the picture I have of his life waiting
for him, another neurotic, pursued by the fear unnameable, is not one
of comfort.

Mare resisted any kind of reading vocabulary until one morn-   52
ing when the Little Ones were all talking at once about what they

were frightened of he let go, "I shoot the bulldog!" Gay's fear was a dog too. Do we realise just how afraid small children are of dogs?

But I have some dirty, thoroughly spoilt children next door who 53 are never held up with fear. Their Key Vocabulary runs from "Daddy," and "kiss" through words like "truck," "hill," and "Mummy" to "love" and "train." How glorious are the dirty spoilt children.

Out press these words, grouping themselves in their own wild 54 order. All boys wanting words of locomotion, aeroplane, tractor, jet, and the girls the words of domesticity, house, Mummy, doll. Then the fear words, ghost, tiger, skellington, alligator, bulldog, wild piggy, police. The sex words, kiss, love, touch, *haka*.* The key words carrying their own illustrations in the mind, vivid and powerful pictures which none of us could possibly draw for them—since in the first place we can't see them and in the second because they are so alive with an organic life that the external pictorial representation of them is beyond the frontier of possibility. We can do no more than supply the captions.

Out push these words. The tendency is for them to gather force 55 once the fears are said, but there are so many variations on character. Even more so in this span of life where personality has not yet been moulded into the general New Zealand pattern by the one imposed vocabulary for all. They are more than captions. They are even more than sentences. They are whole stories at times. They are actually schematic drawing. I know because they tell them to me.

◆ WORKING WITH WORDS

Find the words from the excerpt to match the definitions that follow. The paragraph in which each word appears is indicated in parentheses.

1. Restricted; held back (para. 3)
2. Heartfelt (para. 6)
3. Growing; changing; vital (para. 6)
4. Growing by natural development (para. 6)
5. Suddenly; without warning (para. 7)
6. Exposed; able to be hurt (para. 7)
7. Established by authority (para. 7)

---

haka: Maori war dance

8. A period of change, or the change itself (para. 7)
9. Unable to be reached (para. 10)
10. Core or center or basis (para. 22)

◆ EXAMINING CONTENT

Answer the following questions in complete sentences:

1. What is special about the way in which Ashton-Warner understands children?
2. What does she mean about the five-year-old having both a destructive and creative tendencies?
3. What does the teacher do in order to teach vocabulary?
4. What are some of the words that the students produce? Why are they important?
5. How does Ashton-Warner capture the "inner vision" of children?

◆ RESPONDING TO IDEAS

Choose one of the following and write a three- to five-paragraph draft in response:

1. How did Ashton-Warner's ideas differ from those of more traditional kindergarten teachers?
2. How is the culture of the children evoked through the words that they choose?
3. Why do you think the method is so successful?
4. Can you think of other creative methods that are similar to Ashton-Warner's "Key Vocabulary"?
5. Do you think her method was very popular with the educators of New Zealand? Why or why not?

◆ MORE WRITING TOPICS

1. Using any of the four readings in this chapter, write two detailed descriptions: first, of the school, the class, and the teacher, from the

student's point of view; then, of the school, the class, and the student, from the teacher's point of view.

2. Write a radio play* in which Miss Brown (Esmeralda's teacher), Miss Jones (Eva's teacher), Brother Clint (Mike's teacher), and Ms. Ashton-Warner are together, discussing classroom issues, such as the placement and misplacement of students, or how best to teach the students in their classes. Keep in mind what you know about each of those teachers, based on what you have read in the four excerpts.

3. Write an essay about yourself (or someone you know very well) in a situation such as Eva's, Esmeralda's, or Mike's. (It can be fictional, but if it is, it should not be any less serious or any less real.) Be sure to write about *what* happened, *why* it happened, how the student *felt* inside, and what the *outcome* was.

4. If none of these assignments appeals to you, develop an original one of your own, of similar complexity, and work on that. Make sure you have your teacher's approval of the assignment before you begin work.

Each of the suggested assignments is different, and each calls for a different type of writing approach. They all, however, require you to use your imagination, your familiarity with the readings, your empathy with the people in the readings, and your writing skills. Whether you are writing a dialogue, describing a situation, or explaining an event, use your best writing skills, use complete sentences (with the possible exception of conversations), and be sure, when you are finished, to read over your work. Edit it to the best of your ability, and don't be afraid to make changes and revisions. Make certain that what you hand in is your best work.

◆ MAKING THE FINAL COPY

Go back to your journal and look at all the responses and drafts you have written to readings and questions from this chapter. Choose one of them, or choose one of the assignments in the following section and think about it, develop it, write it, and hand it in for a grade.

---

*A radio play simply means that you only have to write down what each character says; you don't need any description. It's just a four-way conversation.

◆ **STUDENT DRAFT**

Sometimes the most original and creative teachers are not appreciated. Sylvia Ashton-Warner was one of those teachers. She looked at education as a process, a relationship with students, not just as a job. She took her students seriously; yes, you could even say she loved them, even though they came from a different background from hers. You can tell by the way she referred to them in her writing, especially when she says, "Children have two visions, the inner and the outer. Of the two the inner is brighter." (para. 1)

She understood that to really understand children you have to look deeply, listen to what they say, and try to interpret any communication with the child's own perspective. She said that first words have meaning to a child. I agree. My child's first word was the name of his pet, a Siberian Husky named Chekhov. He couldn't pronounce the actual word, so he said something like "Day." He learned this name early because the pet was so important in his world. The same can be true of children learning a second language. That's why words like "Mommy," "Kiss," and "Ghost" were so important. In that child's world, they are what represents love and fear.

Ashton-Warner appreciated the children's naive Maori culture. That's why she let them write their own books using the Key Vocabulary. It is easier to read when the content is something familiar. And these children did not come from educated middle-class culture. They came from an oral tradition, not from a world of books.

Appreciating the need for these children to feel comfortable in a classroom, Ashton-Warner let them begin with the familiar. She let them talk about the fearful words, the ones that once they were exorcised, spoken aloud, would not seem as frightening. The part about Dennis, whose mother thrashed him, made me very sad. Couldn't the teacher have reported the situation of child abuse to the proper authorities? Did Ashton-Warner try?

I wish all teachers were like Ashton-Warner in her dedication, her respect for her job and her students. She understood, like we all should, that any real learning should come from deep within the person, not superficially memorized, soon to be forgotten.

How does this draft differ from your own?

◆ REVISING CHECKLIST

Read over the draft you have completed for the purpose of revising it—that is, improving the content. Use the following questions as a starting point for revision.

- ◆ Does the composition have an introduction? Does the introductory paragraph of the composition make the main idea of the composition clear? Remember, there is more than one way to respond and write an introduction. It must include the most important point, however.
- ◆ Is the development clear and specific? Remember to avoid generality. Be specific. For instance, if you are telling an anecdote remember to include the answers to *Where? When? Who? Why?* Be sure it is clear *how* the anecdote is related to the topic.
- ◆ Is the choice of language appropriate? Be aware of street language, slang and trendy expressions. Academic writing is usually more formal. (Of course, if you are writing dialogue, you have some flexibility in terms of writing in the way your characters would realistically speak.)
- ◆ Are any ideas repeated? Sometimes writers repeat and are not aware of it.
- ◆ Are any ideas not relevant and do these need to be deleted? Sometimes writers digress from the topic. Ask yourself after each sentence, "How does this relate to the ideas preceding and following it?"
- ◆ Is the conclusion appropriate? Does it reflect the main idea and let the reader know that the essay is ending?

◆ EDITING CHECKLIST

Now that you have written and revised your draft, it is time to edit it. Read it over once more, checking for mechanical errors. Use the following questions as a starting point for editing:

- ◆ Is each sentence complete? Avoid fragments. Does each sentence have a subject and a verb and make complete sense?
- ◆ How long are your sentences? Are they too long and contain too many commas? Remember, a comma may not connect two complete sentences. If necessary, refer to an English usage guide.
- ◆ Did you indent each paragraph? Are the paragraphs an appropriate length?

◆ Is your verb tense consistent? If you are telling an anecdote in the past, stay in the past. Do not switch to the present or another tense for no reason.

◆ Does subject and verb agreement exist, especially when the present tense is used? Remember, verbs may consist of more than one word. Make sure the auxiliary verbs are also correct.

◆ Are proper nouns capitalized? Does every sentence begin with a capital?

Read your draft over again one last time, trying to look at it through the eyes of someone completely unfamiliar with it. If you're satisfied, you're through.

◆ EDITING EXERCISE

If you have targeted many errors when you were checking for the fragments listed in the first item of the preceding checklist, you might need the following exercise for practice. Identify the fragments in the following composition:

Maria and Sarah are best friends. Maria from the Dominican Republic, and Sarah was born in the United States. Are in the same classes at the community college they attend in New York City. Because want to transfer to a four-year college, they are trying to maintain a "B" average. On week-ends. They eat seafood at their favorite restaurant in Queens, and they sometimes visit Sarah's aunt on the New Jersey shore. This summer, Maria has invited. Sarah to go to visit her hometown near Bayamon in the Dominican Republic.

Maria makes her best grades in math and science; is studying to be a dental hygienist. She has an older brother who is a dentist and helps her get a job in a dentist's office. She plans to transfer to New York University. After she graduates next fall. Sarah is studying psychology. She loves to practice Spanish. Which is her second language with Maria. She will be a bilingual child psychologist after she her education at Columbia.

Even though they know that people often drift apart. The two young women hope to remain in touch. Want to try and find jobs in the New York City area. Sarah has a boyfriend, Stuart, at Rutgers, and he will start a job near Maria. Who will be finishing graduate school. Sarah has asked Maria to be her maid of honor at her wedding. The two girls have many happy plans for a full and rich future.

The rules for a complete sentence are

1. Each sentence has to have a subject and a verb.
2. Each sentence has to make sense alone, apart from the preceding and following sentences.
3. Every sentence has to begin with a capital letter and end with a period, question mark, or exclamation point.

Now, check the preceding composition you have corrected and make sure that it does not break the rules for a sentence.

Voices
from the Family

◆ PREREADING

1. Different generations of a family may have different customs, values, beliefs—even languages. Do any members of your family differ from one another in one or more of these ways? Describe one such family member.

2. What values do older generations of your family possess that you would like to have? What have you learned from them?

3. What new customs, knowledge, or habits do you and your peers have that older family members do not?

◆ VOCABULARY

hilarious (para. 4)—extremely funny
retrospect (para. 5)—the act of looking back
erupting (para. 7)—spewing out

nostalgia (para. 9)—state of fond remembering

stubbed (para. 13)—hit in a clumsy way

vials (para. 18)—small glass or plastic bottles, such as those used for medicine

Only Daughter
Sandra Cisneros

Sandra Cisneros, a native of Chicago, is internationally acclaimed for her poetry and fiction. Her work has been translated into eight languages. In the following excerpt she examines her relationship with her father, as she recalls confronting him with the information that she has become a writer.

Once, several years ago, when I was just starting out my writing career, I was asked to write my own contributor's note for an anthology I was part of. I wrote: "I am the only daughter in a family of six sons. That explains everything." 1

Well, I've thought about that ever since, and yes, it explains a lot to me, but for the reader's sake I should have written "I am the only daughter in a *Mexican* family of six sons." Or even, "I am the only daughter of a working-class family of nine." All of these had everything to do with who I am today. I was/am the only daughter and *only* a daughter. 2

I was/am the only daughter and *only* a daughter. Being an only daughter in a family of six sons forced me by circumstance to spend a lot of time by myself. Being an only daughter in a family of six sons forced me by circumstance to spend a lot of time by myself because my brothers felt it beneath them to play with a *girl* in public. But that aloneness, that loneliness, was good for a would-be writer— it allowed me time to think and think, to imagine, to read and prepare myself. 3

Being only a daughter for my father meant my destiny would lead me to become someone's wife. That's what he believed. But when I was in the fifth grade and shared my plans for college with him, I was sure he understood. I remember my father saying, "Que bueno, Mi'ja, that's good." That meant a lot to me, especially since my brothers thought the idea hilarious. What I didn't realize was that my father 4 thought college was good for girls—good for finding a husband. After four years in college and two more in graduate school, and still no husband, my father shakes his head even now and says I wasted all that education.

In retrospect, I'm lucky my father believed daughters were   5
meant for husbands. It meant it didn't matter if I majored in something silly like English. After all, I'd find a nice professional eventually, right? This allowed me the liberty to putter about embroidering my little poems and stories without my father interrupting with so much as a "What's that you're writing?"

But the truth is, I wanted him to interrupt. I wanted my father   6
to understand what it was I was scribbling, to introduce me as "My only daughter, the writer." Not as "This is only my daughter. She teaches." *Es maestra*—teacher. Not even profesora.

In a sense, everything I have ever written has been for him, to   7
win his approval even though my father's only reading includes the brown-ink *Esto* sports magazines from Mexico City and the bloody *Alarma!* that feature yet another sighting of *La Virgen de Guadalupe* on a tortilla or a wife's revenge on her philandering husband by bashing his skull in with a *molcajete* (a kitchen mortar made of volcanic rock). Or the *fotonovelas*, the little picture paperbacks with tragedy and trauma erupting from the characters' mouths in bubbles.

My father represents, then, the public majority. A public who is   8
disinterested in reading and yet one whom I am writing about and for, and privately trying to woo.

When we were growing up in Chicago, we moved a lot because   9
of my father. He suffered bouts of nostalgia. Then we'd have to let go of our flat, store the furniture with mother's relatives, load the station wagon with baggage and bologna sandwiches and head south. To Mexico City.

We came back, of course. To yet another Chicago flat, another   10
Chicago neighborhood, another Catholic school. Each time, my father would seek out the parish priest in order to get a tuition break and complain or boast: "I have seven sons."

He meant *siete hijos*, seven children, but he translated it as "sons"   11
"I have seven sons." To anyone who would listen. The Sears Roebuck employee who sold us the washing machine. The short-order cook where my father ate his ham-and-eggs breakfasts. "I have seven sons." As if he deserved a medal from the state.

My papa. He didn't mean anything by that mistranslation, I'm   12
sure. But somehow I could feel myself being erased, I'd tug my father's sleeve and whisper: "Not seven sons. Six! And one daughter."

When my oldest brother graduated from medical school, he ful-   13
filled my father's dream that we study hard and use this—our heads,
instead of this—our hands. Even now my father's hands are thick
and yellow, stubbed by a history of hammer and nails and twine and
coils and springs. "Use this," my father said, tapping his head, "and
not this," showing us those hands. He always looked tired when he
said it.

Wasn't college an investment? And hadn't I spent all those years   14
in college? And if I didn't marry, what was it all for? Why would anyone go to college and then choose to be poor? Especially someone
who had always been poor.

Last year, after ten years of writing professionally, the financial   15
rewards started to trickle in. My second National Endowment for the
Arts Fellowship. A guest professorship at the University of California,
Berkeley. My book, which sold to a major New York publishing house.

At Christmas, I flew home to Chicago. The house was throb-   16
bing, same as always: hot tamales and sweet tamales hissing in my
mother's pressure cooker, and everybody—my mother, six brothers,
wives, babies, aunts, cousins—talking too loud and at the same time.
Like in a Fellini film, because that's just how we are.

I went upstairs to my father's room. One of my stories had just   17
been translated into Spanish and published in an anthology of Chi-
cano writing and I wanted to show it to him. Ever since he recovered
from a stroke two years ago, my father likes to spend his leisure time
horizontally. And that's how I found him, watching a Pedro Infante
movie on Galavision and eating rice pudding.

There was a glass filled with milk on the bedside table. There   18
were several vials of pills and balled Kleenex. And on the floor, one
black sock and a plastic urinal that I didn't want to look at but looked
at anyway. Pedro Infante was about to burst into song, and my father
was laughing.

I'm not sure if it was because my story was translated into Span-   19
ish, or because it was published in Mexico, or perhaps because the
story dealt with Tepeyac, the *colonia* my father was raised in and the
house he grew up in, but at any rate, my father punched the mute
button on his remote control and read my story.

I sat on the bed next to my father and waited. He read it very   20
slowly. As if he were reading each line over and over. He laughed at
all the right places and read lines he liked out loud. He pointed and
asked questions: "Is this So-and-so?" "Yes," I said. He kept reading.

When he was finally finished, after what seemed like hours, my   21
father looked up and asked: "Where can we get more copies of this for
the relatives?"

Of all the wonderful things that happened to me last year, that   22
was the most wonderful.

◆ WORKING WITH WORDS

For each of the following sentences taken from the Cisneros excerpt, write a
sentence that means the same thing, using different words or expressions:

1. "I wanted my father to understand what it was I was scribbling." (para. 7)
2. "He suffered bouts of nostalgia." (para. 10)
3. "My father likes to spend his leisure time horizontally." (para. 18)
4. "The house was throbbing, same as always." (para. 17)

◆ EXAMINING CONTENT

1. Why is the story called "Only Daughter"?
2. What does Cisneros think of her father? How does she describe him?
3. Why did Cisneros's father speak of her as one of his sons, not as a
   daughter?
4. Why did Cisneros's father want her to have a college education?
5. When and why did he eventually accept her as a writer?

◆ RESPONDING TO IDEAS

1. Although Cisneros has success as a writer, she seems to need confirma-
   tion of the value of her work from her father, even though he is not a
   reader of literature. Why is this so important to her?
2. Discuss how you think Cisneros felt when her father would say, "This
   is only my daughter. She teaches," as opposed to, "This is my only
   daughter. She is a writer."

◆ MORE WRITING TOPICS

1. Although much has been written about mother-daughter relationships, not as much has been written about fathers and daughters. Write an essay examining why this is such an important relationship in women's lives, using Cisneros's story as one of your examples.

2. Do you think the Mexican American culture influenced Cisneros's relationship with her father? Explain your response using specific examples.

PREREADING

1. Have you ever had a friend who lost a family member? How did you help him or her?
2. Have you ever felt you were the least favorite member of your family?
3. Have you ever been in a situation where someone you loved was very ill?

◆ VOCABULARY

hear-say (para. 1)—rumor; unverified story
mid-wife (para. 4)—person who helps deliver a baby
indifferent (para. 4)—uncaring
inclination (para. 12)—tendency toward
sow (para. 13)—female pig

Dust Tracks on the Road
Zora Neale Hurston

Zora Neale Hurston was an African American writer and anthropologist who lived from 1891 to 1960. The following is an excerpt from her autobiography, Dust Tracks on the Road. *In this part of her story, Hurston remembers incidents from her childhood, some of which she remembers first hand, and some of which she must have heard in family discussions.*

I Get Born

This is all hear-say. Maybe, some of the details of my birth as told me   1
might be a little inaccurate, but it is pretty well established that I really
did get born.

The saying goes like this. My mother's time had come and my   2
father was not there. Being a carpenter, successful enough to have
other helpers on some jobs, he was away often on building business,
as well as preaching. It seems that my father was away from home for
months this time. I have never been told why. But I did hear that he
threatened to cut his throat when he got the news. It seems that one
daughter was all that he figured he could stand. My sister, Sarah, was

his favorite child, but that one girl was enough. Plenty more sons, but no more girl babies to wear out shoes and bring in nothing. I don't think he ever got over the trick he felt that I played on him by getting born a girl, and while he was off from home at that. A little of my sugar used to sweeten his coffee right now. That is a Negro way of saying his patience was short with me. Let me change a few words with him—and I am of the word-changing kind—and he was ready to change ends. Still and all, I looked more like him than any child in the house. Of course, by the time I got born, I was too late to make any suggestions, so that the old man had to put up with me. He was nice about it in a way. He didn't tie me in a sack and drop me in the lake, as he probably felt like doing.

People were digging sweet potatoes, and then it was hogkilling   3
time. Not at our house, but it was going on in general over the country, like, being January and a bit cool. Most people were either butchering for themselves, or off helping other folks do their butchering, which was almost just as good. It is a gay time. A big pot of hasslits* cooking with plenty of seasoning, lean slabs of fresh-killed pork frying for the helpers to refresh themselves after the work is done. Over and above being neighborly and giving aid, there is the food, the drinks and the fun of getting together.

So there was no grown folks close around when Mama's water   4
broke. She sent one of the smaller children to fetch Aunt Judy, the mid-wife, but she was gone to Weekbridge, a mile and a half away, to eat at a hog killing. The child was told to go over there and tell Aunt Judy to come. But nature, being indifferent to human arrangements, was impatient. My mother had to make it alone. She was too weak after I rushed out to do anything for herself, so she just was lying there, sick in the body, and worried in mind, wondering what would become of her, as well as me. She was so weak, she couldn't even reach down to where I was. She had one consolation. She knew I wasn't dead, because I was crying strong.

Help came from where she never would have thought to look   5
for it. A white man of many acres and things, who knew the family well, had butchered the day before. Knowing that Papa was not at home, and that consequently there would be no fresh meat in our house, he decided to drive the five miles and bring a half of a shoat,

---

*Kind of chitterlings or pig's brains

sweet potatoes and other garden stuff along. He was there a few minutes after I was born. Seeing the front door standing open, he came on in, and hollered, "Hello, there! Call your dogs!" That is the regular way to call in the country because nearly everybody who has anything to watch, has biting dogs.

Nobody answered, but he claimed later that he heard me spreading my lungs all over Orange County, so he shoved the door open and bolted on into the house.   6

He followed the noise and then he saw how things were, and being the kind of a man he was, he took out his Barlow Knife and cut the navel cord, then he did the best he could about other things. When the midwife, locally known as a granny, arrived about an hour later, there was a fire in the stove and plenty of hot water on. I had been sponged off in some sort of way, and Mama was holding me in her arms.   7

As soon as the old woman got there, the white man unloaded what he had brought, and drove off cussing about some blankety-blank people never being where you could put your hands on them when they were needed.   8

He got no thanks from Aunt Judy. She grumbled for years about it. She complained that the cord had not been cut just right, and the belly-band had not been put on tight enough. She was might scared I was going to have a weak back, and that I would have trouble holding my water until I reached puberty. I did.   9

The next day or so a Mrs. Neale, a friend of Mama's, came in and reminded her that she had promised to let her name the baby in case it was a girl. She had a picked up a name somewhere which she thought was very pretty. Perhaps, she had read it somewhere, or somebody back in those woods was smoking Turkish cigarettes. So I became Zora Neale Hurston.   10

There is nothing to make you like other human beings so much as doing things for them. Therefore, the man who grannied me was back next day to see how I was coming along. Maybe it was pride in his own handiwork, and his resourcefulness in a pinch, that made him want to see it through. He remarked that I was a God damned fine baby, fat and plenty of lung power. As time went on, he came infrequently, but somehow kept a pinch of interest in my welfare. It seemed that I was spying noble, growing like a gourd vine, and yelling bass like a gator. He was the kind of a man that had no use for puny things, so I was all to the good with him. He thought my mother was justified in keeping me.   11

But nine months rolled around, and I just would not get on with   12
the walking business. I was strong, crawling well, but showed no inclination to use my feet. I might remark in passing, that I still don't like
to walk. Then I was over a year old, but still I would not walk. They
made allowances for my weight, but yet, that was no real reason for
my not trying.

They tell me that an old sow-hog taught me how to walk. That   13
is, she didn't instruct me in detail, but she convinced me that I really
ought to try.

It was like this. My mother was going to have collard greens for   14
dinner, so she took the dishpan and went down to the spring to wash
the greens. She left me sitting on the floor, and gave me a hunk of
cornbread to keep me quiet. Everything was going along all right,
until the sow with her litter of pigs in convoy came abreast of the
door. She must have smelled the cornbread I was messing with and
scattering crumbs about the floor. So, she came right on in, and began
to nuzzle around.

My mother heard my screams and came running. Her heart   15
must have stood still when she saw the sow in there, because hogs
have been known to eat human flesh.

But I was not taking this thing sitting down. I had been placed   16
by a chair and when my mother got inside the door, I had pulled myself up by that chair and was getting around it right smart.

As for the sow, poor misunderstood lady, she had no interest in   17
me except my bread. I lost that in scrambling to my feet and she was
eating it. She has much less intention of eating Mama's baby, than
Mama had of eating hers.

With no more suggestions from the sow or anybody else, it   18
seems that I just took to walking and kept the thing a'going. The
strangest thing about it was that once I found the use of my feet,
they took to wandering. I always wanted to go. I would wander off
in the woods all along, following some inside urge to go places. This
alarmed my mother a great deal. She used to say that she believed a
woman who was an enemy of hers had sprinkled "travel dust"
around the doorstep the day I was born. That was the only explanation she could find. I don't know why it never occurred to her to connect my tendency with my father, who didn't have a thing on his
mind but this town and the next one. That should have given her a
sort of hint. Some children are just bound to take after their fathers
in spite of women's prayers.

◆ WORKING WITH WORDS

Hurston has a great way of using local expressions to create an ambience for her characters. In other words, she uses colorful language to help the reader get a sense of the world in which her characters live. For example, in the last paragraph she describes her father as a man "who didn't have a thing on his mind but this town and the next one." By this, she means that he was a restless person, someone who always wanted to be off to somewhere else. Find five examples of unusual, colorful or "special" language Hurston uses, and explain in your own words what you think they mean.

⇒ *NOTE:* Did you notice, in the first paragraph in this section, the following:

> *Hurston has a great way of using local expressions.*

You have been taught to use verb tense consistently and accurately. Ms. Hurston, who died in 1960, certainly wrote in the past. Why is her process being described here in the present tense?

When discussing literature, it is a generally accepted practice to describe the writing as though it were being done in the present. This is called the historic present. Thus, we say

> *Hurston* remembers *her childhood*
> *Sandra Cisneros* confronts *her father*
> *Esmeralda Santiago* describes *her first day at school*

But we say

> *Why* did *Sandra's father want her to have a college education?*

and

> *Why* did *the teacher change Eva Hoffman's name?*

because these are actions that characters in the story *did*, in the past.

The historic present (sometimes called the literary present) refers only to the verbs that describe what the author does as author, not what the author does (or did) as a character in the story.

◆ EXAMINING CONTENT

1. Where was Judy the midwife when the baby was born?
2. Who helped with the birth?
3. How did Zora Neale Hurston get her name?
4. How did she learn to walk?
5. In what way does Hurston feel that she is like her father?

◆ RESPONDING TO IDEAS

1. Did you ever have a scary experience when you were young? Describe it in detail.
2. Tell the story of your birth from what others have told you about it.
3. Do you feel you resemble your mother or father? Explain why.
4. Do you feel it is wrong to leave a baby alone for any length of time? When do you think it is safe to do so?

◆ MORE WRITING TOPICS

1. All things considered, which is preferable: having a baby at home or in a hospital? Decide what you think, and discuss why you feel that way.
2. When both parents are not present during the raising of a child, which parent has a greater influence: the one who is present, or the one who is rarely present? Explain.
3. Some people can't settle down and stay in one place for very long. Is this an admirable quality, or one to be avoided?

◆ **PREREADING**

1. Are your grandmothers or grandfathers or anyone from their generation still alive? Describe them.
2. Describe your relationship with your grandparent (or another older relative). Compare it with your relationship with another member of your
   family.
3. Do you think your generation is like or unlike your grandparents' generation? Tell why you believe the way you do.

◆ **VOCABULARY**

> *pterodactyl* (para. 2)—extinct, prehistoric flying reptile
> *affinity* (para. 3)—attraction to
> *gnarled* (para. 3)—twisted
> *profligate* (para. 3)—wildly extravagant
> *Oedipal* (para. 3)—relating to the psychological relationship with one's
>   parents
> *internees* (para. 6)—those detained in an internment camp
> *Nisei* (para. 7)—American-born children of Japanese immigrants

Turning Japanese
David Mura

*David Mura is a Japanese American poet who grew up in the United States and later
went back to Japan to find his ancestral roots. In the following passage from his book*
Turning Japanese, *he tells of how he learns about his grandfather from talking to his
Aunt Ruth.*

Shortly after this talk with Mrs. Hayashe, I began to think about   1
writing a novel about my grandfather. Only by having come to Japan,
I realized, could I even begin to attempt such a novel. Previously I
was able to know only the American side of him, and that only
through the sketchy stories told by my aunt. His Japanese side was beyond my experience. I was just beginning to understand how much
about him I didn't know.

In my clearest memory, my grandfather stands in the hallway of   2
our apartment, talking to my grandmother about the film *Rodan*. He's
wearing a sleeveless undershirt, wire-rim glasses; his silver hair's somewhat long for an old man. His body is slightly bent. I'm sure it's the talk
of the movie and the giant pterodactyl that destroys Tokyo that sustains
this memory, rather than anything about him. I can't recall whether
their talk was translated for me or if they spoke English.

While my father never talked of his father, my Aunt Ruth al-   3
ways seemed willing to talk about him. It's through her stories that
I've constructed an affinity between his sensibility and mine. I know,
for instance, that my grandfather arrived in America around the beginning of the century, fleeing the draft and the Russo-Japanese* wars.
At that time, almost all the Issei, or first generation, were men and
they often sent back to Japan for brides. Sometimes the pictures the
men sent were fakes, and the brides would step from the ships and
find some dwarfish gnome, with crooked teeth and a nose gnarled
as a ginger root. Aunt Ruth took great pleasure in telling me that my
grandfather was so handsome he went back to Shingu** in person to
find a bride. She would tell me about his love of clothes, his gambling
that lost him a pool hall, his bartending days at a hotel in L.A., where
Tom Mix[†] and other stars hung out. In these tales there was something extravagant and profligate about my grandfather, something
to contrast with the rigidness and businesslike attitude of my father,
the Republican ways that I argued against so much of my youth. It
was my grandfather whom I wrote poems about, a dashing, invented
character who probably had more to do with the gamblers in West-
erns and yearning for a romantic past than anything Japanese. I never
really envisioned learning that language, entering its otherness. And
my father, in his second-generation to prove his Americanness, in his
own Oedipal rebellion, gave me no encouragement in this direction.

In Japan, as my interest in my family background awakened, I   4
began to read more about the first Japanese immigrants. When my
grandfather came to America in 1903, the ratio of Japanese men to
Japanese women was about 10 to 1. Although during the 1880's and
1890's most of the trickle of Japanese immigrants were students who

---

*Russo-Japanese: Russian and Japanese
**Shingu: town in Japan
[†]Tom Mix: famous movie cowboy of the 1920s and 1930s

intended to study the ways of the West, by the time my grandfather arrived in the States the greater bulk of immigrants were laborers. My grandfather, a draft dodger, was fairly well educated, but his status was more like that of the laborers than the students. Often second sons without property, these laborers hoped to make enough money in America to return to Japan and buy land. It was not a new world they were seeking but a route back to the old one. And so they brought no women, no family, with them. All that would come later, a reward in the future. . . .

Somehow, behind these acts of fathers and sons lies the backdrop of race and relocation.   5

As the war went on, the internees at the Jerome, Arkansas relocation were given weekend passes. They could travel to Little Rock to eat at a restaurant or watch a movie. My grandfather or grandmother did not go on these trips, only their children. The children spoke English, were enamored of Hollywood's stars.   6

It is summer 1943. On a dust-dry country road, my father waits   7
for the bus with other young Nisei. Behind them, like a bad dream, the fences of barbed wire, the rifle towers, the gates, the barracks filled with mothers, fathers and bawling babies, with aging bachelors, with newlyweds. Down the ridge they can see the sharecropper shacks, more ramshackle than any of the barracks, with gaps in the walls and weather-beaten, cracked boards. Rougher, looser than his older brother Ken—less Japanese, my father and his friends jostle and joke, talk about the baseball game yesterday, about Carol Hiyama or Judy Endo. These boys frighten some of the Issei in camp. They play cards behind the barracks, smoke cigarettes, curse in English.

When the bus comes, it is nearly empty. They take their seats in   8
the front, behind an old white woman with a pillbox hat, a few Negroes, a couple of men in overalls, a mother and her child with pigtails. There's never a question for my father of sitting in the back.

It is the same at the lunch counter where they order hamburgers   9
and malts. Perhaps they notice the stares of the whites around them, but most likely they are too engrossed in their own conversation, in teasing Tosh about his crush on Carol, to notice where the Negroes are sitting. Later these boys will sit below the balcony, below the section for Negroes. The faces of Cary Grant and Katherine Hepburn flow off the screen, borne on light enlarged by glamour and celluloid, becoming part of my father's dreams.

Two years later, he's in college away from the camps, entering   10
the Episcopalian church with Professor Bigelow and his family. It is
a sunny fall morning; the leaves, splashes of red and yellow and orange, swirl down to the street, crackling on the walk. . . . The church
is white, spired, clean in the sunlight. My father has no suit. He's
wearing a white shirt, a tie. It is his first time inside this church.

Had my grandfather been a fervent Buddhist, things might have   11
turned out differently. But my grandfather was too much a man of this
world. Sharing with most Japanese a passive attitude toward religion,
he had grown away from Buddha and the Shinto* gods during his
time in America. My father is an empty vessel, waiting to be filled.

As he ambles along with the Bigelows, he's a little stiff, a bit ner-   12
vous, not knowing what to do. Inside, he's greeted by garden of Geth-
semane, kneeling in prayer, with the cross of his destruction in the
distance; the disciples gathered around him, questioning, listening;
the fish and bread of life laid out in jagged triangles; the haggard
bearded man stretched out on the cross, eyes closed, giving up the
ghost. What strikes my father more, the beautiful colors or this pro-
gression toward suffering? The light or the dark?

He notices in front of the benches a little platform that swings   13
down, cushioned green leather. Just as the children enter the pew,
they suddenly kneel down, facing straight ahead toward the altar;
Mrs. Bigelow and the professor do the same. My father wonders what
he should do. Self-conscious, he does the best he can with a halfway
gesture, the way seventh graders in our parish years later used to
bow. The professor smiles and tries to reassure him, but my father,
watching the altar boy light the candles on the altar, hearing the organ
and the voices of the choir, is again wondering what to do. As the ser-
vice continues and the members in the pews rise up to speak in uni-
son kneel, rise, kneel, over and over at exactly the right time, my father
is disoriented. He feels a slight ache in his back, is thankful at least for
the cushioned platform.

"This is the body and blood which is shed for you and the New   14
Testament. Take this and drink. Do this often in remembrance of me."

Thank God he thinks, I understand the words. And in all of this   15
there is a music that takes over my father, something beyond sense,

---

*Shinto: indigenous religion of Japan

beyond God or Christ. What attracts him is a sense of belonging, of crossing some line, a way out of the Buddhist temples and streets of L.A., something he first felt in the radios and comic books, the very language that poured from his mouth, in the games of mumbletypeg, marbles, and baseball, in the pledge he recited in school each morning. Something that wasn't foreign, that did not keep him out.

He will convert, he will take up the cross, he will bring us to 16 church all through my childhood, up until the time we move from our middle-class home in Morton Grove to our upper-class one in Northbrook, a time when he is finally a vice-president, when religion is no longer needed. By then I will be estranged from the church, an atheist, wondering what brought him to think a white man must be God.

Growing up, I had the usual complaints of most Asian kids 17 about their hard-driving parents. There were never enough excellents, enough hundreds on tests; there were always errors I'd made on the field, tackles I missed. When I was seven, my father took me to the sidewalk on Lake Shore Drive. He pushed me off on my bike, screamed, "Pedal, pedal," and quickly became disgusted when I fell, yelling that I didn't listen to him. Ten years later, when I learned to drive, it was the same; sitting beside me in our Buick, he slammed on some imaginary brake in front of him and shook my arm. A terrible teacher, he always ended up screaming and shouting, muttering about my lack of concentration, my refusal to perform.

Perhaps the problem was how I took all this. I believed whatever 18 it was that reddened his face, that clenched it so tight, that coiled his fist into a tight ball, must have come from me. I must have created this force, it was what I deserved. I was simply unable to brush it off.

Years later when I confronted my infidelities, my own harangues 19 at Susie, it seemed difficult—no, almost impossible—to take my sexuality and the rage it contained and connect it with my father and his rage. The equation did not compute.

I see my father now as a successful executive, writing speeches 20 for other executives, writing videos, public-relations campaigns, giving speeches at conventions and meetings, splicing bits of information with familiar corn-pone jokes. I see him at evening striding down the fairway in back of his house, shading his eyes as his drive soars into the sun, the tiny white ball disappearing in the last blaze of orange light, the first crickets of evening gnats scribbling their mad circles around his head. His body looks ten years younger, hardened by weights, by Nautilus, though it has begun to stoop just a touch to descend toward earth. He is sixty, he is content, the fairway stretches out before him, he wants no other life than this. He has no problems with identity, with the past or race. He has been freed from history.

And I am still his son.   21

◆ WORKING WITH WORDS

Mura's piece is enhanced by his use of adjectives that describe things vividly. In each of the following examples, explain what he meant by the adjectives indicated. If you are not immediately clear on the meaning, use the dictionary, although it won't always be enough to help you. In some cases, you must rely on your sense of the word from the context in which it is used. Go back to the paragraphs indicated for the context.

1. "*sketchy* stories" (para. 1)
2. "*dwarfish* gnome" (para. 3)
3. "*ramshackle* . . . shacks" (para. 7)
4. "*fervent* Buddhist" (para. 11)
5. "*haggard* bearded man" (para. 12)
6. "*hard-driving* parents" (para. 17)
7. "*corn-pone* jokes" (para. 20)

◆ EXAMINING CONTENT

1. How did Mura learn about his grandfather?
2. What does the term *first-generation* mean, as it is used to describe an immigrant?
3. How was Mura's father's world different from his grandfather's?
4. Why did his father love going to church? Why did he become Presbyterian instead of Buddhist?
5. Was there racial prejudice in the world of David Mura's father and grandfather? Refer to the parts of the reading selection that suggest this.
6. What kind of relationship did David Mura have with his father? Read aloud the passages that tell us.

◆ **RESPONDING TO IDEAS**

1. In the next to last paragraph, Mura says that his father is "freed from history." What does he mean by this? In what way can someone be tied to history or freed from it?
2. Do people belong to a religion for reasons other than belief in a theology? Why?
3. Are people influenced by the way their parents treated them? Give your opinion and specific examples. You may use your own experience or that of others.
4. David Mura's father's generation did not seem to have as much trouble with identity as did Mura's. Give reasons why.

◆ **MORE WRITING TOPICS**

1. Much has been written recently about the influence of a father in a son's personality. Do you believe fathers can be blamed for a son's behavior? Please explain your response with specific examples.
2. Sometimes people go to a church because it is near their home. Sometimes people become a member of a specific religion because it is the dominant one of the culture in which they are living. Are these valid choices? Why or why not?

◆ PREREADING

1. Do you have a relative who really meant a lot to you when you were growing up? Who is this person?
2. How can a relative be influential in a child's life, even when the parents are present?
3. How important are role models in the life of a child?

◆ VOCABULARY

synonymous (para. 1)—same as
peered (para. 1)—looked at
spinster (para. 3)—a woman who has never married
privileged (para. 7)—given special rights
bizarre (para. 13)—strange

Remembering Lobo
Pat Mora

Pat Mora of Texas is a Chicana educator, poet and lecturer. She has written poetry, essays, and children's books. The following, a remembrance of her favorite aunt, appeared in Nepantla, *a collection of essays she published in 1993.*

Remembering Lobo

We called her *Lobo.* The word means "wolf" in Spanish, an odd name   1
for a generous and loving aunt. Like all names it became synonymous
with her, and to this day returns me to my child self. Although the
name seemed perfectly natural to us and to our friends, it did cause
frowns from strangers throughout the years. I particularly remember
one hot afternoon when on a crowded streetcar between the border
cities of El Paso and Juarez, I momentarily lost sight of her. "Lobo!
Lobo!" I cried in panic. Annoyed faces peered at me, disappointed at
such disrespect to a white-haired woman.

    Actually the fault was hers. She lived with us for years, and   2
when she arrived home from work in the evening, she'd knock

on the front door and ask, *"Donde estan mis lobitos?"* "Where are my little wolves?"

Gradually she became our lobo, a spinster aunt who gathered   3
the four of us around her, tying us to her for life by giving us all she had. Sometimes to tease her we would call her by her real name. *"Donde esta Ignacia?"* we would ask. Lobo would laugh and say, "She is a ghost."

To all of us in nuclear families today, the notion of an extended   4
family under one roof seems archaic, complicated. We treasure our private space. I will always marvel at the generosity of my parents, who opened their door to both my grandmother and Lobo. No doubt I am drawn to the elderly because I grew up with two entirely different white-haired women who worried about me, tucked me in at night, made me tomato soup or hot *hierbabuena* (mint tea) when I was ill.

Lobo grew up in Mexico, the daughter of a circuit judge, my   5
grandfather. She was a wonderful storyteller and over and over told us about the night her father, a widower, brought his grown daughters on a flatbed truck across the Rio Grande at the time of the Mexican Revolution. All their possessions were left in Mexico. Lobo had not been wealthy, but she had probably never expected to have to find a job and learn English.

When she lived with us, she worked in the linens section of a   6
local department store. Her area was called "piece goods and bedding." Lobo never sewed, but she would talk about materials she sold, using words I never completely understood, such as *pique* and *broadcloth.* Sometimes I still whisper such words just to remind myself of her. I'll always savor the way she would order "sweet mild" at restaurants. The precision of a speaker new to the language.

Lobo saved her money to take us out to dinner and a movie, to   7
take us to Los Angeles in the summer, to buy us shiny black shoes for Christmas. Though she never married and never bore children, Lobo taught me much about one of our greatest challenges as human beings: loving well. I don't think she ever discussed the subject with me, but through the years she lived her love and I was privileged to watch.

She died at ninety-four. She was no sweet, docile Mexican   8
woman dying with perfect resignation. Some of her last words before drifting into semiconsciousness were loud words of annoyance at the incompetence of nurses and doctors.

"*No sirven.*" "They're worthless," she'd say to me in Spanish.   9
"They don't know what they're doing. My throat is hurting and they're
taking X rays. Tell them to take care of my throat first."

I was busy striving for my cherished middle-class politeness.   10
"Shh, shh," I'd say. "They're doing the best they can."

"Well, it's not good enough," she'd say, sitting up in anger.   11

She was a woman who literally whistled while she worked. The   12
best way to cheer her when she'd visit my young children was to ask
for her help. Ask her to make a bed, fold laundry, set the table or dry
dishes, and the whistling would begin as she moved about her task.
Like all of us, she loved being needed. Understandable, then, that she
muttered in annoyance when her body began to fail her. She was a
woman who found self-definition and joy in visibly showing her family her love for us by bringing us hot *te de canela* (cinnamon tea) in
the middle of the night to ease a cough, by bringing us comics and
candy whenever she returned home. A life of giving.

One of my last memories of her is a visit I made to her on   13
November 2, *El Dia de los Muertos,* or All Souls' Day. She was sitting
in her rocking chair, smiling wistfully. The source of the smile may
seem a bit bizarre to a U.S. audience. She was fondly remembering
past visits to the local cemetery on this religious feast day.

"What a silly old woman I have become," she said. "Here I sit   14
in my rocking chair all day on All Souls Day, sitting when I should
be out there. At the cemetery. Taking good care of *mis muertos,* my
dead ones.

"What a time I used to have. I'd wake while it was still dark   15
outside. I'd hear the first morning birds, and my fingers would almost itch to begin. By six I'd be having a hot bath, dressing carefully
in black, wanting *mis muertos* to be proud of me, proud to have me
looking respectable and proud to have their graves taken care of. I'd
have my black coffee and plenty of toast. You know the way I like it.
Well browned and well buttered. I wanted to be ready to work hard.

"The bus ride to the other side of town was a long one, but I'd   16
say a rosary and plan my day. I'd hope that my perfume wasn't too
strong and yet would remind others that I was a lady.

"The air at the cemetery gates was full of chrysanthemums: that   17
strong, sharp, fall smell. I'd buy tin cans full of the gold and wine
flowers. How I liked seeing aunts and uncles who were also there to
care for the graves of their loved ones. We'd hug. Happy together.

"Then it was time to begin. The smell of chrysanthemums was 18
like a whiff of pure energy. I'd kneel on a few patches of grass, and I'd
scrub and scrub, shining the gray stones, leaning back on my knees
to rest for a bit and then scrubbing again. Finally a relative from
nearby would say, '*Ya ya Nacha,*' and laugh. Enough. I'd stop, blink my
eyes to return from my trance. Slightly dazed, I'd stand slowly, place
a can of chrysanthemums before each grave.

"Sometimes I would just stand there in the desert sun and lis- 19
ten. I'd hear the quiet crying of people visiting new graves; I'd hear
families exchanging gossip while they worked.

"One time I heard my aunt scolding her dead husband. She'd 20
sweep his gravestone and say '*Porque?* Why did you do this, you
thoughtless man? Why did you go and leave me like this? You know
I don't like to be alone. Why did you stop living?' Such a sight to see
my aunt with her proper black hat and her fine dress and her carefully
polished shoes muttering away for all to hear.

"To stifle my laughter, I had to cover my mouth with my hands." 21

◆ WORKING WITH WORDS

In addition to the vocabulary list, look up these words from the excerpt you
just read, and recheck how they are used in context. (The paragraph numbers
are given.) Then answer the questions that follow.

1. Explain the difference between what is meant by the two phrases *nuclear family* and *extended family* (para. 4).
2. Give examples of three things you might *marvel* (para. 4) at, and tell why.
3. Describe what a person is like if he or she could be called *docile* (para. 8).
4. Under what circumstances might you smile *wistfully* (para. 13)?
5. Give an example of something besides laughter that can be *stifled* (para. 21).

◆ EXAMINING CONTENT

1. How did Lobo get her name?
2. Describe the way she got to the United States.
3. What was Lobo's talent?
4. What kind of job did she have?

5. How was the author able to cheer her up?
6. Describe *El Dia de Los Muertos*.

◆ RESPONDING TO IDEAS

1. Why do you think the author picked this particular relative to write about?
2. What lessons do you think the author learned from Lobo?
3. What relative do you have who reminds you of Lobo?
4. What traditions did you learn about the Mexican culture from this reading?

◆ MORE WRITING TOPICS

Write an essay on either of the following topics. Use examples from the text we just read to develop your essay.

1. "Remembering the Dead in Mexican Culture"
2. "The Importance of the Extended Family"

◆ **PREREADING**

1. In small groups, share a story about growing up with one of your parents or an older relative or caretaker.
2. Write the stories down, and read them aloud to the class.
3. List on the board the common and different characteristics of each story.

◆ **VOCABULARY**

rancor (para. 1)—anger; resentment
grimace (para. 18)—make an angry face
nozzle (para. 23)—part of a garden hose that spews water
coax (para. 23)—persuade
maudlin (para. 23)—overly sentimental
menace (para. 23)—threat
spartan (para. 24)—not luxurious
mediocre (para. 25)—average; of unexceptional quality

Native Speaker
Chang-Rae Lee

This Korean American novelist wrote Native Speaker, *a novel about a man in New York who, in addition to being Korean and American, has another secret identity. He works as a private investigator—a spy. In the following excerpt, Lee describes an episode in which the protagonist remembers growing up with his father in suburbia.*

During high school I used to wander out to the garage from the house to read or just get away after one of the countless arguments I had with my father. Our talk back then was in fact one long and grave contention, an incessant quarrel, though to hear it now would be to recognize the usual forms of homely rancor and still homelier devotion, involving all the dire subjects of adolescence—my imperfect studies, my unworthy friends, the driving of his car, smoking and drinking, the whatever and whatever. One of our worst nights of talk was after he suggested that the girl I was taking to the eighth-grade Spring Dance didn't—or couldn't—find me attractive.

"What do you think she like?" he asked, or more accurately said,   2
shaking his head to tell me I was a fool. We had been watching the late
news in his study.

"She likes *me*," I told him defiantly. "Why is that so hard for you   3
to take?"

He laughed at me. "You think she like your funny face? Funny   4
eyes? You think she dream you at night?"

"I really don't know, Dad," I answered. "She's not even my girl-   5
friend or anything. I don't know why you bother so much."

"Bother?" he said. *"Bother?"*   6

"Nothing, Dad, nothing."   7

"Your mother say exact same," he decreed.   8

"Just forget it."   9

"No, no, *you* forget it," he shot back, his voice rising. "You don't   10
know nothing! This American girl, she nobody for you. She don't know
nothing about you. You Korean man. So so different. Also, she know we
live in expensive area."

"So what!" I gasped.   11

"You real dummy, Henry. Don't you know? You just free dance   12
ticket. She just using you." Just then the housekeeper shuffled by us
into her rooms on the other side of the pantry.

"I guess that's right," I said. "I should have seen that. You   13
know it all. I guess I still have much to learn from you about deal-
ing with women."

"What you say!" he exploded. "What you say!" He slammed   14
his palm on the side lamp table, almost breaking the plate of smoked
glass. I started to leave but he grabbed me hard by the neck as if to
shake me and I flung my arm back and knocked off his grip. We were
turned on each other, suddenly ready to go, and I could tell he was as
astonished as I to be glaring this way at his only blood. He took a step
back, afraid of what might have happened. Then he threw up his
hands and just muttered, "Stupid."

A few weeks later I stumbled home from the garage apartment   15
late one night, drunk on some gin filched from a friend's parents'
liquor cabinet. My father appeared downstairs at the door and I
promptly vomited at his feet on the newly refinished floors. He
didn't say anything and just helped me to my room. When I struggled down to the landing the next morning the mess was gone. I still
felt nauseous. I went to the kitchen and he was sitting there with his

tea, smoking and reading the Korean-language newspaper. I sat across from him.

"Did she clean it up?" I asked, looking about for the woman. He looked at me like I was crazy. He put down the paper and rose and disappeared into the pantry. He returned with a bottle of bourbon and glasses and he carefully poured two generous jiggers of it. It was nine o'clock on Sunday morning. He took one for himself and then slid the other under me.   16

"*Mah-shuh!*" he said firmly. *Drink!* I could see he was serious. "*Mah-shuh!*"   17

He sat there, waiting. I lifted the stinking glass to my lips and could only let a little of the alcohol seep onto my tongue before I leaped to the sink and dry-heaved uncontrollably. And as I turned with tears in my eyes and the spittle hanging from my mouth I saw my father grimace before he threw back his share all at once. He shuddered, and then recovered himself and brought the glasses to the sink. He was never much of a drinker. *Clean all this up well so she doesn't see it*, he said hoarsely in Korean. *Then help her with the windows.* He gently patted my back and then left the house and drove off to one of his stores in the city.   18

The woman, her head forward and bent, suddenly padded out from her back rooms in thickly socked feet and stood waiting for me, silent.   19

I knew the job, and I did it quickly for her. My father and I used to do a similar task together when I was very young. This before my mother died, in our first, modest house. Early in the morning on the first full warm day of the year he carried down from the attic the bug screens sandwiched in his brief, powerful arms and lined them up in a row against the side of the house. He had me stand back a few yards with the sprayer and wait for him to finish scrubbing the metal mesh with an old shoe brush and car soap. He squatted the way my grandmother did (she visited us once in America before she died), balancing on his flat feet with his armpits locked over his knees and his forearms working between them in front, the position so strangely apelike to me even then that I tried at night in my bedroom to mimic him, to see if the posture came naturally to us Parks, to us Koreans. It didn't.   20

When my father finished he rose and stretched his back in several directions and then moved to the side. He stood there straight   21 as if at attention and then commanded me with a raised hand to fire away.

"*In-jeh!*" he yelled. *Now!*   22

I had to pull with both hands on the trigger, and I almost lost   23 hold of the nozzle from the backforce of the water and sprayed wildly at whatever I could hit. He yelled at me to stop after a few seconds so he could inspect our work; he did this so that he could make a big deal of bending over in front of me, trying to coax his small boy to shoot his behind. When I finally figured it out I shot him; he wheeled about with his face all red storm and theater and shook his fists at me with comic menace. He skulked back to a safe position with his suspecting eyes fixed on me and commanded that I fire again. He shouted for me to stop and he went again and bent over the screens; again I shot him, this time hitting him square on the rump and back, and he yelled louder, his cheeks and jaw wrenched maudlin with rage. I threw down the hose and sprinted for the back door but he caught me from behind and swung me up in what seemed one motion and plunked me down hard on his soaked shoulders. My mother stuck her head out the second-floor kitchen window just then and said to him, *You be careful with that bad boy.*

My father grunted back in that low way of his, the vibrato from   24 his neck trickling my thighs, his voice all raw meat and stones, and my mother just answered him, *Come up right now and eat some lunch.* He marched around the side of the house with me hanging from his back by my ankles and then bounded up the front stairs, inside, and up to the kitchen table, where she had set out bowls of noodles in broth with half-moon slices of pink and white fish cake and minced scallions. And as we sat down, my mother cracked two eggs into my father's bowl, one into mine, and then took her seat between us at the table before her spartan plate of last night's rice and kimchee and cold mackerel (she only ate leftovers at lunch), and then we shut our eyes and clasped our hands, my mother always holding mine extra tight, and I could taste on my face the rich steam of soup and the call of my hungry father offering up his most patient prayers to God.

None of us even dreamed that she would be dead six years   25 later from a cancer in her liver. She never even drank or smoked. I have trouble remembering the details of her illness because she and my father kept it from me until they couldn't hide it any longer. She was buried in a Korean ceremony two days afterward, and for me it was more a disappearance than a death. During her illness they said her regular outings on Saturday mornings were to go to "meetings" with her old school friends who were living down in the city. They said her constant weariness and tears were from her concern over my mediocre studies. They said, so calmly, that the rotten pumpkin color of her face and neck and the patchiness of her once rich hair were due to a skin condition that would get worse before it became better. They finally said, with hard pride, that she was afflicted with a "Korean fever" that no doctor in America was able to cure.

A few months after her death I would come home from school   26
and smell the fishy salty broth of those same noodles. There was the woman, Ahjuhma, stirring a beaten egg into the pot with long chopsticks; she was wearing the yellow-piped white apron that my mother had once sewn and prettily embroidered with daisies. I ran straight up the stairs to my room on the second floor of the new house, and Ahjuhma called after me in her dialect, "Come, there is enough for you." I slammed the door as hard as I could. After a half hour there was a knock and I yelled back in English, "Leave me alone!" I opened the door hours later when I heard my father come in, and the bowl of soup was at my feet, sitting cold and misplaced.

After that we didn't bother much with each other.   27

I still remember certain things about the woman: she wore white   28
rubber Korean slippers that were shaped exactly like miniature canoes. She had bad teeth that plagued her. My father sent her to the dentist, who fitted her with gold crowns. Afterward, she seemed to yawn for people, as if to show them off. She balled up her hair and held it with a wooden chopstick. She prepared fish and soup every night; meat or pork every other; at least four kinds of *namool*, prepared vegetables, and then always something fried.

She carefully dusted the photographs of my mother the first   29
thing every morning, and then vacuumed the entire house.

For years I had no idea what she did on her day off; she'd   30
go walking somewhere, maybe the two miles into town though I couldn't imagine what she did there because she never learned three words of English. Finally, one dull summer before I left for college, a friend and I secretly followed her. We trailed her on the road into the center of the town, into the village of Ardsley. She went into Rocky's Corner newsstand and bought a glossy teen magazine and a red Popsicle. She flipped through the pages, obviously looking

only at the pictures. She ate the Popsicle like it was a hot dog, in three large bites.

"She's a total alien," my friend said. "She's completely bizarre." 31

She got up and peered into some store windows, talked to no 32 one, and then she started on the long walk back to our house.

She didn't drive. I don't know if she didn't wish to or whether 33 my father prohibited it. He would take her shopping once a week, first to the grocery and then maybe to the drugstore, if she needed something for herself. Once in a while he would take her to the mall and buy her some clothes or shoes. I think out of respect and ignorance she let him pick them out. Normally around the house she simply wore sweatpants and old blouses. I saw her dressed up only once, the day I graduated from high school. She put on an iridescent dress with nubbly flecks in the material, which somehow matched her silvery heels. She looked like a huge trout. My father had horrible taste.

Once, when I was back from college over spring break, I heard 34 steps in the night on the back stairwell, up and then down. The next night I heard them coming up again and I stepped out into the hall. I caught the woman about to turn the knob of my father's door. She had a cup of tea in her hands. Her hair was down and she wore a white cotton shift and in the weak glow of the hallway night-light her skin looked almost smooth. I was surprised by the pretty shape of her face.

"Your papa is thirsty," she whispered in Korean, "go back to 35 sleep." . . .

◆ WORKING WITH WORDS

1. Find the sentence in the reading in which each of the words in the Vocabulary section appears.
2. Write a synonym and antonym for each of the words listed in the Vocabulary section.

◆ EXAMINING CONTENT

1. What was Henry Park's father's response to Henry's having a white girlfriend?

2. Describe the kind of playing that father and son did while cleaning the screens. What is its significance?
3. Describe Henry's father.
4. What did his father do when he found that Henry had been drinking alcohol?

◆ RESPONDING TO IDEAS

1. Do you think that Henry was afraid of his father?
2. In your opinion, did Henry and his father have a good relationship?
3. Do you know anyone in your family who is like Henry's father? In what ways are they similar?
4. What effect do you think this experience will have on Henry when he is grown?
5. In the book *Native Speaker*, Henry Park grew up, fell in love, and married a white woman, Lelia. Do you think the preceding episode, in which his father expresses doubt that an Anglo girl would like Henry, influenced him in his choice of a spouse?

◆ MORE WRITING TOPICS

1. Write a composition comparing Henry Park's account of his father with that of David Mura. Reread both texts and use specific examples to flesh out your comparison.
2. Do you agree or disagree that rebelling against one's parents' wishes is a normal part of growing up? Use some aspect of personal experience to support your point of view.

PREREADING

1. Tell about a time you were reunited with a family member after a long absence.
2. Did you or anyone you know ever move to a large city, having lived only in a small town or in a rural setting? Describe the first impression of the new surroundings.

◆ **VOCABULARY**

> *scrawny* (para. 10)—very skinny
> *wobbling* (para. 12)—moving unsurely or unsteadily
> *tattered* (para. 13)—torn, worn out
> *peered* (para. 13)—looked over
> *spindly* (para. 19)—long and skinny
> *skulked* (para. 23)—moved slowly
> *maudlin* (para. 23)—tearful
> *vibrato* (para. 24)—a quivering sound
> *mediocre* (para. 25)—average
> *daffodil* (para. 68)—a kind of yellow flower

Breath, Eyes, Memory
Edwidge Danticat

Edwidge Danticat was born in Haiti in 1969, where she was raised by her aunt. She was reunited with her parents in the United States at age twelve. She published her first writings after receiving a degree in French literature from Barnard College and an MFA from Brown University. Her short stories have appeared in more than twenty periodicals and national magazines.

In the following excerpt from Breath, Eyes, Memory, *she describes the reunion of her adolescent character Sophie with her mother in New York City.*

"I cannot believe that I am looking at you," she said. "You are my little girl. You are here."   1

She pinched my cheeks and patted my head.   2

"Say something," she urged. "Say something. Just speak to me.   3
Let me hear your voice."

She pressed my face against hers and held fast.   4

"How are you feeling?" she asked. "Did you have a nice plane   5
flight?"

I nodded.   6

"You must be very tired," she said. "Let us go home."   7

She grabbed my suitcase with one hand and my arm with the   8
other.

Outside it was overcast and cool.   9

"My goodness." Her scrawny body shivered. "I didn't even   10
bring you something to put over your dress."

She dropped the suitcase on the sidewalk, took off the denim   11
jacket she had on and guided my arms through the sleeves.

A line of cars stopped as we crossed the street to the parking   12
lot. She was wobbling under the weight of my suitcase.

She stopped in front of a pale yellow car with a long crack across   13
the windshield glass. The paint was peeling off the side door that she
opened for me. I peered inside and hesitated to climb onto the tat-
tered cushions on the seats.

She dropped the suitcase in the trunk and walked back to me.   14

"Don't be afraid. Go right in."   15

She tried to lift my body into the front seat but she stumbled   16
under my weight and quickly put me back down.

I climbed in and tried not to squirm. The sharp edge of a loose   17
spring was sticking into my thigh.

She sat in the driver's seat and turned on the engine. It made a   18
loud grating noise as though it were about to explode.

"We will soon be on our way," she said.   19

She rubbed her hands together and pressed her head back   20
against the seat. She did not look like the picture Tante Atie had on her
night table. Her face was long and hollow. Her hair had a blunt cut
and she had long spindly legs. She had dark circles under her eyes and,
as she smiled, lines of wrinkles tightened her expression. Her fingers
were scarred and sunburned. It was as though she had never stopped
working in the cane fields after all.

"It is ready now," she said.   21

She strapped the seatbelt across her flat chest, pressing herself   22
even further into the torn cushions. She leaned over and attached my
seatbelt as the car finally drove off.

Night had just fallen. Lights glowed everywhere. A long string of cars   23
sped along the highway, each like a single diamond on a very long
bracelet.

"We will be in the city soon," she said.   24

I still had not said anything to her.   25

"How is your Tante Atie?" she asked. "Does she still go to night   26
school?"

"Night school?"   27

"She told me once in a cassette that she was going to start night   28
school. Did she ever start it?"

"*Non.*"   29

"The old girl lost her nerve. She lost her fight. You should have   30
seen us when we were young. We always dreamt of becoming important women. We were going to be the first women doctors from my
mother's village. We would not stop at being doctors either. We were
going to be engineers too. Imagine our surprise when we found out
we had limits."

All the street lights were suddenly gone. The streets we drove   31
down now were dim and hazy. The windows were draped with bars;
black trash bags blew out into the night air.

There were young men standing on street corners, throwing   32
empty cans at passing cars. My mother swerved the car to avoid a
bottle that almost came crashing through the windshield.

"How is Lotus?" she asked. "Donald's wife, Madame Augustin."   33

"She is fine," I said.   34

"Atie has sent me cassettes about that. You know Lotus was not   35
meant to marry Donald. Your aunt Atie was supposed to. But the
heart is fickle, what can you say? When Lotus came along, he did not
want my sister anymore."

There was writing all over the building. As we walked towards it,   36
my mother nearly tripped over a man sleeping under a blanket of
newspapers.

"Your schooling is the only thing that will make people respect   37
you," my mother said as she put a key in the front door.

The thick dirty glass was covered with names written in graffiti   38
bubbles.

"You are going to work hard here," she said, "and no one is   39
going to break your heart because you cannot read or write. You have
a chance to become the kind of woman Atie and I have always wanted
to be. If you make something of yourself in life, we will all succeed.
You can *raise our heads.*"

A smell of old musty walls met us at the entrance to her apart-   40
ment. She closed the door behind her and dragged the suitcase inside.

"You wait for me here," she said, once we got inside. I stood on   41
the other side of a heavy door in the dark hall, waiting for her.

She disappeared behind a bedroom door. I wandered in and slid   42
my fingers across the table and chairs neatly lined up in the kitchen.
The tablecloth was shielded with a red plastic cover, the same blush
red as the sofa in the living room.

There were books scattered all over the counter. I flipped   43
through the pages quickly. The books had pictures of sick old people
in them and women dressed in white helping them.

I was startled to hear my name when she called it. "Sophie,   44
where are you?"

I ran back to the spot where she had left me. She was standing   45
there with a tall well-dressed doll at her side. The doll was caramel-
colored with a fine pointy noise.

"Come," she said. "We will show you to your room."   46

I followed her through a dark doorway. She turned on the light   47
and laid the doll down on a small day-bed by the window.

I kept my eyes on the blue wallpaper and the water stains that   48
crept from the ceiling down to the floor.

She kept staring at my face for a reaction.   49

"Don't you like it?" she asked.   50

"Yes. I like it. Thank you."   51

Sitting on the edge of the bed, she unbraided the doll's hair, tak-   52
ing out the ribbons and barrettes that matched the yellow dress. She
put them on a night table near the bed. There was a picture of her
and Tante Atie there. Tante Atie was holding a baby and my mother
had her hand around Tante Atie's shoulder.

I moved closer to get a better look at the baby in Tante Atie's   53
arms. I had never seen an infant picture of myself, but somehow
I knew that it was me. Who else could it have been? I looked
for traces in the child, a feature that was my mother's but still
mine too. It was the first time in my life that I noticed that I looked
like no one in my family. Not my mother. Not my Tante Atie. I
did not look like them when I was a baby and I did not look like
them now.

"If you don't like the room," my mother said, "we can always   54
change it."

She glanced at the picture as she picked up a small brush and   55
combed the doll's hair into a ponytail.

"I like the room fine," I stuttered.   56

She tied a rubber band around the doll's ponytail, then reached   57
under the bed for a small trunk.

She unbuttoned the back of the doll's dress and changed her   58
into a pajama set.

"You won't resent sharing your room, will you?" She stroked   59
the doll's back. "She is like a friend to me. She kept me company while
we were apart. It seems crazy, I know. A grown woman like me with
a doll. I am giving her to you now. You take good care of her."

She motioned for me to walk over and sit on her lap. I was not   60
sure that her thin legs would hold me without snapping. I walked
over and sat on her lap anyway.

"You're not going to be alone," she said. "I'm never going to be   61
farther than a few feet away. Do you understand that?"

She gently helped me down from her lap. Her knees seemed to   62
be weakening under my weight.

"Do you want to eat something? We can sit and talk. Or do you   63
want to go to bed?"

"Bed."   64

She reached over to unbutton the back of my dress.   65

"I can do that," I said.   66

"Do you want me to show you where I sleep, in case you need   67
me during the night?"

We went back to the living room. She unfolded the sofa and   68
turned it into a bed.

"This is where I'll be. You see, I'm not far away at all."   69

When we went back to the bedroom, I turned my back to her as   70
I undressed. She took the dress from me, opened the closet door, and
squeezed it in between some of her own.

The rumpled Mother's Day card was sticking out from my   71
dress pocket.

"What is that?" she asked, pulling it out.   72

She unfolded the card and began to read it. I lay down on the   73
bed and tried to slip under the yellow sheets. There was not enough
room for both me and the doll on the bed. I picked her up and laid her
down sideways. She still left little room for me.

My mother looked up from the card, walked over, and took the   74
doll out of the bed. She put her down carefully in a corner.

"Was that for me?" she asked looking down at the card.   75

"Tante Atie said I should give it to you."   76

"Did you know how much I loved daffodils when I was a girl?"   77

"Tante Atie told me."   78

She ran her fingers along the cardboard, over the empty space   79
where the daffodil had been.

"I haven't gone out and looked for daffodils since I've been here.   80
For all I know, they might not even have them here."

She ran the card along her cheek, then pressed it against her chest.   81

"Are there still lots of daffodils?"   82

"Oui," I said. "There are a lot of them."   83

Her face beamed even more than when she first saw me at the   84
airport. She bent down and kissed my forehead.

"Thank God for that," she said.   85

I couldn't fall asleep. At home, when I couldn't sleep, Tante Atie would   86
stay up with me. The two of us would sit by the window and Tante
Atie would tell me stories about our lives, about the way things had
been in the family, even before I was born. One time I asked her how
it was that I was born with a mother and no father. She told me the
story of a little girl who was born out of the petals of roses, water from
the stream, and a chunk of the sky. That little girl, she said was me.

As I lay in the dark, I heard my mother talking on the phone.   87

"Yes," she said in Creole. "She is very much here. In bone and   88
flesh. I cannot believe it myself."

Later that night, I heard that same voice screaming as though   89
someone was trying to kill her. I rushed over, but my mother was

alone thrashing against the sheets. I shook her and finally woke her up. When she saw me, she quickly covered her face with her hands and turned away.

"*Ou byen?* Are you all right?" I asked her.   90

She shook her head yes.   91

"It is the night," she said. "Sometimes, I see horrible visions in   92
my sleep."

"Do you have any tea you can boil?" I asked.   93

Tante Atie would have known all the right herbs.   94

"Don't worry, it will pass," she said, avoiding my eyes. "I will   95
be fine. I always am. The nightmares, they come and go."

There were sirens and loud radios blaring outside the building.   96

I climbed on the bed and tried to soothe her. She grabbed my   97
face and squeezed it between her palms.

"What is it? Are you scared too?" she asked. "Don't worry." She   98
pulled me down into the bed with her. "You can sleep here tonight if
you want. It's okay. I'm here."

She pulled the sheet over both our bodies. Her voice began to   99
fade as she drifted off to sleep.

I leaned back in the bed, listening to her snoring.   100

Soon, the morning light came creeping through the living room   101
window. I kept staring at the ceiling as I listened to her heart beating
along with the ticking clock.

"Sophie," she whispered. Her eyes were still closed. "Sophie, I   102
will never let you go again."

Tears burst out of her eyes when she opened them.   103

"Sophie, I am glad you are with me. We can get along, you and   104
me. I know we can."

She clung to my hand as she drifted back to sleep.   105

The sun stung my eyes as it came through the curtains. I slid   106
my hand out of hers to go to the bathroom. The grey linoleum felt
surprisingly warm under my feet. I looked at my red eyes in the
mirror while splashing cold water over my face. New eyes seemed
to be looking back at me. A new face all together. Someone who
had aged in one day, as though she had been through a time machine, rather than an airplane. Welcome to New York, this face
seemed to be saying. Accept your new life. I greeted the challenge,
like one greets a new day. As my mother's daughter and Tante
Atie's child.

◆ WORKING WITH WORDS

Most past tense verbs end in -ed. List past tense verbs in the text that do not end in -ed. (For example, *bent* [not *bended*] is the past tense of *bend*.)

◆ EXAMINING CONTENT

1. Describe Sophie's mother. You may use vocabulary from the story, but describe her in your own words.
2. How did Sophie know how to find her mother?
3. How did Tante Atie tell Sophie's mother about night school? Why?
4. Describe Sophie's impressions of the city.
5. What kind of card did Sophie make for her mother?
6. How had Sophie been able to fall asleep in Haiti?

◆ RESPONDING TO IDEAS

1. How do we know Sophie's mother was glad to have her back?
2. How do you think Sophie felt when she saw her mother?
3. Why do you think her mother had nightmares?
4. Do you think Sophie will miss Tante Atie?
5. What do you think was meant by the following: "*Your schooling is the only thing that will make people respect you*"?

◆ MORE WRITING TOPICS

1. Many relationships are important for a growing teenager, but a strong female role model is most important for a teenage girl. Agree or disagree, and support your point of view with personal or anecdotal evidence.
2. The most difficult time to have to adopt a new culture is early childhood? Adolescence? Young adulthood? Middle age? Old age? Make a good case to support your opinion.
3. Politicians and many others invoke the term *family values* frequently, as if it always meant the same thing to all people. What are family values? Are they the same in every family? Are they the same in every culture? Are they the same today as they were thirty or fifty years ago?

◆ MAKING THE FINAL COPY

Go back to your journal and look at the responses you have written to read-ings and questions from this chapter. After you have done that, select one of the following assignments; think about it, develop it, write it, and hand it in for a grade.

1. Write an essay about a member of your family in which you describe that person and her or his relationship to you. Wherever possible, use comparisons with some of the characters we discussed in this chapter.
2. Select one of the readings and write a play with the characters in it. Then perform the play for your classmates.
3. Write an essay agreeing or disagreeing with one of the following ideas:
   - ◆ Parents can have a strong influence on the personality development of their child.
   - ◆ People should take a course in parenting before they decide to have children.
   - ◆ All children, even adults, need approval from their parents.
4. Write an essay on the theme, "The Member of My Family Who Influ-enced Me the Most."
5. Write a letter to any one of the parents in any of the readings in this chapter. The purpose of the letter should be to try to tell them some-thing important that their own child could not or would not tell them.

If none of these assignments appeals to you, develop one of your own, of similar complexity, and work on that. Make sure you have your instruc-tor's approval of the assignment before you begin work.

Each of the suggested assignments is different, and each calls for a dif-ferent type of writing approach. All, however, require you to use your imag-ination, your familiarity with the reading, your empathy with the people in the readings, and your writing skills. Whether you are writing a dialogue, de-scribing a person, or explaining an event, use your best writing skills, and use complete sentences (with the possible exception of conversations). When you are finished, be sure to read over your work, edit it to the best of your ability, and don't be afraid to make changes and revisions. Do not hand it in until it is your best work.

◆ REVISING CHECKLIST

Read over the draft you have completed for the purpose of revising it—that is, improving the content. Use the questions below as a starting point for revision.

◆ Does the composition have an introduction? Does the introductory paragraph of the composition make the main idea of the composition clear? Remember, there is more than one way to respond and write an introduction. However, it must include the most important point.

◆ Is the development clear and specific? Remember to avoid generality. Be specific. For instance, if you are telling an anecdote remember to include the answers to *Where? When? Who? Why?* Be sure it is clear *how* the anecdote is related to the topic.

◆ Is the choice of language appropriate? Be aware of street language, slang and trendy expressions. Academic writing is usually more formal. (Of course, if you are writing dialogue, you have some flexibility in terms of writing in the way your characters would realistically speak.)

◆ Are any ideas repeated? Sometimes writers repeat and are not aware of it.

◆ Are any ideas not relevant and do these need to be deleted? Sometimes writers digress from the topic. Ask yourself after each sentence, "How does this relate to the ideas preceding and following it?"

◆ Is the conclusion appropriate? Does it reflect the main idea and let the reader know that the essay is ending?

◆ EDITING CHECKLIST

Now that you have written and revised your draft, it is time to edit it. Read it over once more, checking for mechanical errors. Use the following questions as a starting point for editing.

◆ Is each sentence complete? Avoid fragments. Does each sentence have a subject and a verb and make complete sense?

◆ How long are your sentences? Are they too long and contain too many commas? Remember, a comma may not connect two complete sentences. If necessary, refer to an English usage guide.

◆ Did you indent each paragraph? Are the paragraphs an appropriate length?

◆ Is your verb tense consistent? If you are telling an anecdote in the past, stay in the past. Do not switch to the present or another tense for no reason.

◆ Does subject and verb agreement exist, especially when the present tense is used? Remember, verbs may consist of more than one word. Make sure the auxiliary verbs are also correct.

◆ Are proper nouns capitalized? Does every sentence begin with a capital?

Read your draft over one last time before handing it in for a grade.

◆ EDITING EXERCISE

Always remember the following rules:

> Singular subject takes a verb ending with -s in the present tense.
> *The* **mother takes** *her children to the library every Sunday.*
> Plural subject takes a verb not ending in s in the present tense.
> *The* **mothers take** *their children to the library every Sunday.*
> Where there is an auxiliary, the auxiliary becomes plural or singular.
> *The* **father does** *play baseball with his sons on Sunday.*

Check the following sentences for errors in subject verb agreement. Make corrections if necessary.

1. The difference between Moira and Janet are remarkable.
2. One of my parents are coming to pick me up.
3. My family live in Quito, Ecuador.
4. Each of my cousins write an editorial for the school paper each week.
5. One of the books that my parents gave me are boring.
6. Half of the money that Fred and Gloria earned are gone.
7. The members of the family does not like each other.
8. There are a great deal of controversy as to who is the leader in my family.

◆ STUDENT DRAFT

Here is a student draft which is a response to "Remembering Lobo." Read it over and use the preceding checklists to make suggestions as to how to improve the composition for the final draft. Write a list of suggestions down and share them with the group.

"Remembering Lobo" is an outstanding short story to which   1
any Latino would respond favorably because it describe, almost
to perfection, how in every family there is that special someone
who is not your mother or father, but that has done more for
you than them. In this piece many Mexican customs are made
understandable for other people which are from a different
culture. Such is the case of "El Dia de los Muertos" that is the

day in which many Latinos, especially Mexicans honor and show their love and respect to those significant people in their lives that have passed away.

Another issue presented are the case of a family member who decides to dedicate her life to her niece and her brothers without expecting to receive anything in exchange but love. I believe that this situation is very common in my culture because many men and women don't accept the responsibility of being a parent. For this reason after the children are born they sometimes fall into the care of an older relative that usually do not have children. This relative takes it upon himself to raise the children and teach them well about how they should behave and most of the time they do so through their actions.

My grandmother is an example of a relative that sacrificed her time and had the patience to raise some one else's child: me. The circumstances for which I went to live with her were not because of my parents absence but even though my father was still alive she opened the doors of her heart, and gave a home to me. My "mama" teach all the good things that I have learned in learn and warned me about those that were bad. In fact, though we didn't always agree, she never left my side during bad times.

Nourishing me with her love, she gives me all the best that she had, but never hesitated to reprimand against the bad actions that I committed. As I grew, I learned what a treasure I had a home. She became my model and my inspiration. Today I have a family of my own and her teachings have helped me understand my own children. Without knowing it, my grandmother molded me into the woman I am today.

The author also highlights important issues of our life situation, specifically age. She tries to explain how elderly people don't want to feel like a burden others. Sometimes it is hard to interact with the elderly because they may become stubborn and even defensive. I believe that when we have a member of the family that is old and just wants to feel useful we should ease the environment and kind of humor that person. By acting that way we will be returning some of the love that we received.

Finally, there are always that special someone in everyone's life. From that person, that may not even share a blood bond with us, but we will always reap a lot of reward from that person and take our identity from him or her. These special people might not always say what we want them to, but they will nearby offering the support we need.

Questions for Discussion

1. What are the strengths of the preceding draft?
2. What are its weaknesses?
3. Compare this draft with your own.
4. Select the checklist questions that point out ways for improvement. Read them aloud and tell how you would answer these concerns.
5. Is the language always specific enough to discuss the ideas in "Remembering Lobo"? How could references to the text itself or specific instances in the writer's life strengthen the preceding draft?

4 Voices from Many Cultures

1. One definition of culture is "the systematic body of learned behavior that is transmitted from parents to children." What is *your* definition of culture?
2. What is your cultural heritage? What languages do you speak?
3. How has your family's cultural background affected your thoughts and habits? For example, what cultural traditions do you honor?
4. What did you learn from the preceding chapter ("Voices from the Family") about culture?

◆ **VOCABULARY**

gladiolus (para. 47)—an iris plant with large flowers
flout (para. 55)—to act with disregard or scorn toward someone or something

graveyard shift (para. 55)—night shift (for example, midnight until 8 A.M.) at a job

defected (para. 57)—turned against a cause, a party, or a people

translucent (para. 68)—able to pass light through, but not clearly or transparently

Homeland
Barbara Kingsolver

In the title story from her collection Homeland, *Barbara Kingsolver's eleven-year-old narrator remembers the time and wisdom shared with her elderly grandmother. In Great Mam's last summer, the poor coal-mining family takes a trip from Kentucky to Great Mam's Cherokee birthplace. The young girl's consciousness of the trip and of that time resonates in her memory, as does her special relationship with the woman whose background and wisdom distinguished her.*

To look at her, you would not have thought her an Indian. She 1
wore blue and lavender flowered dresses with hand-tatted collars, and brown lace-up shoes with sturdy high heels, and she smoked a regular pipe. She was tall, with bowed calves and a faintly bent-forward posture, spine straight and elbows out and palms forward, giving the impression that she was at any moment prepared to stoop and lift a burden of great bulk or weight. She spoke with a soft hill accent, and spoke properly. My great-grandfather had been an educated man, more prone in his lifetime to errors of judgment than errors of grammar.

Great Mam smoked her pipe mainly in the evenings, and al- 2
ways on the front porch. For a time I believed this was because my mother so vigorously objected to the smell, but Great Mam told me otherwise. A pipe had to be smoked outdoors, she said, where the smoke could return to the Beloved Old Father who gave us tobacco. When I asked her what she meant, she said she meant nothing special at all. It was just the simplest thing, like a bread-and-butter note you send to an aunt after she has fed you a meal.

I often sat with Great Mam in the evenings on our porch swing, 3
which was suspended by four thin, painted chains that squeaked. The air at night smelled of oil and dust, and faintly of livestock, for the man at the end of our lane kept hogs. Great Mam would strike a

match and suck the flame into her pipe, lighting her creased face in brief orange bursts.

"The small people are not very bright tonight," she would say, meaning the stars. She held surprising convictions, such as that in the daytime the small people walked among us. I could not begin to picture it.   4

"You mean down here in the world, or do you mean right here in Morning Glory?" I asked repeatedly. "Would they walk along with Jack and Nathan and me to school?"   5

She nodded. "They would."   6

"But why would they come *here*?" I asked.   7

"Well, why wouldn't they?" she said.   8

I thought about this for a while, entirely unconvinced.   9

"You don't ever have to be lonesome," she said. "That's one thing you never need be."   10

"But mightn't I step on one of them, if it got in my way and I didn't see it?"   11

Great Mam said, "No. They aren't that small."   12

She had particular names for many things, including the months. February she called "Hungry Month." She spoke of certain animals as if they were relatives our parents had neglected to tell us about. The cowering white dog that begged at our kitchen door she called "the sad little cousin." If she felt like it, on these evenings, she would tell me stories about the animals, their personalities and kindnesses and trickery, and the permanent physical markings they invariably earned by doing something they ought not to have done. "Remember that story," she often commanded at the end, and I would be stunned with guilt because my mind had wandered onto crickets and pencil erasers and Black Beauty.   13

"I might not remember," I told her. "It's too hard."   14

Great Mam allowed that I might *think* I had forgotten. "But you haven't. You'll keep it stored away," she said. "If it's important, your heart remembers."   15

I had known that hearts could break and sometimes even be attacked, with disastrous result, but I had not heard of hearts remembering. I was eleven years old. I did not trust any of my internal parts with the capacity of memory.   16

When the seasons changed, it never occurred to us to think to ourselves, "This will be Great Mam's last spring. Her last June apples.   17

Her last fresh roasting ears from the garden." She was like an old pine, whose accumulated years cause one to ponder how long it has stood, not how soon it will fall. Of all of us, I think Papa was the only one who believed she could die. He planned the trip to Tennessee. We children simply thought it was a great lark.

This was in June, following a bad spring during which the whole 18 southern spine of the Appalachians had broken out in a rash of wild-cat strikes. Papa was back to work at last, no longer home taking up kitchen-table space, but still Mother complained of having to make soups of neckbones and cut our school shoes open to bare our too-long toes to summer's dust, for the whole darn town to see. Papa pointed out that the whole darn town had been on the picket lines, and wouldn't pass judgment on the Murray kids if they ran their bare bottoms down Main Street. And what's more, he said, it wasn't his fault if John L. Lewis had sold him down the river.

My brothers and I thrilled to imagine ourselves racing naked 19 past the Post Office and the women shopping at Herman Ritchie's Market, but we did not laugh out loud. We didn't know exactly who Mr. John L. Lewis was, or what river Papa meant, but we knew not to expect much. The last thing we expected was a trip.

My brother Jack, because of his nature and superior age, was 20 suspicious from the outset. While Papa explained his plan, Jack made a point of pushing lima beans around his plate in single file to illustrate his boredom. It was 1955. Patti Page and Elvis were on the radio and high school boys were fighting their mothers over ducktails. Jack had a year to go before high school, but already the future was plainly evident.

He asked where in Tennessee we would be going, if we did go. 21 The three of us had not seen the far side of a county line.

"The Hiwassee Valley, where Great Mam was born," Papa said. 22

My brother Nathan grew interested when Jack laid down his 23 fork. Nathan was only eight, but he watched grownups. If there were no men around, he watched Jack.

"Eat your beans, Jack," Mother said. "I didn't put up these limas 24 last fall so you could torment them."

Jack stated, "I'm not eating no beans with guts in them." 25

Mother took a swat at Jack's arm. "Young man, you watch your 26 mouth. That's the insides of a hog, and a hog's a perfectly respectable animal to eat." Nathan was making noises with his throat. I tried not to make any face one way or the other.

Great Mam told Mother it would have been enough just to have   27
the limas, without the meat. "A person can live on green corn and
beans, Florence Ann," she said. "There's no shame in vegetables."

We knew what would happen next, and watched with interest.   28
"If I have to go out myself and throw a rock at a songbird," Mother
said, having deepened to the color of beetroot, "nobody is going to say
this family goes without meat!"

Mother was a tiny woman who wore stockings and shirt-   29
waists even to hoe the garden. She had yellow hair pinned in a
tight bun, with curly bangs in front. We waited with our chins
cupped in our palms for Papa's opinion of her plan to make a soup
of Robin Redbreast, but he got up from the table and rummaged
in the bureau drawer for the gas-station map. Great Mam ate
her beans in a careful way, as though each one had its own private
importance.

"Are we going to see Injuns?" Nathan asked, but no one an-   30
swered. Mother began making a great deal of noise clearing up the
dishes. We could hear her out in the kitchen, scrubbing.

Papa unfolded the Texaco map on the table and found where   31
Tennessee and North Carolina and Georgia came together in three
different pastel colors. Great Mam looked down at the colored lines
and squinted, holding the sides of her glasses. "Is this the Hiwassee
River?" she wanted to know.

"No, now those lines are highways," he said. "Red is interstate.   32
Blue is river."

"Well, what's this?"   33

He looked. "That's the state line."   34

"Now why would they put that on the map? You can't see it."   35

Papa flattened the creases of the map with his broad hand,   36
which were crisscrossed with fine black lines of coal dust, like a map
themselves, no matter how clean. "The Hiwassee Valley's got a town
in it now, it says 'Cherokee.' Right here."

"Well, those lines make my eyes smart," Great Mam said. "I'm   37
not going to look anymore."

The boys started to snicker, but Papa gave us a look that said   38
he meant business and sent us off to bed before it went any farther.

"Great Mam's blind as a post hole," Jack said once we were in   39
bed. "She don't know a road from a river."

"She don't know beans from taters," said Nathan.   40

"You boys hush up, I'm tired," I said. Jack and Nathan slept   41
lengthwise in the bed, and I slept across the top with my own blanket.

"Here's Great Mam," Nathan said. He sucked in his cheeks   42
and crossed his eyes and keeled over backward, bouncing us all on
the bedsprings. Jack punched him in the ribs, and Nathan started to
cry louder than he had to. I got up and sat by the bedroom door
hugging my knees, listening to Papa and Mother. I could hear them
in the kitchen.

"As if I hadn't put up with enough, John. It's not enough that   43
Murrays have populated God's earth without the benefit of marriage," Mother said. This was her usual starting point. She was legally
married to my father in a Baptist Church, a fact she could work into
any conversation.

"Well, I don't see why," she said, "if we never had the money to   44
take the kids anyplace before."

Papa's voice was quieter, and I couldn't hear his answers.   45

"Was this her idea, John, or yours?"   46

When Nathan and Jack were asleep I went to the window and   47
slipped over the sill. My feet landed where they always did, in the
cool mud of Mother's gladiolus patch alongside the house. Great
Mam did not believe in flower patches. Why take a hoe and kill all the
growing things in a piece of ground, and then plant others that have
been uprooted from somewhere else? This was what she asked me.
She thought Mother spent a fearful amount of time moving things
needlessly from one place to another.

"I see you, Waterbug," said Great Mam in the darkness, though   48
what she probably meant was that she heard me. All I could see was
the glow of her pipe bowl moving above the porch swing.

"Tell me the waterbug story tonight," I said, settling onto the   49
swing. The fireflies were blinking on and off in the black air above
the front yard.

"No, I won't," she said. The orange glow moved to her lap, and   50
faded from bright to dim. "I'll tell you another time."

The swing squeaked its sad song, and I thought about Ten-   51
nessee. It had never occurred to me that the place where Great Mam
had been a child was still on this earth. "Why'd you go away from
home?" I asked her.

"You have to marry outside your clan," she said. "That's law.   52
And all the people we knew were Bird Clan. All the others were gone.

So when Stewart Murray came and made baby eyes at me, I had to go with him." She laughed. "I liked his horse."

I imagined the two of them on a frisking, strong horse, crossing   53
the mountains to Kentucky. Great Mam with black hair. "Weren't you afraid to go?" I asked.

"Oh, yes I was. The canebrakes were high as a house. I was   54
afraid we'd get lost."

We were to leave on Saturday after Papa got off work. He   55
worked days then, after many graveyard-shift years during which we rarely saw him except asleep, snoring and waking throughout the afternoon, with Mother forever forced to shush us; it was too easy to forget someone was trying to sleep in daylight. My father was a soft-spoken man who sometimes drank but was never mean. He had thick black hair, no beard stubble at all nor hair on his chest, and a nose he called his Cherokee nose. Mother said she thanked the Lord that at least He had seen fit not to put that nose on her children. She also claimed he wore his hair long to flout her, although it wasn't truly long, in our opinion. His nickname in the mine was "Indian John."

There wasn't much to get ready for the trip. All we had to do in   56
the morning was wait for afternoon. Mother was in the house scrubbing so it would be clean when we came back. The primary business of Mother's life was scrubbing things, and she herself looked scrubbed. Her skin was the color of a clean boiled potato. We didn't get in her way.

My brothers were playing a ferocious game of cowboys and In-   57
dians in the backyard, but I soon defected to my own amusements along the yard's weedy borders, picking morning glories, pretending to be a June bride. I grew tired of trying to weave the flowers into my coarse hair and decided to give them to Great Mam. I went around to the front and came up the three porch steps in one jump, just exactly the way Mother said a lady wouldn't do.

"Surprise," I announced. "These are for you." The flowers were   58
already wilting in my hand.

"You shouldn't have picked those," she said.   59

"They were a present." I sat down, feeling stung.   60

"Those are not mine to have and not yours to pick," she said,   61
looking at me, not with anger but with intensity. Her brown pupils

were as dark as two pits in the earth. "A flower is alive, just as much as you are. A flower is your cousin. Didn't you know that?"

I said, No ma'am, that I didn't.   62

"Well, I'm telling you now, so you will know. Sometimes a per-   63
son has got to take a life, like a chicken's or a hog's when you need it. If you're hungry, then they're happy to give their flesh up to you because they're your relatives. But nobody is so hungry they need to kill a flower."

I said nothing.   64

"They ought to be left where they stand, Waterbug. You need to   65
leave them for the small people to see. When they die they'll fall where they are, and make a seed for next year."

"Nobody cared about these," I contended. "They weren't but   66
just weeds."

"It doesn't matter what they were or were not. It's a bad thing   67
to take for yourself something beautiful that belongs to everybody. Do you understand? To take it is a sin."

I didn't, and I did. I could sense something of wasted life in the   68
sticky leaves, translucent with death, and the purple flowers turning wrinkled and limp. I'd once brought home a balloon from a Ritchie child's birthday party, and it had shriveled and shrunk with just such a slow blue agony.

"I'm sorry," I said.   69

"It's all right." She patted my hands. "Just throw them over the   70
porch rail there, give them back to the ground. The small people will come and take them back."

I threw the flowers over the railing in a clump, and came back,   71
trying to rub the purple and green juices off my hands onto my dress. In my mother's eyes, this would have been the first sin of my afternoon. I understood the difference between Great Mam's rules and the Sunday-school variety, and that you could read Mother's Bible forward and backward and never find where it said it's a sin to pick flowers because they are our cousins.

"I'll try to remember," I said.   72

"I want you to," said Great Mam. "I want you to tell your children."   73

"I'm not going to have any children," I said. "No boy's going to   74
marry me. I'm too tall. I've got knob knees."

"Don't ever say you hate what you are." She tucked a loose sheaf   75
of black hair behind my ear. "It's an unkindness to those that made

you. That's like a red flower saying it's too red, do you see what
I mean?"

"I guess," I said.   76

"You will have children. And you'll remember about the flow-   77
ers," she said, and I felt the weight of these promises fall like a deer-
skin pack between my shoulder blades.

By four o'clock we were waiting so hard we heard the truck   78
crackle up the gravel road. Papa's truck was a rustcolored Ford with
complicated cracks hanging like spider webs in the corners of the
windshield. He jumped out with his long, blue-jean strides and patted the round front fender.

"Old Paint's had her oats," he said. "She's raring to go." This   79
was a game he played with Great Mam. Sometimes she would say,
"John Murray, you couldn't ride a mule with a saddle on it," and
she'd laugh, and we would for a moment see the woman who raised
Papa. Her bewilderment and pleasure, to have ended up with this
broad-shouldered boy.

Today she said nothing, and Papa went in for Mother. There   80
was only room for three in the cab, so Jack and Nathan and I climbed
into the back with the old quilt Mother gave us and a tarpaulin in
case of rain.

"What's she waiting for, her own funeral?" Jack asked me.   81

I looked at Great Mam, sitting still on the porch like a funny old   82
doll. The whole house was crooked, the stoop sagged almost to the
ground, and there sat Great Mam as straight as a schoolteacher's ruler.
Seeing her there, I fiercely wished to defend my feeling that I knew
her better than others did.

"She doesn't want to go," I said. I knew as soon as I'd spoken   83
that it was the absolute truth.

"That's stupid. She's the whole reason we're going. Why   84
wouldn't she want to go see her people?"

"I don't know, Jack," I said.   85

Papa and Mother eventually came out of the house, Papa in a   86
clean shirt already darkening under the arms, and Mother with her
Sunday purse, the scuff marks freshly covered with white shoe polish. She came down the front steps in the bent-over way she walked
when she wore high heels. Papa put his hand under Great Mam's
elbow and she silently climbed into the cab.

When he came around to the other side I asked him, "Are you   87
sure Great Mam wants to go?"

"Sure she does," he said. "She wants to see the place where she   88
grew up. Like what Morning Glory is to you."

"When I grow up I'm not never coming back to Morning Glory,"   89
Jack said.

"Me neither." Nathan spat over the side of the truck, the way   90
he'd seen men do.

"Don't spit, Nathan," Papa said.   91

"Shut up," Nathan said, after Papa had gotten in the truck and   92
shut the door.

The houses we passed had peeled paint and slumped porches   93
like our own, and they all wore coats of morning-glory vines, deli-
ciously textured and fat as fur coats. We pointed out to each other the
company men's houses, which had bright white paint and were
known to have indoor bathrooms. The deep ditches along the road,
filled with blackberry brambles and early goldenrod, ran past us like
rivers. On our walks to school we put these ditches to daily use prac-
ticing Duck and Cover, which was what our teachers felt we ought to
do when the Communists dropped the H-bomb.

"We'll see Indians in Tennessee," Jack said. I knew we would.   94
Great Mam had told me how it was.

"Great Mam don't look like an Indian," Nathan said.   95

"Shut up, Nathan," Jack said. "How do you know what an In-   96
dian looks like? You ever seen one?"

"She does so look like an Indian," I informed my brothers. "She   97
is one."

According to Papa we all looked like little Indians, I especially.   98
Mother hounded me continually to stay out of the sun, but by each
summer's end I was so dark-skinned my schoolmates teased me, saying I ought to be sent over to the Negro school.

"Are we going to be Indians when we grow up?" Nathan asked.   99

"No, stupid," said Jack. "We'll just be the same as we are now."   100

◆ WORKING WITH WORDS

Read each of the following phrases from the story, and explain in your own
words what each means.

1. *The small people* are not very bright tonight. (para. 4)
2. "the *sad little cousin.*" (para. 13)
3. We children simply thought it was *a great lark.* (para. 17)
4. "She *don't know beans from taters,*" said Nathan. (para. 40)
5. Stewart Murray came and *made baby eyes* at me. (para. 52)
6. "Old Paint's had her oats," he said. "*She's raring to go.*" (para. 79)

◆ EXAMINING CONTENT

1. When does this story take place?
2. Where is the family going and why?
3. Why did Great Mam marry outside her clan?
4. What were some of Great Mam's rules? Give an example from the story.
5. Why did Great Mam have unusual names for things? What were some of them?
6. How did Great Mam's rules differ from Sunday school rules?

◆ RESPONDING TO IDEAS

1. Describe the relationship the protagonist has with Great Mam.
2. What does the granddaughter learn from listening to her grandmother's stories?
3. What kind of stereotypes do people have about Native Americans?
4. What kind of cultural values are described in this story? How would you compare the culture of Great Mam with that of her eleven-year-old grandchild?
5. How significant is the gender of the narrator for the perspective of the story?

◆ MORE WRITING TOPICS

Read each of the following questions, and think about how to answer them. Then write a response essay suggested by these questions and answers.

1. What is culture?
2. What do all human beings have in common?
3. Is there such a thing as a common human culture?
4. How are traditions in a culture is handed down from generation to generation?

PREREADING

1. Can you think of cultural customs that are related to gender?
2. Do you know of any customs that discriminate against a group within a culture in a negative way? Describe them.
3. Ethnocentrism has been called "judging another culture by the values of one's own culture." Can you cite examples of this kind of thinking about cultural traditions and cultures?

◆ **VOCABULARY**

amah (para. 2)—a Chinese nurse
glutinous (para. 4)—sticky
concubine (para. 5)—mistress
pomegranates (para. 7)—a fruit with many seeds
jibes (para. 19)—mocking gestures or comments

Bound Feet and Western Dress
Pang-Mei Natasha Chang

In the following excerpt, Pan-Mei Natasha Chang tells about her experience with the Chinese custom of binding the feet of girls to make them more attractive according to an ancient cultural tradition.

You ask me about my childhood. In China there is a legend that says that the moon used to be inhabited by two sisters. Their brother lived in the sun. The sisters, who were very beautiful, became embarrassed because people gazed at them so much during the night. They asked their brother to change homes with them. He laughed and told them that there were many more people about in the daytime than at night, so that even more eyes would be turned upward toward them. The sisters assured him that they had a plan to prevent people from looking at them. So they changed places. The two sisters went to live in the sun and their brother in the moon. Now, if a person tries to look at the sisters, the two women immediately prick at his eyes with their seventy-two embroidery needles which are the sun's rays.

That is the full legend, but there are many versions. Sometimes the tale is told as if the sisters never leave the moon, and other times the story is told as if the sisters' only home is in the sun. These are the versions of the story I heard from my amah and my mama when I was little. My amah, who had grown up in the country and worked in the fields as a young girl, showed me the sisters in the moon and made me marvel at the beauty of their flowing silk robes and tiny embroidered slippers. Mama, who changed my life with one brave decision when I was three years old, taught me to imagine the sisters in the sun and to trust in the truth of things beyond sight.

My vision of the sky was filled with both pairs of sisters. At   3
night, when my amah undressed me and combed out the braids she had plaited for me in the morning, I looked out my window for the moon sisters and fell asleep with the comfort that they were there. Playing in the back courtyard during the day, I felt a glowlike heat at the top of my head and middle of my back and knew that the sisters in the sun were watching over me too. Because I had heard the two parts of the story separately as a child, both sides entered my heart; I saw the sisters in the sun, and I saw them in the moon.

On the twenty-third day of the twelfth lunar month of my third   4
year, six days before the New Year Festival, my family celebrated the Little New Year called the Festival of the Kitchen God. We were not country folk but observed this custom for the servants who believed in the folklore of the gods. During the year we hung the image of the Kitchen God above the cooking stove in the kitchen, lit incense and provided fresh fruit for him every day. On the day of the festival, the Kitchen God ascended to the heavens to note for the Supreme God the virtues and vices of the household he governed. To ensure a favorable report from the Kitchen God, the servants prepared a feast in his honor and placed especially sticky glutinous rice dumplings on the shrine before his image so his lips would remain closed upon reaching the heavens.

Because these dumplings, filled with red bean paste, are mushy   5
and tender, they are also supposed to soften the feet of little girls. It was the custom when I was little for a woman to have tiny, tiny feet. Westerners call them bound feet, but we call them something so much prettier in China: new moon or lotus petals, after the Tang Dynasty concubine who started the tradition. So beautiful a dancer was she that the Emperor had a larger-than-life lotus complete with pond constructed for her of metal and jewels, and, for his entertainment, asked

her to wrap her feet in strips of silk cloth and dance among the petals of the lotus. Her graceful dance steps were like the new moon flitting among the clouds in the reflection of a lotus pond. The Emperor was so impressed that other women began to wrap their feet and bend their arches in the crescent shape of the new moon. That is how the tradition began.

How small, how beautiful, then, the bounded foot. Give me your hand so you might see how it is done, how the toes of the feet are taught to curve gently around the sole of the foot until they touch your heel. Imagine your palm as the sole and your fingers as the toes. See how your fingers in your palm make a loose fist in the shape of a new moon? That is the bound foot—you end up walking on your heels and the knuckles of your toes—and if it is perfectly formed, you can slide three fingers into the niche between the toes and the heels.

My mother had three-inch feet that she had wrapped in fresh bandages every morning and bathed in perfumed water in the evening. When she walked, stiff-legged and sway-hipped, the tips of her embroidered slippers peeped out, first one and then the other, from the edge of her robe. My amah, who came from the countryside and whose feet were big like a man's, said if I was good I would grow up to be like my mother, pale and beautiful like one of the sisters in the moon. I had first seen these sisters at Moon Festival, the harvest celebration on the fifteenth day of the eighth month of the year, when the family ate round-layered pastries called mooncakes and pome-granates, which were in season. We then rose in the middle of the night to gather in the back courtyard, shivering in our nightclothes, and admire the harvest moon hanging full and heavy above us. I was two when my amah first bundled me in blankets in her arms and took me outside for the evening festivities. She told me to watch closely, to observe the swirl of mist around the moon and the faint craters in its surface. These were the signs of the sisters, she said, a hush of won-der in her voice. Then I saw them floating above me in the moon: two women in long lustrous robes and tiny silk slippers. Closing my eyes later that night, I still felt the luminous glare of the moon like a bright star in my head, and the two sisters drifted above me in my dreams.

On my third Festival of the Kitchen God, when I was three, my amah instructed me to eat an entire glutinous rice dumpling by myself. She said that it would help to soften me, but I did not know what she meant until the next morning. Mama and my amah arrived

6

7

8

at my bedside with a basin of warm water and strips of heavy white cotton. They soaked my feet in the water and then proceeded to bind them with the thick wet bandages. When the bandages completed their first tight wraps around my feet, I saw red in front of my eyes and could not breathe. It felt as if my feet had shrunk into tiny insects. I began shrieking with pain; I thought I would die.

"What are you crying for?" my amah scolded me. "Every little girl wants to have her feet bound." 9

Mama said I would grow used to it, that there was nothing she 10 could do. To keep me occupied, she set up a little chair in the kitchen so that I could spend the day watching the cook prepare the meals. Only the day before, I had taken it all for granted, run across this very floor. That day, my screams filled the household as long as my strength permitted. Before lunch, my father and brothers had come by to comfort me, but as the afternoon progressed only Mama and my amah appeared in the kitchen to calm me. I could not be silenced. I watched Cook's cleaver glint up and down, heard the chicken's bones crunch beneath his blows and shrieked at the sound of it. It was as if my own toes were breaking us as they curved beneath my soles.

Bound feet takes years of wrapping. The toe bones have to be 11 broken slowly, carefully. Even after a young girl's feet are perfectly formed, she has to keep them wrapped so they will stay in that shape. Prospective in-laws ask: "Did she complain much during her foot-binding years?" If yes, then they would think twice. She was a complainer, then, not obedient enough. Even at age three, I knew. If I was good, Mama and Baba would say that my feet were perfectly formed golden lilies, that I had been even-tempered and docile during those difficult years. But if this were not true, everyone would know. The Kitchen God would tell the Supreme God. The matchmaker would warn prospective families. The servants would gossip about me to other servants in the town. Everyone in Jiading knew the Chang family. If I was bad, no one would want me. I would not marry and would become a disgrace to my family. And still, I cried.

For three days I sat before my amah and Mama, enduring the 12 ritual: the removal of bloody bandages, the soaking, the rewrapping and tightening. But on the fourth morning something miraculous happened. Second Brother, who could no longer bear my screams, told Mama to stop hurting me.

"Take the bandages off," he said to Mama. "It is too painful   13
for her."

"If I weaken now," Mama said, "Yu-i will suffer in the end. Who   14
will marry her with big feet?"

Second Brother said that foot binding was a custom that was no   15
longer beautiful.

Mama asked Second Brother again who would marry me if she   16
let my feet alone. Second Brother then said: "I will take care of Yu-i if
no one marries her."

Second Brother was only fifteen at the time, but he had been   17
raised to be true to his word, and Mama relented. She called my amah
over to help undo the bindings, and from that day forth I never had
my feet bound again.

Shen jing bing. Crazy, my amah said about Mama's decision.   18
Even a few years later, when the Empress Dowager passed a series of
reforms banning foot binding, and Mama allowed my two younger
sisters to grow their feet, my amah worried for our future. Who would
marry us with big feet? We were *bu san, bu si,* neither three nor four.
We could not work in the fields all day long and do the chores of a
man. But neither could we just sit still and stay quiet like ladies in the
female quarters.

Flat and soundless, my feet became my talisman, guiding me   19
through a new, large, open world. In the kitchen I followed the cook
around from chopping block to stove and stood easily while peeling
shrimp or performing other chores; Mama sat in a chair far from the
fires and wearily gave orders. The power of my feet shielded me
from the jibes of my cousins; when they called me "little peasant
girl," I teased them back and ran away as fast as I could. Stalking
hard-shelled beetles in the back courtyard, I crushed them beneath
my heel if they tried to escape.

When I was twelve, Mama gave birth to the twelfth and last   20
child, Fourth Sister. Mama fainted during the delivery, and Baba, who
was the doctor, thought we were going to lose both her and the child.
He called Seventh and Eighth Brothers upstairs to Mama's room and
had the two of them urinate into a bowl, which he then passed directly under Mama's nose. Young boys' urine is strong like ammo-
nia, and Mama woke up. But we were all scared, and Mama remained
weak during Fourth Sister's early years, so I was the one who chewed

up rice for the baby to eat and took her out to play so that Mama could rest quietly in the house.

One day, as I was playing with Fourth Sister in the back court- 21 yard, I dropped her hard on the ground. Stunned, she burst out crying after a few seconds. My father, who happened to see her fall, immediately came running from the house. He scooped up Fourth Sister, then hit me hard across my face and said that I had to be more careful, that I ran around wild like a country girl.

It was the only time in my life that my father ever hit me, and I 22 stayed in the courtyard, crying, long after Baba had returned to the house with Fourth Sister. Later that afternoon Mama, who was still weak and almost never dirtied the soles of her slippers, came out of the house to sit beside me. Wiping away my tears with her hand, she held me close and said that it was hard to be as free as the sisters in the sky. No man could see them, Mama said, looking up at the sun with her half-closed eyes, but the sisters were there, dancing and playing happily in their new home.

◆ WORKING WITH WORDS

As you know, it is *very* important, particularly in academic writing, to use complete sentences. In some circumstances, however, you will see incomplete sentences, particularly in creative writing such as the piece from which the preceding excerpt was taken. For example, paragraph 6 begins with:

> How small, how beautiful, then, the bound foot.

Technically, this is an incomplete sentence; it has, after all, no verb. And yet, we understand the meaning, and the author's intent. Although it has no exclamation point at the end, it can be thought of as an exclamation. The author could easily have inserted a verb:

> How small, how beautiful, then, *is* the bound foot.

She obviously did not leave it out accidentally, but rather to achieve an effect.

Look at each of the exclamations that follow, and decide which are technically complete sentences. Rewrite the ones that are not, adding whatever is needed to complete them. Then be sure to examine the subtle differences between the two different ways of saying (essentially) the same thing.

1. Ow, my thumb!
2. The Yankees rule!
3. Oh, how completely and utterly ridiculous!
4. Excellent.
5. Good job, my friend!
6. What a jerk!

(Remember, for academic compositions, you want to write entirely in complete sentences, with an appropriate subject and verb. In creative assignments, particularly ones in which you are writing dialogue, you may want to use exclamations that are not complete sentences, because that is the way that people sometimes speak.)

✔ *A TIP:* Imperative sentences, also called commands, may *appear* to lack a subject:

> Take out your books.
> Go to hell.
> Call me Ishmael.
> Pass the biscuits, please.

They do have a subject. The convention in English is that the subject of each of these sentences is *You,* and the *You* is implied. There is an invisible *you* at the beginning of each of these imperative sentences. (If you reread them with a *You* in front, they make sense, although they sound a bit odd.)

◆ **EXAMINING CONTENT**

1. Summarize the legend about the sisters in the sky. What is its significance in the context of the story?
2. How did the tradition of foot-binding begin? Describe the process.
3. When was it outlawed? Why?
4. What was the author's response to having her feet bound?
5. Who rescued her? How will he help her if no one marries her?
6. After her feet were unbound, what was her response to having larger feet? What was her amah's response?

◆ RESPONDING TO IDEAS

1. What is your interpretation of the sisters who lived in the moon and the sisters who lived in the sun?
2. What does the tradition of foot-binding say about women's role in traditional Chinese society?
3. What effect do you think having unbound feet had on the author's sense of self? And if she had left her feet bound?
4. Can you think of cultural traditions from other countries that have to do with beauty and aesthetic values? Can you think of a cultural tradition that some people find normal or typical, but that other people find strange, or even shocking?

◆ MORE WRITING TOPICS

When several cultures exist within close proximity of one another, confusion, offense, and disruption often occur, particularly when the members of the different groups know very little about each other.

    With this in mind, read each of the following statements, and develop one into a response essay by agreeing or disagreeing with it:

1. Anything is acceptable if it is part of a culture's beliefs.
2. Mutilating the body for beauty is acceptable in a culture.
3. Ethnocentrism is learned at home.

◆ **PREREADING**

1. Do you ever worry about the effect of pollution on the environment?
2. Do you ever wish life could be simplified so that there was less waste of everything?
3. Have you ever been in a situation where you had to "make do" with what you had for an extended period?
4. Can you remember a time when people were happier and the world seemed safer? Do you think there ever was such a time?
5. Have you ever wondered about how it would be to live in a society that would be more peaceful?

◆ **VOCABULARY**

winnowing (para. 2)—getting rid of inferior elements of grain
ploughed [plowed] (para. 3)—turned the soil over, by means of a plow
mischievously (para. 4)—in the manner of good-natured fun
prosperity (para. 6)—state of being well off
sentient (para. 6)—conscious
fodder (para. 12)—food reserved for farm animals
ecology (para. 15)—a system of interrelationships between organisms within an environment

Ancient Futures: Learning from the Ladakh
Helen Norberg-Hodge

Helen Norberg-Hodge has long been a friend of the Ladakh people, a self-contained enclave of Buddhists in the Himalayas. She is also a student of their culture. In the following excerpt from Ancient Futures: Learning from the Ladakh, *she writes about the self-sufficient, frugal society in which the people seem to have a deep appreciation of interdependent community, where individual responsibility is considered a highly important trait. Crime, waste, and pollution are virtually unknown; people seem happy and peaceful and thus have much to teach the rest of the world. Norberg-Hodge, a linguist and researcher, was awarded the Alternative Nobel Prize, the Right Livelihood Award, in 1986. She is currently director of the Ladakh Project, founded in 1978, and its parent organization, the International Society for Ecology and Culture.*

Sonam had invited me home for Skangsol, the harvest festival. 1
I woke to the fragrant smell of burning *shukpa,* or juniper. Uncle
Phuntsog was walking from room to room carrying an incense burner,
the scent wafting into every corner. This daily ceremony ensures a
spiritual cleansing and is performed in all Buddhist houses.

I walked out onto the balcony. Whole families—grandfathers, 2
parents, children—were working in the fields, some cutting, some
stacking, others winnowing. Each activity had its own particular song.
The harvest lay in golden stacks, hundreds to a field, hardly allowing
the bare earth to show through. A clear light bathed the valley with
an intense brilliance. No ugly geometry had been imposed on this
land, no repetitive lines. Everything was easy to the eye, calming to
the soul.

Farther down the valley, a man sang to his animals as they 3
ploughed his fields:

Oh, you two great bulls, sons of the wild yak!
Your mother may be a cow, but you are like the tiger and the lion!
You are like the eagle, the king of birds!
Aren't you the dancers of the high peaks?
Aren't you the ones who take the mountains on your lap?
Aren't you the ones who drink the ocean in one gulp?
Oh, you two great bulls, Pull! Pull!

Above me on the roof, the deep, rumbling sound of the 4
zangstung, eight-foot-long copper horns, signaled that the ceremony
was about to begin. Like all religious occasions, this was a social event
too, and several guests had already arrived. Men and women were
being entertained in separate rooms. They were sitting at low tables
intricately carved with dragons and lotus flowers; on the walls were
frescoes many generations old. The men wore long homespun robes
(*gonchas*), some a natural beige color, some dyed the deep maroon of
the hills. Many wore a large turquoise earring and the traditional hairstyle—a plait at the back, with the front of the head shaved. The
women were dressed in fuller robes, topped with a waistcoat of bro-
cade. They wore magnificent jewelry—bracelets, rings, necklaces—
and dazzling *peraks,* headdresses studded with dozens of turquoises
and corals. An older man waved me over to sit down next to him.
"This is my new daughter-in-law," he said, introducing me to the others. His eyes sparkled mischievously as they all laughed.

Sonam circled his guests repeatedly, serving tea and *chang*.* As   5
he came to fill your glass, you were expected to refuse again and
again, even withdrawing your glass a few inches to prevent him from
pouring anything into it, and only then give way. Such polite refusal
(*dzangs choches*) sometimes takes the form of a song between the host
and his guest:

> *I shall not drink more* chang.
> *Only if someone can take the blue skies on his lap will I take* chang.
>
> *The Sun and Moon take the blue skies on their lap.*
> *Drink cool* chang! *Drink! Drink!*
>
> *I shall not drink more* chang.
> *Only if someone can braid the water of the streams will I take*
>   chang.
>
> *The fish with golden eyes braid the water of the streams.*
> *Drink cool* chang! *Drink! Drink!*

The monks were performing the ceremony in the family's altar   6
room, or *tchotkhang*. They had made pyramids of barley dough dec-
orated with butter and flower petals (*storma*) as offerings to the five
Dharmapalas, the protective deities of Buddhism. For two days now,
Sonam's family would celebrate *skangsol*; the harvest was completed,
and the farmer's year was starting a new cycle. Prayers were offered
for the happiness and prosperity not only of this one family, but for
every sentient being in the universe. The muted sounds of the monks'
chanting and the rhythmic beat of the drums could be heard throughout the village until dark.

Soon after I had arrived in Ladakh, I was washing some clothes in   7
a stream. Just as I was plunging a dirty dress into the water, a little girl,
no more than seven years old, came by from a village upstream. "You
can't put your clothes in that water," she said shyly. "People down there
have to drink it." She pointed to a village at least a mile farther down-
stream. "You can use that one over there; that's just for irrigation."

I was beginning to learn how Ladakhis manage to survive in   8
such a difficult environment. I was also beginning to learn the meaning of the word *frugality*. In the West, *frugality* conjures up images of

---

*chang (n.)—a fermented barley drink

old aunts and padlocked pantries. But the frugality you find in Ladakh, which is fundamental to the people's prosperity, is something quite different. Using limited resources in a careful way has nothing to do with miserliness; this is frugality in its original meaning of "fruitfulness": getting more out of little.

Where we would consider something completely worn out, exhausted of all possible worth, and would throw it away, Ladakhis will find some further use for it. Nothing whatever is just discarded. What cannot be eaten can be fed to the animals; what cannot be used as fuel can fertilize the land.   9

Sonam's grandmother, Abi-le, did not throw away the barley after making *chang* from it. She had already poured water over the boiled and fermented grain to make four separate brews. Then, instead of discarding it, she spread the grain on a yak-hair blanket to dry so it could later be ground for eating. She molded the crushed remains of apricot kernels, a dark brown paste from which oil had already been carefully squeezed, into the form of a small cup; later, when it had hardened, she would use the cup to turn her spindles. She even saved the dishwater, with its tiny bits of food, to provide a little extra nourishment for the animals.   10

Ladakhis patch their homespun robes until they can be patched no more. When winter demands that they wear two or three on top of each other, they put the best one on the inside to keep it in good condition for special occasions. When no amount of stitching can sustain a worn-out robe, it is packed with mud into a weak part of an irrigation channel to help prevent leakage.   11

Virtually all the plants, shrubs, and bushes that grow wild, either around the edges of irrigated land or in the mountains—what we would call "weeds"—are gathered and serve some useful purpose. *Burtse* is used for fuel and animal fodder; *yagdzas,* for the roofs of houses; the thorny *tsermang,* for building fences to keep animals out of fields and gardens; *demok,* as a red dye. Others are used for medicine, food, incense, and basket weaving.   12

The soil in the stables is dug up to be used as fertilizer, thus recycling animal urine. Dung is collected not only from the stables and pens, but also from the pastures. Even human night soil is not wasted. Each house has composting latrines consisting of a small room with a hole in the floor built above a vertical chute, usually one floor high. Earth and ash from the kitchen stove are added, thus aiding chemical   13 decomposition, producing better fertilizer, and eliminating smells. Once a year the latrine is emptied at ground level and the contents used on the fields.

In such ways Ladakhis traditionally have recycled everything. 14 There is literally no waste. With only scarce resources at their disposal, farmers have managed to attain almost complete self-reliance, dependent on the outside world only for salt, tea, and a few metals for cooking utensils and tools.

With each day and new experience in Ladakh, I gained a deeper 15 understanding of what this self-reliance meant. Concepts like "sustainability" and "ecology" had meant little to me when I first arrived. With the years, I not only came to respect the Ladakhis' successful adaptation to nature, but was also forced to reassess the Western lifestyle I had been accustomed to.

Some of my best memories of living closer to nature come from 16 experiences at the high pastures, or *phu*. For the animals too, the *phu* is the promised land. Earlier in the spring, the farmer has sung to them of the pleasures to come:

> *Oh, you beautiful beast, you strong beast!*
> *Your tail is long, and your horns reach to the sky!*
> *Please plough our fields,*
> *Please work hard for us now,*
> *And we will take you to the pastures*
> *Where you can eat long grass and flowers*
> *And do nothing all day!*
> *Oh, you beautiful beast!*

To reach the *phu* at Nyimaling, the "meadow of sun," we had to 17 cross the high Gongmaru La, a 17,500-foot pass. It would be a long day's journey. My friend Tsering and I would be coming back soon, but her sister, Deskit, and the children would stay up there with her uncle Norbu, making butter and cheese and collecting brushwood and dung. Over the summer, they would collect at least a tone of dried dung, to be used for cooking and basic heating in the coldest months of winter. The rest of the family would travel up and back every now and then to bring up bread, flour, and *chang* and to take back to the village what had been gathered.

The morning of our departure we were up early. We loaded the 18 donkeys with things we would need: warm clothes and blankets, sacks of barley flour, salt, tea, and dried apricots. By lunchtime we were nearing the head of the valley and stopped by the side of a melt-water stream. The mountain walls that rose steeply on both sides had shielded us from the harsh sun all morning, so we had made good time. But now it was getting hotter, and everyone welcomed the rest. Some twigs and dung were collected from the side of the path, and Tsering made a small fire. The salty butter tea was particularly wel-come; by now I had come to appreciate it. After a long walk in the dry heat, you feel the need to replenish the salt in your body, while your parched lips cry out for the butter to moisten them.

During the afternoon, as we climbed steadily upward, the ex-   19 traordinary beauty of the silent landscape filled me with a sense of exhilaration and profound joy. Nonetheless exertion at high altitude was difficult and, straining for breath and feeling light-headed, I had to stop for rests. Tsering, Deskit, and the children stopped too, though they all could have easily run up the slope. At sunset, we reached the top of the pass. We stood spellbound, gazing out on a vista of endless peaks and ranges burnished by the last rays of evening sun. We gave the customary cry, "*Kiki soso, lhar gyalo*" ("May the gods be victori-ous"), and took a few moments' rest at the *lhato*, the cairn with prayer flags that is the beacon of every mountain pass in Ladakh.

We arrived at the first houses of the *phu* in semidarkness; the   20 sun had set, but a glow remained for more than an hour, silhouetting the peaks in Zanskar a hundred miles away. With the darkening sky, stars began to appear. Standing in a doorway, Uncle Norbu surveyed the valley, checking that he had rounded up all the goats; they should be shut away in their pens before nightfall.

◆ WORKING WITH WORDS

Many of the English words that are used to describe the activities of farming have developed double meanings or have been generalized for use in our everyday lives. For example, *plowing* refers to the energetic, sometimes diffi-cult task of pushing or turning the soil. Have you ever heard anyone say that they are "plowing through their work" when they weren't referring to farm work at all? If you haven't heard anyone say that, can you figure out what was meant? We know what *planting a seed* means, but what about *planting an idea?*

It is likely that farming has given us so many words that are used figu-ratively in our language because at one time farming was a basic activity that touched everyone's lives more directly than it does today, especially in the modern industrial world.

Select five other words (not necessarily from the reading) that are related to farming, and show how they are sometimes used in a nonfarming figurative sense. (HINT: If you have difficulty beginning, try just making a long list of words that have something to do with farming. Afterwards, read through your list, and try to find "double meanings" in some of the words.)

◆ EXAMINING CONTENT

1. How did the author describe her impression of the valley in which Sonam lived?
2. Describe the ceremony of the harvest.
3. What is frugality according to the Ladakhis? Describe in your own words the examples Norberg-Hodge gives of frugal living among the Ladakhis.
4. Why would the Ladakhis wear their best robes under more worn-out robes in the winter?
5. What were the only items that the Ladakhis needed from the outside world?

◆ RESPONDING TO IDEAS

1. Why do you think the Ladakhis have learned to live so simply and conservatively?
2. How do you think we can learn from the Ladakhis with respect to ecological conservation?
3. The Ladakh religion, Tibetan Buddhism, teaches people to accept life's impermanence and that all living things are sacred. As the author puts it in a later section of the book,

   Rather than clinging to an idea of how things should be, they seem blessed with the ability to actively welcome things as they are. (p. 81)

   In what ways do you think this influences the way they live as described in the text?
4. In your opinion, will the Ladakhis survive as they are or will they change to be more like the rest of the world?
5. Can you imagine spending an extended period of time living with the Ladakhis, as Norberg-Hodge did? Why or why not?

◆ MORE WRITING TOPICS

Take a position, either pro or con, on one of the following topics, and develop it into an essay:

1. Ecological planning can save the planet.
2. One culture can learn from another culture.
3. It is wrong to eat meat, because animals, like all living creatures, are sacred.

◆ PREREADING

1. What holidays do you celebrate in your native culture?
2. Do you ever wonder how major religious holidays, such as Christmas, are celebrated in different cultures? Do you think it would be difficult to have fun at a celebration in a culture very different from your own?
3. Tell about a tradition related to food from a culture other than your own.

◆ VOCABULARY

disparity (para. 2)—inequality, marked difference

viscera (para. 4)—guts

grossness (para. 4)—great size and weight

expansively (para. 13)—with high spirits or generosity

rhapsodized (para. 35)—praised lavishly

kudu, gemsbok (para. 42), *duiker, steenbok* (para. 64)—game animals native to southern Africa: the gemsbok is a type of goat; the other three are types of antelope

corroborate (para. 66)—to support a statement by means of a second statement which agrees with the first

cryptic (para. 68)—puzzling; coded

manipulation (para. 75)—the act of moving something; by extension, influencing or effecting the behavior of others

viable (para. 76)—capable of living; capable of serving a particular purpose

Eating Christmas in the Kalahari
Richard Borshay Lee

The following essay was published in the scientific journal Anthropology, 98/99. *The author, Richard Borshay Lee, is a professor of anthropology at the University of Toronto. In this fascinating piece he tells about his experience sharing the celebration of Christmas while doing fieldwork among the !Kung Bushmen of the Kalahari.*

The !Kung Bushmen's knowledge of Christmas is thirdhand.   1
The London Missionary Society brought the holiday to the southern Tswana tribes in the early nineteenth century. Later, native catechists spread the idea far and wide among the Bantu-speaking pastoralists,

⇒ *NOTE:* The native language of the Bushmen of the Kalahari in southern Africa includes many sounds that are unique to it and are virtually impossible to render into the standard characters of the English alphabet. Anthropologists and linguists have developed a number of codes, such as the use of an exclamation point (!) or slash mark (/) to indicate some of these sounds, which include clicks made at the back of the throat.

even in the remotest corners of the Kalahari Desert. The Bushmen's idea of the Christmas story, stripped to its essentials, is "praise the birth of white man's god-chief"; what keeps their interest in the holiday high is the Tswana-Herero custom of slaughtering an ox for his Bushmen neighbors as an annual goodwill gesture. Since the 1930's, part of the Bushmen's annual round of activities has included a December congregation at the cattle posts for trading, marriage brokering, and several days of trance-dance feasting at which the local Tswana headman is host.

As a social anthropologist working with !Kung Bushmen, I   2
found that the Christmas ox custom suited by purposes. I had come to the Kalahari to study the hunting and gathering subsistence economy of the !Kung, and to accomplish this it was essential not to provide them with food, share my own food, or interfere in any way with their food-gathering activities. While liberal handouts of tobacco and medical supplies were appreciated, they were scarcely adequate to erase the glaring disparity in wealth between the anthropologist, who maintained a two-month inventory of canned goods, and the Bushmen, who rarely had a day's supply of food on hand. My approach, while paying off in terms of data, left me open to frequent accusations of stinginess and hard-heartedness. By their lights, I was a miser.

The Christmas ox was to be my way of saying thank you for the   3
cooperation of the past year; and since it was to be our last Christmas in the field, I determined to slaughter the largest, meatiest ox that money could buy, insuring that the feast and trance-dance would be a success.

Through December I kept my eyes open at the wells as the cat-   4
tle were brought down for watering. Several animals were offered, but none had quite the grossness that I had in mind. Then, ten days before the holiday, a Herero friend led an ox of astonishing size and mass up to our camp. It was solid black, stood five feet high at the

shoulder, had a five-foot span of horns, and must have weighed 1,200 pounds on the hoof. Food consumption calculations are my specialty, and I quickly figured that bones and viscera aside, there was enough meat—at least four pounds—for every man, woman, and child of the 150 Bushmen in the vicinity of /ai/ai who were expected at the feast.

Having found the right animal at last, I paid the Herero £20 ($56)   5
and asked him to keep the beast with his herd until Christmas day. The next morning word spread among the people that the big solid black one was the ox chosen by /ontah (my Bushman name; it means, roughly, "whitey") for the Christmas feast. That afternoon I received the first delegation. Ben!a, an outspoken sixty-year-old mother of five, came to the point slowly.

"Where were you planning to eat Christmas?"   6

"Right here at /ai/ai," I replied.   7

"Alone or with others?"   8

"I expect to invite all the people to eat Christmas with me."   9

"Eat what?"   10

"I have purchased Yehave's black ox, and I am going to slaugh-   11
ter and cook it."

"That's what we were told at the well but refused to believe it   12
until we heard it from yourself."

"Well, it's the black one," I replied expansively, although won-   13
dering what she was driving at.

"Oh, no!" Ben!a groaned, turning to her group. "They were   14
right." Turning back to me she asked, "Do you expect us to eat that bag of bones?"

"Bag of bones! It's the biggest ox at /ai/ai."   15

"Big, yes, but old. And thin. Everybody knows there's no meat   16
on that old ox. What did you expect us to eat off it, the horns?"

Everybody chuckled at Ben!a's one-liner as they walked away,   17
but all I could manage was a weak grin.

That evening it was the turn of the young men. They came to sit   18
at our evening fire. /gaugo, about my age, spoke to me man-to-man.

"/ontah, you have always been square with us," he lied. "What   19
has happened to change your heart? That sack of guts and bones of Yehave's will hardly feed one camp, let alone all the Bushmen around ai/ai." And he proceeded to enumerate the seven camps in the /ai/ai vicinity, family by family. "Perhaps you have forgotten that we are not few, but many. Or are you too blind to tell the

difference between a proper cow and an old wreck? That ox is thin to the point of death."

"Look, you guys," I retorted, "that is a beautiful animal, and   20
I'm sure you will eat it with pleasure at Christmas."

"Of course we will eat it; it's food. But it won't fill us up to the   21
point where we will have enough strength to dance. We will eat and go home to bed with stomachs rumbling."

That night as we turned in, I asked my wife, Nancy: "What did   22
you think of the black ox?"

"It looked enormous to me. Why?"   23

"Well, about eight different people have told me I got gypped;   24
that the ox is nothing but bones."

"What's the angle?" Nancy asked. "Did they have a better one   25
to sell?"

"No, they just said that it was going to be a grim Christmas be-   26
cause there won't be enough meat to go around. Maybe I'll get an in-dependent judge to look at the beast in the morning."

Bright and early, Halingisi, a Tswana cattle owner, appeared at   27
our camp. But before I could ask him to give me his opinion on Yehave's black ox, he gave me the eye signal that indicated a confi-dential chat. We left the camp and sat down.

"/ontah, I'm surprised at you: you've lived here for three years   28
and still haven't learned anything about cattle."

"But what else can a person do but choose the biggest, strongest   29
animal one can find?" I retorted.

"Look, just because an animal is big doesn't mean that it has   30
plenty of meat on it. The black one was a beauty when it was younger, but now it is thin to the point of death."

"Well I've already bought it. What can I do at this stage?"   31

"Bought it already? I thought you were just considering it. Well,   32
you'll have to kill and serve it, I suppose. But don't expect much of a dance to follow."

My spirits dropped rapidly. I could believe that Ben!a and   33
/gaugo just might be putting me on about the black ox, but Halingisi seemed to be an impartial critic. I went around that day feeling as though I had bought a lemon of a used car.

In the afternoon it was Tomazo's turn. Tomazo is a fine hunter,   34
a top trance performer . . . and one of my most reliable informants. He approached the subject of the Christmas cow as part of my continu-ing Bushman education.

"My friend, the way it is with us Bushmen," he began, "is that   35
we love meat. And even more than that, we love fat. When we hunt we
always search for the fat ones, the ones dripping with layers of white
fat: fat that turns into a clear, thick oil in the cooking pot, fat that slides
down your gullet, fills your stomach and gives you a roaring diar-
rhea," he rhapsodized.

"So, feeling as we do," he continued, "it gives us pain to be   36
served such a scrawny thing as Yehave's black ox. It is big, yes, and
no doubt its giant bones are good for soup, but fat is what we really
crave and so we will eat Christmas this year with a heavy heart."

The prospect of a gloomy Christmas now had me worried, so I   37
asked Tomazo what I could do about it.

"Look for a fat one, a young one . . . smaller, but fat. Fat enough   38
to make us //gom ('evacuate the bowels'), then we will be happy."

My suspicions were aroused when Tomazo said that he hap-   39
pened to know of a young, fat, barren cow that the owner was willing to part with. Was Tomazo working on commission, I wondered?
But I dispelled this unworthy thought when we approached the
Herero owner of the cow in question and found that he had decided
not to sell.

The scrawny wreck of a Christmas ox now became the talk of the   40
/ai/ai water hole and was the first news told to the outlying groups
as they began to come in from the bush for the feast. What finally convinced me that real trouble might be brewing was the visit from u!au,
an old conservative with a reputation for fierceness. His nickname
meant spear and referred to an incident thirty years ago in which he
had speared a man to death. He had an intense manner; fixing me
with his eyes, he said in clipped tones:

"I have only just heard about the black ox today, or else I would   41
have come here earlier. /ontah, do you honestly think you can serve
meat like that to people and avoid a fight?" He paused, letting the
implications sink in. "I don't mean fight you, /ontah; you are a white
man. I mean a fight between Bushmen. There are many fierce ones
here, and with such a small quantity of meat to distribute, how can
you give everybody a fair share? Someone is sure to accuse another
of taking too much or hogging all the choice pieces. Then you will
see what happens when some go hungry while others eat."

The possibility of at least a serious argument struck me as all   42
too real. I had witnessed the tension that surrounds the distribution
of meat from a kudu or gemsbok kill, and had documented many

arguments that sprang up from a real or imagined slight in meat distribution. The owners of a kill may spend up to two hours arranging and rearranging the piles of meat under the gaze of a circle of recipients before handing them out. And I also knew that the Christmas feast at /ai/ai would be bringing together groups that had feuded in the past.

Convinced now of the gravity of the situation, I went in earnest to search for a second cow; but all my inquiries failed to turn one up.   43

The Christmas feast was evidently going to be a disaster, and the incessant complaints about the meagerness of the ox had already taken the fun out of it for me. Moreover, I was getting bored with the wisecracks, and after losing my temper a few times, I resolved to serve the beast anyway. If the meat fell short, the hell with it. In the Bushmen idiom, I announced to all who would listen: 44

"I am a poor man and blind. If I have chosen one that is too old and too thin, we will eat it anyway and see if there is enough meat there to quiet the rumbling of our stomachs."   45

On hearing this speech, Ben!a offered me a rare word of comfort. "It's thin," she said philosophically, "but the bones will make a good soup."   46

At dawn Christmas morning, instinct told me to turn over the butchering and cooking to a friend and take off with Nancy to spend Christmas alone in the bush. But curiosity kept me from retreating. I wanted to see what such a scrawny ox looked like on butchering and if there *was* going to be a fight, I wanted to catch every word of it. Anthropologists are incurable that way.   47

The great beast was driven up to our dancing ground, and a shot in the forehead dropped it in its tracks. Then, freshly cut branches were heaped around the fallen carcass to receive the meat. Ten men volunteered to help with the cutting. I asked /gaugo to make the breast bone cut. This cut, which begins the butchering process for most large game, offers easy access for removal of the viscera. But it also allows the hunter to spot-check the amount of fat on the animal. A fat game animal carries a white layer up to an inch thick on the chest, while in a thin one, the knife will quickly cut to bone. All eyes fixed on his hand as /gaugo, dwarfed by the great carcass, knelt to the breast. The first cut opened a pool of solid white in the black skin. The second and third cut widened and deepened the creamy white. Still no bone. It was pure fat; it must have been two inches thick.   48

"Hey /gau," I burst out, "that ox is loaded with fat. What's this   49
about the ox being too thin to bother eating? Are you out of your mind?"

"Fat?" /gau shot back, "You call that fat? This wreck is thin,   50
sick, dead!" And he broke out laughing. So did everyone else. They
rolled on the ground, paralyzed with laughter. Everybody laughed
except me; I was thinking.

I ran back to the tent and burst in just as Nancy was getting up.   51
"Hey, the black ox. It's fat as hell! They were kidding about it being
too thin to eat. It was a joke or something. A put-on. Everyone is really
delighted with it!"

"Some joke," my wife replied. "It was so funny that you were   52
ready to pack up and leave /ai/ai."

If it had indeed been a joke, it had been an extraordinarily con-   53
vincing one, and tinged, I thought, with more than a touch of malice
as many jokes are. Nevertheless, that it was a joke lifted my spirits
considerably, and I returned to the butchering site where the shape of
the ox was rapidly disappearing under the axes and knives of the
butchers. The atmosphere had become festive. Grinning broadly, their
arms covered with blood well past the elbow, men packed chunks of
meat into the big cast-iron cooking pots, fifty pounds to the load, and
muttered and chuckled all the while about the thinness and worth-
lessness of the animal and /ontah's poor judgment.

We danced and ate that ox two days and two nights; we cooked   54
and distributed fourteen potfuls of meat and no one went home hungry and no fights broke out.

But the "joke" stayed in my mind. I had a growing feeling that   55
something important had happened in my relationship with the Bushmen and that the clue lay in the meaning of the joke. Several days
later, when most of the people had dispersed back to the bush camps,
I raised the question with Hakekgose, a Tswana man who had grown
up among the !Kung, married a !Kung girl, and who probably knew
their culture better than any other non-Bushman.

"With us whites," I began, "Christmas is supposed to be the day   56
of friendship and brotherly love. What I can't figure out is why the
Bushmen went to such lengths to criticize and belittle the ox I had
bought for the feast. The animal was perfectly good and their jokes
and wisecracks practically ruined the holiday for me."

"So it really did bother you," said Hakekgose. "Well, that's the   57
way they always talk. When I take my rifle and go hunting with them,

if I miss, they laugh at me for the rest of the day. But even if I hit and bring one down, it's no better. To them, the kill is always too small or too old or too thin; and as we sit down on the kill site to cook and eat the liver, they keep grumbling, even with their mouths full of meat. They say things like, 'Oh this is awful! What a worthless animal! Whatever made me think that this Tswana rascal could hunt!' "

"Is this the way outsiders are treated?" I asked.   58

"No, it is their custom; they talk that way to each other too. Go   59
and ask them."

/gaugo had been one of the most enthusiastic in making me feel   60
bad about the merit of the Christmas ox. I sought him out first.

"Why did you tell me the black ox was worthless, when you   61
could see that it was loaded with fat and meat?"

"It is our way," he said smiling. "We always like to fool people   62
about that. Say there is a Bushman who has been hunting. He must not come home and announce like a braggard, 'I have killed a big one in the bush!' He must first sit down in silence until I or someone else comes up to his fire and asks, 'What did you see today?' He replies quietly, 'Ah, I'm no good for hunting. I saw nothing at all [pause] just a little tiny one.' Then I smile to myself," /gaugo continued, "because I know he has killed something big."

"In the morning we make up a party of four or five people to cut   63
up and carry the meat back to the camp. When we arrive at the kill we examine it and cry out, 'You mean to say you have dragged us all the way out here in order to make us cart home your pile of bones? Oh, if I had known it was this thin I wouldn't have come.' Another one pipes up, 'People, to think I gave up a nice day in the shade for this. At home we may be hungry but at least we have nice cool water to drink.' If the horns are big, someone says, 'Did you think that some-how you were going to boil down the horns for soup?'

"To all this you must respond in kind. 'I agree,' you say, 'this   64
one is not worth the effort; let's just cook the liver for strength and leave the rest for the hyenas. It is not too late to hunt today and even a duiker or a steenbok would be better than this mess.'

"Then you set to work nevertheless; butcher the animal, carry   65
the meat back to the camp and everyone eats," /gaugo concluded.

Things were beginning to make sense. Next, I went to Tomazo.   66
He corroborated /gaugo's story of the obligatory insults over a kill and added a few details of his own.

"But," I asked, "why insult a man after he has gone to all that 67
trouble to track and kill an animal and when he is going to share the
meat with you so that your children will have something to eat?"

"Arrogance," was his cryptic answer. 68

"Arrogance?" 69

"Yes, when a young man kills much meat he comes to think of 70
himself as a chief or a big man, and he thinks of the rest of us as his
servants or inferiors. We can't accept this. We refuse one who boasts,
for someday his pride will make him kill somebody. So we always
speak of his meat as worthless. This way we cool his heart and make
him gentle."

"But why didn't you tell me this before?" I asked Tomazo with 71
some heat.

"Because you never asked me," said Tomazo, echoing the re- 72
frain that has come to haunt every field ethnographer.

The pieces now fell into place. I had known for a long time that 73
in situations of social conflict with Bushmen I held all the cards. I
was the only source of tobacco in a thousand square miles, and I was
not incapable of cutting an individual off for non-cooperation.
Though my boycott never lasted longer than a few days, it was an in-
dication of my strength. People resented my presence at the water
hole, yet simultaneously dreaded my leaving. In short I was a perfect target for the charge of arrogance and for the Bushmen tactic of
enforcing humility.

I had been taught an object lesson by the Bushmen; it had come 74
from an unexpected corner and had hurt me in a vulnerable area. For
the big black ox was to be the one totally generous, unstinting act of my
year at /ai/ai, and I was quite unprepared for the reaction I received.

As I read it, their message was this: There are no totally gener- 75
ous acts. All "acts" have an element of calculation. One black ox
slaughtered at Christmas does not wipe out a year of careful manipulation of gifts given to serve your own ends. After all, to kill an animal and share the meat with people is really no more than Bushmen
do for each other every day and with far less fanfare.

In the end, I had to admire how the Bushmen had played out 76
the farce—collectively straight-faced to the end. Curiously, the episode
reminded me of the *Good Soldier Schweik* and his marvelous encounters
with authority. Like Schweik, the Bushmen had retained a thorough-
going skepticism of good intentions. Was it this independence of spirit,

I wondered, that had kept them culturally viable in the face of generations of contact with more powerful societies, both black and white? The thought that the Bushmen were alive and well in the Kalahari was strangely comforting. Perhaps, armed with that independence and with their superb knowledge of their environment, they might yet survive the future.

◆ WORKING WITH WORDS

It is interesting to note that the essay you just read was "a Christmas story," yet there could hardly be found a single word in it that westerners, Christian or non-Christian, would associate with that holiday. Think about an article about Christmas (or any major holiday) that you might read in your current environment or in any other culture with which you are familiar. Make a list of ten vocabulary words that you might expect to find in such an article, words that might be challenging for a nonwestern reader, someone who has never celebrated the holiday in the manner of your imagined article. (For example, a !Kung Bushman reading an article about Christmas in the United States or England might be mystified by the word Christmas *carol*.) Define those words for such a reader.

◆ EXAMINING CONTENT

1. How did the Bushmen of the Kalahari learn to celebrate Christmas?
2. Why did Lee normally not share his food with the people he was studying?
3. How was Lee going to say thank you for the cooperation of the Bushmen?
4. What was the reaction of the people to the author's Christmas offering?
5. Why was Lee perplexed and confused?
6. Why did the Bushmen laugh?
7. How did the celebration end? Was it successful?

◆ RESPONDING TO IDEAS

1. Would you have reacted differently from the author to the experience of offering the Christmas gift?
2. Would you describe the author as patient or impatient? Why?

3. What manipulative practices did the author use with the !Kung during his stay? How do you think this affected the way they thought of him?
4. Did the author admire the Bushmen after the incident was over? Why or why not?
5. What can we learn from this story about culture and human interaction?
6. What do you think the Bushmen learned about the researcher's culture?
7. What is your overall impression of the author?

◆ MORE WRITING TOPICS

Respond to one of the following, either supporting it or contradicting it, by using evidence gained from your readings and/or your experiences:

1. Humor is cultural. What is funny in one culture may not be in another.
2. Although it is difficult, it is essential for people from different cultures to communicate carefully with one another.

◆ **PREREADING**

1. Do you believe that some people, like shamans, have special powers to affect a person's health?
2. Have you ever heard of someone being cured by unorthodox methods?
3. Do you think that the "success" of such methods is an accident?
4. Tell about a mysterious event that happened in your life.

◆ **VOCABULARY**

barrio (para. 6)—neighborhood, especially an Hispanic ghetto (loan word from Spanish)
racket (para. 9)—illegal scheme
badmouth (para. 14)—make negative remarks about, spread gossip
bombarded (para. 16)—to be bombed or hit repeatedly
paraphernalia (para. 23)—equipment

Doña Toña of Nineteenth Street
Louie "the Foot" Gonzalez

The following story is by the Mexican American writer from Sacramento, California, called Louie "the Foot" Gonzalez. The author remembers an experience when a neighborhood curandera—*a shamanistic wisewoman who cures by means of herbs and supernatural methods—helped his sick mother, an experience that speaks volumes about his culture.*

Her name was Doña Toña and I can't help but remember the   1
fear I had of the old lady. Maybe it was the way all the younger kids
talked about her:

"Ya, man. I saw her out one night and she was pulling some   2
weeds near the railroad tracks and her cat was meowing away like it
was ready to fight that big black dog and, man, she looked just like a
witch, like the Llorona trying to dig up her children."

"Martin's tellin' everybody that she was dancin' aroun' real slow   3
and singin' some witch songs in her backyard when it was dark and
everybody was asleep."

Doña Toña was always walking somewhere . . . anywhere . . .   4
even when she had no particular place to go. When she walked, it
was as though she were making a great effort because her right leg
was kind of funny. It dragged a little and it made her look as if her foot
were made of solid metal.

Her face was the color of lightly creamed coffee. The wrinkles   5
around her forehead and eyes were like the rings of a very old tree.
They gave her age as being somewhere around seventy-five years
old, but as I was to discover later, she was really eighty-nine. Even
though her eyes attracted much attention, they always gave way to
her mouth. Most of the people that I had observed looking at her directed their gaze at her mouth. Doña Toña had only one tooth to her
name and it was the strangest tooth I had ever seen. It was excep-
tionally long and it stuck out from her upper gum at a forty-five degree angle. What made it even stranger was that it was also twisted.
She at one time probably had an overabundance of teeth, until they
began to push against each other, twisting themselves, until she had
only one last tooth left. It was the toughest of them all, the king of the
hill, 'el mero chingón.'*

Doña Toña was born in 1885 in one of the innumerable little   6
towns of México. The Mexican Revolution of 1910 drove her from her
little-town home when she was twenty-seven years old. She escaped
the mass bloodshed of the Revolution by crossing the border into the
United States and living in countless towns from Los Angeles to Sacramento, where she became the most familiar sight in Barrio Cinco. She
was one of the barrio's landmarks; when you saw her, you knew that
you were in the barrio. She had been there longer than anyone else
and yet no one, except perhaps her daughter María, knew very much
about her. Some people said that was the way she wanted it. But as far
as I could see, she didn't show signs of wanting to be alone.

Whenever Doña Toña caught someone watching her during   7
one of her never-ending strolls, she would stop walking and look at
that person head-on. No one could keep staring at her once she had
started to stare back. There was something in Doña Toña's stare that

---

el mero chingón (Span.)—literally, "The Big Fish"

could make anybody feel like a child. Her crow-black eyes could hypnotize almost anybody. She could have probably put an owl to sleep with her stare.

Doña Toña was Little Feo's grandmother. She lived with her daughter, María, who was Little Feo's mother. All of Little Feo's ten years of life had passed without the outward lovingness that grandmothers are supposed to show. But the reason for it was Little Feo's own choice. 8

Whenever Little Feo, who was smaller, thinner, and darker than the rest of the barrio ten years old, was running around with us (Danny, Fat Charlie, Bighead, Joe Nuts, and a few other guys that lived close by) nobody would say anything about his "abuelita."* Before, whenever anybody used to make fun of her or use her for the punchline of a joke, Little Feo would get very quiet; his fists would begin to tighten and his face would turn a darker shade as all his blood rushed to his brain. One time when Fat Charlie said something like, "What's black and flies at night? Why . . . it's Feo's granny," Little Feo pounced on him faster than I had ever seen anybody pounce on someone before. Fat Charlie kicked the hell out of Little Feo, but he never cracked another joke like that again, at least not about Doña Toña. 9

Doña Toña was not taken very seriously by very many people until someone in the barrio got sick. Visits to Doctor Herida when someone got sick were common even though few people liked to go to him because he would just look at the patient and then scribble something on a prescription form and tell the sick one to take it next door to McAnaws Pharmacy to have it filled. Herida and the pharmacist had a racket going. When the medicine Herida prescribed didn't have the desired effect, the word was sent out in the barrio that Doña Toña was needed somewhere. Sometimes it was at the Osorio house, where Jaime was having trouble breathing, or the Canaguas place, where what's-her-name was gaining a lot of weight. Regardless of the illness, Doña Toña would always show up, even if she had to drag herself across the barrio to get to where she was needed; and, many times, that's exactly what she did. Once at the place of need, 10

---

abuelita (n., Span.)—literally, little grandmother

she did whatever it was she had to and then she left, asking nothing of anyone. Usually, within a short time of her visit—hours (if the illness were a natural one) or a day or two (if it were supernatural)—the patient would show signs of improvement.

Doña Toña was never bothered about not receiving any credit for her efforts.   11

"You see, comadre, I tol' you the medicina would estar' to work."   12

"Ándale, didn't I tell you that Doctor Herida knew what he was doing?"   13

"I didn't know what that stupid old lady thought she was going to accomplish by doing all the hocus-pocus with those useless herbs and plants of hers. Everybody knows that an old witch's magic is no match for a doctor's medicine. That crazy old WITCH."   14

And that's how it was. Doña Toña didn't seem to mind that they called on her to help them and, after she had done what she could, they proceeded to badmouth her. But that's the way it was and she didn't seem to mind.   15

I remember, perhaps best of all, the time my mother got sick. She was very pale and her whole body was sore. She went to see Doctor Herida and all he did was ask *her* what was wrong and, without even examining her, he prescribed something that she bought at McAnaws. When all the little blue pills were gone, the soreness of her bones and the paleness of her skin remained. Not wanting to go back to Herida's, my mother asked me to go get Doña Toña. I would have never gone to get the old lady, but I had never before seen my mother so sick. So I went.   16

On the way to Little Feo's house, which was only three blocks from my own, I saw Doña Toña walking towards me. When she was close enough to hear me, I began to speak but she cut me off, saying that she knew my mother was sick and had asked for her. I got a little scared because there was no way that she could have known that my mother had asked for her, yet she knew. My head was bombarded with thoughts that perhaps she might be a witch after all. I had the urge to run away from her but I didn't. I began to think that if she were a witch, why was she always helping people? Witches were bad people. And Doña Toña wasn't. It was at this point that my fear of her disappeared and, in its place, sprouted an intense curiosity.   17

Doña Toña and I reached my house and we climbed the ten steps   18
that led to the front door. I opened the door and waited for her to step
in first, but she motioned with her hand to me to lead the way.

Doña Toña looked like a little moving shadow as we walked   19
through the narrow hallway that ended at my mother's room. Her
leg dragged across the old faded linoleum floor making a dull scrap-
ing sound. I reached the room and opened the door. My mother was
half-asleep on the bed as Doña Toña entered. I walked in after her because I wanted to see what kind of magic she was going to have to
perform in order to save my mother; but as soon as Doña Toña began
taking some candles from her sack, my mother looked at me and told
me to go outside to play with the other kids.

I left the room but had no intentions of going outside to play.   20
My mother's bedroom was next to the bathroom and there was a
door that connected both of them. The bathroom could be locked
only from the inside, so my mother usually left it unlocked in case
some unexpected emergency came up. I went into the bathroom and,
without turning on the light, looked through the crack of the slightly
open door.

My mother was sprawled on the bed, face down. Her night   21
gown was open exposing her shoulder blades and back. Doña Toña
melted the bottoms of two candles and then placed one between the
shoulder blades and the other at the base of the spine. Doña Toña
began to pray as she pinched the area around the candles. Her move-
ments were almost imperceptible. The candlelight made her old
brown hands shine and her eyes looked like little moons. Doña Toña's
voice got louder as her hands moved faster across my mother's back.
The words she prayed were indecipherable even with the increase in
volume. The scene reminded me of a priest praying in Latin during
Mass, asking God to save us from damnation while no one knew what
he was saying. The wax from the candles slid down onto my mother's
back and shoulder blades, forming what looked like roots. It looked
as though there were two trees of wax growing out of her back.

About a half an hour went by before the candles had burned   22
themselves into oblivion, spreading wax all over my mother's back.
Doña Toña stopped praying and scraped the wax away. She reached
into the sack and pulled out a little baby food jar half-filled with something that resembled lard. She scooped some of the stuff out with her
hand and rubbed it over the areas that had been covered by the wax.

Next, she took from the sack a coffee can filled with an herb that looked like oregano. She sprinkled the herb over the lardlike substance and began rubbing it into the skin.

When she was almost finished, Doña Toña looked around the   23
room and stared straight into the dark opening of the bathroom. I felt that she knew I was behind the door but I stayed there anyway. She turned back to face my mother, bent down, and whispered something in her ear.

Doña Toña picked up all her paraphernalia and returned it to its   24
place in the sack. As she started to leave, she headed for the bathroom door. The heart in my chest almost exploded before I heard my mother's voice tell Doña Toña that she was leaving through the wrong door.

I hurried from the bathroom and ran through the other rooms   25
in the house so that I could catch Doña Toña to show her the way out. I reached her as she was closing the door to my mother's room and led her to the front of the house. As she was making her way down the stairs I heard her mumble something about "learning the secrets" then she looked up at me and smiled. I couldn't help but smile back because her face looked like a brown jack-o-lantern with only one strange tooth carved into it. Doña Toña turned to walk down the remaining four stairs. I was going to ask her what she had said, but by the time I had the words formed in my mind, she had reached the street and was on her way home.

I went back inside the house and looked in on my mother. She   26
was asleep. I knew that she was going to be all right and that it was not going to be because the "medicina" was beginning to work or because Doctor Herida knew what he was doing.

◆ WORKING WITH WORDS

Languages borrow from one another all the time. *Barrio* is a Spanish word that has been borrowed by the English language. In Spanish, the word for sweater is *sueter*. Make a list of as many words as you can that have been borrowed by English from other languages, and note which language they come from.

◆ EXAMINING CONTENT

1. Who is Doña Toña? What kind of reputation does she have?

2. When was Doña Toña called for?
3. Were the people who called her grateful?
4. What was wrong with the author's mother?
5. Describe how Doña Toña tried to cure her.
6. Was the author's mother cured?

◆ RESPONDING TO IDEAS

1. Why do you think people were not grateful for the *curandera*'s help?
2. What opinion does the author seem to have of Doña Toña?
3. Explain Little Feo's reaction to teasing about his *abuelita*.
4. Explain what is meant by this sentence in para. 10: "Herida and the pharmacist had a racket going." Have you ever heard of a racket like that before?
5. Why is the author curious as to what Doña Toña does while she is in the room with his mother?
6. Do you think that the *curandera* made a lasting impression on young Gonzalez? Why?
7. Can you think of any counterparts to the *curandera* in other cultures?

◆ MORE WRITING TOPICS

Respond to one or more of the following in a well-organized essay:

1. Some people have special powers.
2. Healers are common in many of the world's cultures.
3. There are many kinds of knowledge.

◆ MAKING THE FINAL COPY

In groups with your classmates, brainstorm (talk about and write down the first ideas that come to mind spontaneously) about the following topics. Take your brainstorming notes and develop them into a composition on the topic of culture.

◆ Describe parallel holidays, celebrations, or events in several cultures, comparing how the events differ according to the context.

◆ Every culture has its nonverbal signals. Compare two or more cultures with respect to their nonverbal signals.

◆ People often like to use shortcuts in describing people from a particular culture, categorizing them in stereotypes. Discuss common stereotypes, positive and negative, of several cultures. Be specific and give examples.

◆ Take any idea from the section in the chapter called "Responding to Ideas" and develop it into a four-paragraph composition.

◆ REVISING CHECKLIST

Read over the draft you have completed for the purpose of revising it—that is, improving the content. Use the following questions as a starting point for revision.

◆ Does the composition have an introduction? Does the introductory paragraph of the composition make the main idea of the composition clear? Remember, there is more than one way to respond and write an introduction. It must include the most important point, however.

◆ Is the development clear and specific? Remember to avoid generality. Be specific. For instance, if you are telling an anecdote, remember to include the answers to *Where? When? Who? Why?* Be sure it is clear *how* the anecdote is related to the topic.

◆ Is the choice of language appropriate? Be aware of street language, slang and trendy expressions. Academic writing is usually more formal. (Of course, if you are writing dialogue, you have some flexibility in terms of writing in the way your characters would realistically speak.)

◆ Are any ideas repeated? Sometimes writers repeat and are not aware of it.

◆ Are any ideas not relevant and do these need to be deleted? Sometimes writers digress from the topic. Ask yourself after each sentence, "How does this relate to the ideas preceding and following it?"

◆ Is the conclusion appropriate? Does it reflect the main idea and let the reader know that the essay is ending?

◆ EDITING CHECKLIST

Now that you have written and revised your draft, it is time to edit it. Read it over once more, checking for mechanical errors. Use the following questions as a starting point for editing.

◆ Is each sentence complete? Avoid fragments. Does each sentence have a subject and a verb and make complete sense?

◆ How long are your sentences? Are they too long and contain too many commas? Remember, a comma may not connect two complete sentences. If necessary, refer to an English usage guide.

◆ Did you indent each paragraph? Are the paragraphs an appropriate length?

◆ Is your verb tense consistent? If you are telling an anecdote in the past, stay in the past. Do not switch to the present or another tense for no reason.

◆ Does subject and verb agreement exist, especially when the present tense is used? Remember, verbs may consist of more than one word. Make sure the auxiliary verbs are also correct.

◆ Are proper nouns capitalized? Does every sentence begin with a capital?

◆ EDITING EXERCISE

Transition expressions signal a relationship between two ideas expressed in independent clauses. They help make writing logical and can be moved around within an independent clause. Take the word *however.*

> He enjoyed his travel among the Tibetans; *however,* he was glad to return home.
>
> OR
>
> *However,* the Tibetans seemed friendly and he decided to stay several weeks.

Here are common transitional expressions:

> *Adding an idea:* also, in addition, further, furthermore, moreover
> *Contrasting:* however, nevertheless, on the other hand, in contrast, still, on the contrary, rather, conversely
> *Providing an alternative:* instead, alternatively, otherwise
> *Showing similarity:* similarly, likewise
> *Showing a logical order:* first, second, third, then, next, later, subsequently, meanwhile, previously, finally, eventually

Showing results: as a result, consequently, therefore, accordingly, for this reason, thus

Affirming: of course, in fact, certainly, obviously, to be sure, undoubtedly, indeed

Giving examples: for example, for instance

Explaining: in other words

Adding more information: incidentally, by the way, besides

Summarizing: in short, generally, overall, all in all, in conclusion

---

⇒ *NOTE:* There is much flexibility in the placement of transitional phrases within a sentence. For example, here is a sentence (borrowed from a paragraph you will read in a moment) containing the common transitional phrase *on the other hand:*

> On the other hand, Japanese speakers believe that a quieter person might be able to empathize more easily by sensing the feelings of another person.

Observe what happens when the phrase is moved to a variety of locations within the same sentence.

◆ Japanese speakers, *on the other hand*, believe that a quieter person might be able to empathize more easily by sensing the feelings of another person.

◆ Japanese speakers believe, *on the other hand*, that a quieter person might be able to empathize more easily by sensing the feelings of another person.

◆ Japanese speakers believe that a quieter person, *on the other hand*, might be able to empathize more easily by sensing the feelings of another person.

◆ Japanese speakers believe that a quieter person might be able to empathize more easily, *on the other hand*, by sensing the feelings of another person.

Notice the subtle differences in the emphasis of the sentence that are conveyed by the different placement of the transitional phrase. Each of the preceding sentences means approximately the same thing; however, the emphasis of each is slightly different.

In the following paragraph, examine the transitional expressions and words that help link one idea to the other. (Refer to the meanings in the preceding list.)

> Americans, *in general,* find it difficult to remain silent for any length of time. *On the other hand,* Japanese speakers believe that a quieter person might be able to empathize more easily by sensing the feelings of another person. A Japanese speaker, *for example,* might trail sentences off rather than complete them because expressing ideas before knowing how they will be received seems rude. According to Lebra, a Japanese-born anthropologist, American businessmen will find such a style harder to take than the American up-front, more direct form of communication. *In addition,* Deborah Tannen, a linguist, has also found that female and masculine styles of communication follow these trends, with women tending to be indirect and men direct.

◆ STUDENT DRAFT

Here is a student draft responding to one of the suggested topics. Examine it in light of the previous exercise, as well as the revising and editing checklists. Meet with one or more classmates and suggest changes. Be sure to include the strengths of the composition, as well as its weaknesses, in your discussion.

> Nonverbal signals vary from culture to culture. For example, I am Mexican, and in my culture it is considered impolite to look someone directly in the face when you are speaking to them. Here in the United States, it is considered, in conclusion, rude when you don't look at a person's eyes when you speak to him or her.
> Subsequently, another difference is touching. In Latin countries, it is considered appropriate to touch someone as a sign of affection. When people meet, they kiss each other's cheek. Similarly, in England, however, this would be considered fresh. Another difference that I can cite is laughing. When someone laughs, it does not always mean he or she is having fun. Thirdly, in Asian countries, a laugh can mean embarrassment. A smile can mean someone doesn't understand what is said in Puerto Rico.

On the contrary, people have many different ways of dressing, standing, sitting, and holding their limbs that make a difference in meaning, depending on the culture. Furthermore, this makes living on the planet fun; we can always learn something new from someone from another culture.

✔ *A TIP:* Be careful not to *over*use transitional expressions. It is generally not a good idea to put one in sentence after sentence in a row. This can make your writing sound awkward or stilted. Read your work over and make sure it "sounds right" to you.

CHAPTER

5 Voices of Society

1. Have you ever moved away from one neighborhood to another? How did you feel about the change?
2. Can you think of a crossroads in your life, when you or someone in your family had a difficult decision to make that would improve your lifestyle? Describe it.
3. When a family has to move to another place, who suffers more, the children or the adults? Why?

◆ VOCABULARY

> *metamorphosis* (para. 10)—dramatic change
> *impeccably* (para. 12)—without flaws; perfectly
> *penchant* (para. 13)—preference

bourgeoisie (para. 29)—middle class

elite (para. 41)—upper class, or (adj.) having upper class or superior
characteristics

Only Twice I've Wished for Heaven
Dawn Turner Trice

Chicago Tribune *editor Dawn Turner Trice published her first novel,* Only Twice
I've Wished for Heaven, *in 1997. In the following excerpt from Chapter Three of
that book, she describes the protagonist Temmy's struggle with a dramatic change in
her life.*

I was only eleven years old but deeply rooted in our South Side   1
bungalow when my father moved my mother and me across town to
Lakeland. Our move took place in early September 1975. I remember
sitting in the backseat of our well-aged Volvo, which Daddy had spit-
shined himself the night before, picking at the tear in the vinyl between my legs. The more I picked and pulled at the wadding, the
easier it was to forget about the itchy ankle socks and the pleated skirt
my father had forced me to wear.

"Daughter of mine," he said, glaring at me over his shoulder.   2
"Daughter of mine" was his new way of referring to me. The words
fell clankety on my ears and felt completely inappropriate for two
people who had swapped bobbers and minnows and baseball cards,
including a 1968 Ernie Banks number that only I could have made
him part with. That particular one I kept by itself, wrapped in wax
paper in one of Daddy's old tackle boxes under my bed. Though my
mother never understood why a little girl would need such things—
including several pairs of All Stars that Mama made me lace in pink,
explaining only, "Because I said so!"—when cleaning my bedroom,
she always, always cleaned around them. She also demanded that
my father, from time to time, bring me roses in addition to model air-
planes and finely crafted fishing rods with walnut stock handles.

"Daughter of mine," Daddy continued. This time, he squinted   3
into the rearview mirror. "I won't ask you again to stop picking at
that seat. Sit up straight, dear."

"But—"   4

"No buts, Temmy, and close your legs. You're a young lady.   5
Didn't our talk last night mean anything? Weren't you listening?
We're almost there now. Sit up straight, I said."

I suppose my father's metamorphosis didn't happen all at once.   6
But it seemed that way to me. In truth, it was probably a gradual thing,
like an apple left sitting on a counter. One day it's all red and softly
curved and the next you find yourself slicing off sections, trying to
find places the mold and sunken-in dark spots haven't yet reached.
As we drove closer to Lakeland, I wanted just to shake my father, make
him wake up and come back to himself. I wanted him to shave off that
silly mustache he'd recently scratched out of his face and toss off
that too-tight striped necktie. The house, though sold, was still empty.
We could move back in, patch it up, make it pretty again, I thought. But
of course my thinking was simplistic. My father would never again
see the house at 13500 South Morrison Street as our home.

For me, our bungalow, our neighborhood, was the only home I'd   7
ever wanted to know. From the day I'd learned our address and our
telephone number by heart, it had become as much a part of me as my
name. My parents had created a life that was sturdy and robust, ex-
isting as so much color: yellow-and-blue-trimmed bungalows that
lined perfectly square city blocks; Miss Jane's red compact—the size
of Daddy's hand—which Mama said Miss Jane held like a shield
while sitting where the sunlight was best on her front porch, warding
off the years; and Mr. Jenkins's broad purple boxers that were always
line-drying on his back fence across the alley. How the prospect of
ivory towers and debutante balls could ever compare to this world
was completely beyond my understanding. I also wondered how my
father could not only choose Lakeland but yearn for it. It was a
lifestyle he'd once believed to be too "one size fits all," and as loosely
woven and thin as tissue paper.

At stoplights, Daddy busied himself by flicking lint off my   8
mother's sky blue cardigan and attempting to blot her perfectly
smudged lipstick. Mama batted his hand away, warning with side
glances that he was acting a fool.

"Thomas, you'll draw back a stub," she said calmly, refusing a   9
full head turn to her left. So, after Daddy pulled the radio's knob and
Mama pushed it back in (saying the static, all that popping and cracking, was trying her nerves), he folded several sheets of Kleenex and
wiped his loafers. These, I must say, were the same loafers that just one

year before he swore pinched his toes and were fit for nothing more than pulling weeds in our garden.

It used to be, before night school transformed my father from a   10
cabdriver into a teacher, that Daddy watched me with a sense of ceremony as I played in our backyard. He would watch as I skipped around our partially painted picnic table and climbed the bottom branches of our apple tree. He clapped when I completed a somersault; he cheered when I shattered the Coke bottle with the slingshot he'd seen me eye in the Woolworth two blocks from our house. And with him and often my mother as my audience, that tiny backyard—with its thick rows of collards and cramped tomato vines— grew under endless possibilities. Back then, Daddy admired my socks that rarely matched, and my prickly hair, his shade of red, which he once chuckled with Saville pride was so wild, a comb would break its neck getting through.

But on that morning, when my father reached a heavy hand   11
back toward me, it was only to brush wayward strands, forcing them, too, into submission.

The night before our move, Daddy rummaged through the house,   12
deciding what was fitting and proper to take to the kingdom of the drab and what was best left behind. We had packed most of our things and sent them ahead. What remained, the movers would take the following morning. There wasn't much need for furniture because Lakeland's apartments, Daddy said, were "impeccably" furnished. The only redeeming quality about that final night was that Mama allowed my friend Gerald Wayne to sleep over with me. We spent the early-evening hours in the backyard in my tent before going inside. It was one last opportunity to listen to all the crickets and grasshoppers and the pitter-patter of alley rats, whose size often put some cats to shame.

Gerald Wayne and I had been friends since the second grade.   13
Though I had seen him often in school, we met one Saturday while he was sitting on the curb in front of Wilson's Fix-It shop, playing by himself, as he often had. (I inherited both my parents' penchant for the down-and-out.) I just happened to be walking by, when he looked up at me, smiled, exposing two vacant spaces where front teeth should have been, and said in a most sincere voice, "You dare me eat this worm?" Had he given me ample time, I suppose I would indeed have considered the question. Only he didn't. Before I could utter a word,

he dangled the worm over his mouth, let the squirmy little thing stare into his tonsils, then scarfed it down. Oh, he was nasty. He didn't even flinch.

Children always teased Gerald because of his dietary habits. But   14
he had yet another unbearable affliction: He reeked—smelled just like a goat. None of us truly understood why, especially with his family living on the west side of the el train tracks, near the old soap factory. I suppose we thought proximity alone would have an impact on his condition. Even back then, Gerald was the cutest little boy in the second grade. He had smooth brown skin, dark brown eyes that twinkled, and a smile that sometimes made even me feel faint. But he had this black cloud that formed a capsule around his entire body. It was as if no other part of the atmosphere would allow it to enter, so it clung to Gerald for dear life. It even shimmied in the moonlight. Mama said all the child needed was a bath. Daddy later obliged him with one and threatened that if he didn't make "dipping" himself part of his daily routine, he would be banned from our house. Gerald liked having a friend, so he washed, religiously.

The night before we moved, Gerald and I sat in my tent with   15
our legs crossed and the flashlight dimming between us as we sighed, grasping for topics that didn't smack of corny recollections or mushy farewells.

"My dad said you guys are lucky to be moving to Lakeland,"   16
Gerald said, interrupting several seconds of silence. "The construction company he works for helped build it. 'Yep,' he said, 'the Savilles are some lucky black people.' "

"Oh, shut up, Gerald," I said, choking back tears. "Nobody's   17
lucky to be going, nowhere—I mean, anywhere." Daddy had begun to drill me on my double negatives.

Outside the tent, a soft breeze nudged the wind chimes on the   18
back porch, which alone held many of my childhood memories. It was there where Gerald helped me dig a hole to bury the horrendous Cinderella dress our neighbor Miss Jane had bought one Christmas, expecting me to wear it to church with her. Mama knew I had buried it back there. She pretended not to see one of the bells jutting up from the ground. But she never said anything, because she hated it, too. In the knotholes in the pine of the banister I had stuffed so many wads of purple and green bubble gum that after several years, they seemed to hold the old rickety thing together. And once I had even caught

Mama and Daddy under that porch, moaning and touching one another in places that made me giggle.

Feeling sick, I opened the flap of the tent. I told Gerald I had to use   19
the bathroom, then went into the house to find my father. I didn't want
Gerald to see one teardrop. I don't know when it happened, but Gerald considered himself my protector, my shadow and shield. No, I'm
not sure when it happened, because I was the one who often protected
him. Like the day I had rubbed his head when Sandy Roberts shoved
him to the ground. Daddy had told him that it was never acceptable
for a boy to fight a girl, so Gerald couldn't hit her back. But I could.

In the house, I saw my father scurrying about and I wondered   20
what was lifting him, when my mother and I felt to leave was one of
the most wrenching things that could happen to us. One final box,
marked Garvey, Du Bois, Merton, and Robeson sat in the hallway.
My father had so many books that the movers had to make two trips
for them alone. He was about to prop the box against the door when
he noticed me staring at him.

"Hey, princess," he said.   21

"Hey," I said, picking at the newly painted lime green wall. I   22
unpigeoned my feet, remembering my mother's warnings about them
one day turning completely inward.

"You okay? Seems like you got something on your mind. At   23
least I hope you aren't so rude that you'd leave my boy out there by
himself for nothing. Come here." He reached out to me with those
huge arms of his and made me sit on his lap.

"I don't want to leave," I muttered.   24

"Daughter of mine," he said. "I thought we talked about this. It's   25
a once-in-a-lifetime opportunity, dear. There's a waiting list a mile
long to get into Lakeland. And our name"—he thumped my chest,
then his—"our name was pulled in the lottery. Where we're going is
a much better place than this."

He brushed his hair back in frustration, revealing a row of red-   26
dish gray strands. Then he looked up at the top of the stairs, where
Mama was standing, folding towels. She, too, was listening; she, too,
needed another dose of convincing. At first, my father looked everywhere except directly at me. I followed his gaze to the empty living
room. Without furniture, it was all too apparent the floor sloped too
much toward the fake fireplace, and oddly, the room seemed smaller
than it had before.

"Lakeland is a wonderful place," he said finally. "That apart-   27
ment will be three times the size of this old place. You'll have your
own huge bedroom with your own balcony. . . ." He paused. "Temmy,
you're too young to understand this, but soon this neighborhood will
have gone to pot. Already young boys are hanging out on the corners. It won't be long before this place won't be worth half of what we
paid for it."

"I don't care," I moaned.   28

"You haven't heard one word, have you, honey?" Daddy took   29
a long, deep breath. "There was a time, when I first met your mama,
that I would never have been considering living among the 'bourgeoisie.' But there comes a time when you have to mix some ideas.
You get older and understand that nothing is all good; nothing is all
bad. You know why I decided to go back to school? I wanted to give
you somebody who does more than drive a cab, and write letters to
newspapers and hand our pamphlets in his spare time. I had to ask
myself, What more could I offer my wife, my daughter? In a few
months, you'll be twelve years old. Soon, you'll be going off to college.
I want you to be proud of where you come from and I want you to be
proud of me. I'll be a teacher, honey. Your old man a teacher at a fine,
fine school."

As I walked back to the tent, I wondered what I had done. I had   30
always been proud of my father, and I wondered when he thought I'd
begun to feel otherwise.

Down the hall from the stairs was a small, pantry-sized room   31
that my father had used as his office. There were no windows, just his
cold marble-topped desk and his favorite leather chair, cracked and
worn, tired-looking from years and years of our weight. Daddy had
found the set in an alley in the downtown legal district one afternoon
while picking up a fare. He brought it home and dusted it off, and
many nights I would stop in just before bed. Though I rarely understood the depth of Emerson or Tolstoy, I knew it was nearly impossible for me to find slumber without the melody of his baritone rocking
me to sleep. Those nights, I believed with all my heart that as the
years passed and my legs would begin to dangle far below my father's lap, below the final bar of missing gold tacks, we would always fit into the perfectly molded cushion that we'd created. That
was until my father decided to leave the set behind.

Gerald had fallen asleep. I knew this as soon as I reached the   32
kitchen, which led to the back porch. For such a small child, he had

a tremendous snore, thunderous snatches of gasping and wheezing. Mama and I stood on the porch for a second, listening to him, watching his figure, silhouetted by the light, heave up and down.

"You know everything's going to be okay, don't you, Temmy?"   33
she asked. For years I told myself—I suppose because everybody seemed to agree—I looked just like my father. But that was because of the hair. The red hair tended to blind people to the rest of my features. The truth was that I had a lot of my mother's face, her broad eyes, olive-brown complexion, and heavy, good-for-whistling lips. That night, Mama didn't wait for an answer. I suppose she knew I didn't have one.

"Stay out fifteen more minutes, Tem," she said. "Then I'll come   34
get you both ready for bed." She smiled at me, then kissed me on the lips.

The next morning, I awoke to the scent of my mother's coun-   35
try bacon. I jumped out of bed and ran to wake Gerald in the guest room. By the time I got there, he was already watching the sun rise over the Jenkinses' tree house across the alley, and the garbagemen, sweaty, their pants sliding down their butts, hurl huge barrels of our un-Lakeland-like belongings into their truck. Too soon afterward, it was time to leave. I gave him my new address and he promised to write and visit as soon as he could. From my backseat in the car, I watched my friend, hands crammed into the pockets of his baggy jeans, turn and head for his side of the tracks. I waved, but he didn't see me. Still, I continued until we turned the corner at Alexander Street, and soon the house, Gerald, the Woolworth, everything, leaned in the distance and eventually was completely out of sight.

The clock on the gate showed 10:00 A.M. when our car pulled   36
up. My father made certain it was ten exactly. The guard said, "Good morning and welcome to Lakeland." He checked Daddy's driver's license against a clipboard of notes, then handed him a map and showed us how to maneuver Lakeland's labyrinth of twists and turns to the Five forty-five building, our new home. Finally, he opened a massive iron gate that groaned as it parted, and we were allowed in.

As I looked out the car window, my fingers began to tingle and   37
turn cold. Let my father tell it: This place was straight out of a fairy tale. One square mile of rich black soil carved out of the ghetto. One square mile of ivory towers, emerald green grass, and pruned oaks and willows so stately, they rivaled those in the suburbs and made the

newly planted frail trees in the projects beyond the fence blend into the shade. The four high-rise apartment buildings were the tallest structures I'd ever seen, and already janitors were hanging from scaffolds, washing beveled-glass windows, making sure everything shined in tandem.

Men, women, and children were out in droves, reading under the trees, sitting on hand-carved wooden benches, or walking dogs along winding cobblestone streets—appropriately named Martin Luther King, Jr., Drive, Langston Hughes Parkway, Ida B. Wells Lane. When we passed a field of children taking turns riding a pony, I got on my knees to look out the back window. Then, remembering my father's warnings, I slid back down the vinyl. I was surprised to see him smiling at me in the rearview mirror. We turned onto a path that followed the lake, and a flock of white gulls flew over the car. I scooted from one side of the seat to the other to watch their pearl gray wings stretching across the sky as they squawked like restless, hungry babies, back and forth between the rocks and a lighthouse in the middle of the water. 38

In Lakeland, Daddy said, was the world's wealth of top black professionals: surgeons, engineers, politicians. Lakeland had begun in the early 1960s as part of Chicago's Life Incentive Project. As an apology to the rat-infested and blighted tenement houses blacks had to endure during the migration, the mayor garnered support from the state capital to the White House to build this urban utopia. It was an idyllic community, stripped of limitations and bounds. According to the *Sentinel*'s annual obligatory article, Lakeland had every amenity: a twenty-seven-hole golf course, an Olympic-size swimming pool, coffeehouses with the classics lining oak shelves, and an academy whose students were groomed and pointed, some said from the womb, in the direction of either Morehouse, Spelman, Harvard, or Yale. Even Lakeland's section of Lake Michigan was different from that of every other community that bordered the shore. In Lakeland, the water was heavily filtered and chlorinated—sometimes even helped along by food coloring—to look the aqua blue of dreams. 39

This generation of residents, once removed from salt pork, fatback, and biscuits, now dined on caviar and escargot. Neatly draped Battenberg lace scarves on marcelled heads replaced dingy do-rags and stocking caps. And plump, curved saffron to dark brown behinds that once jiggled like jelly and made little boys long 40 to be men were now girdled and clamped down, as stiff and rigid as paddleboards.

Despite what lay outside the fence on Thirty-fifth Street, what-   41
ever the world had told black people they couldn't do or be or wish for, it didn't apply to the residents of Lakeland. Within the confines of that ivy-lined wrought-iron fence lived this elite group of people who had been allowed to purge their minds of all those things that re-minded them of what it meant to be poor and downtrodden. Once here, Lakelandites didn't look back. They surely didn't want to go back. All they had to do was sign a two-part contract in which they agreed to pay a monthly rent that was lower than the average mort-gage. And they vowed to put their bodies and their beliefs into this great blender and leave it there until the whitewashed folk who came out no longer resembled the pageant of folk who had entered. The women made the Stepford Wives look like members of the Rainbow Coalition. The men, with their expensive pipes, plaid pants, and stiff white collars, were about as individual as the curds in white milk.

"This is Lakeland," Daddy said, pulling up in front of our build-   42
ing. He beamed almost as if he had built the place, or, worse yet, birthed it.

He patted the steering wheel and told the Volvo to be nice. For   43
his sake, I was hoping it wouldn't sputter and spit the way it usually did when he turned it off. I was happy it didn't embarrass him. A doorman rushed the car, opening the door for my mother, then for me. Solemnly, Mama and I walked up a slight incline to the oak dou-ble doors, which led to a lobby of glittering marble and crystal. Daddy, however, floated in on air.

◆ WORKING WITH WORDS

Which three of the vocabulary words listed for this selection are derived from the French language? Look them up in a dictionary that provides the ety-mology of words, and explain their derivations.

◆ EXAMINING CONTENT

1. What is a "1968 Ernie Banks number"? (para. 2)

2. How did Temmy feel about the home she was leaving? How did she anticipate her new home?

3. Why did her father feel it was best to move?

4. Tell two things Gerald Wayne was known to do (or *not* do) in order to attract attention to himself.

5. What was in the boxes "marked Garvey, Du Bois, Merton, and Robeson"? (para. 20)

◆ RESPONDING TO IDEAS

1. How do you think Temmy's age affects her response to moving to a new neighborhood?

2. Why did Temmy's father begin to call her "daughter of mine"? Why did her mother insist on pink laces in her All-Star sneakers?

3. Temmy's father went from working as a cab driver to being a teacher. When he was younger, he disdained living in a place like Lakeland; now he insisted they move there. Why? What other changes was he going through? How do you know?

4. Why were Temmy's father's desk and chair being left behind?

5. Explain the sentence, "The women made the Stepford Wives look like members of the Rainbow Coalition." (para. 41) Who are the Stepford Wives, what is the Rainbow Coalition, and what do these references mean in this context?

6. Explain the meaning and references in this sentence: "This generation of residents, once removed from salt pork, fatback, and biscuits, now dined on caviar and escargot." (para. 40)

◆ MORE WRITING TOPICS

Read the following questions, and choose one to answer in an essay:

1. Which is more important for a growing child: economic stability and security or strong family ties?

2. Do teenagers receive their values more from their contemporaries or from their family?

3. True or false: Without stability, rootedness, and a permanent home, it's almost impossible to have a successful, happy childhood.

PREREADING

1. Have you ever been in a situation in which the color of someone's skin was used to discriminate against that person or in which appearance led to stereotyping?
2. Are there any other ways that society sometimes tries to unfairly categorize people?
3. Do you believe that social class and skin color are linked in any way? Explain.

◆ **VOCABULARY**

elixir (para. 4)—a medicine in liquid form
disparagingly (para. 4)—in a manner that belittles something or someone
relegation (para. 7)—the act of assigning to an inferior position
menial labor (para. 7)—low-wage, untrained work

Hunger of Memory
Richard Rodriguez

In the following excerpt from Hunger of Memory, *Mexican American author Richard Rodriguez remembers the significance of the color of skin in his family, and what color and other external characteristics indicate about a person's class and position in society.*

Regarding my family, I see faces that do not closely resemble   1
my own. Like some other Mexican families, my family suggests Mexico's confused colonial past. Gathered around a table, we appear to be from separate continents. My father's face recalls faces I have seen in France. His complexion is white—he does not tan; he does not burn. Over the years, his dark wavy hair has grayed handsomely. But with time his face has sagged to a perpetual sigh. My mother, whose surname is inexplicably Irish—Moran—has an olive complexion. People have frequently wondered if, perhaps, she is Italian or Portuguese. And, in fact, she looks as though she could be from southern Europe. My mother's face has not aged as quickly as the rest of her body; it remains smooth and glowing—a cool tan—which her gray hair cleanly

accentuates. My older brother has inherited her good looks. When he was a boy people would tell him that he looked like Mario Lanza, and hearing it he would smile with dimpled assurance. He would come home from high school with girl friends who seemed to me glamorous (because they were) blonds. And during those years I envied him his skin that burned red and peeled like the skin of the *gringos*. His complexion never darkened like mine. My youngest sister is exotically pale, almost ashen. She is delicately featured, Near Eastern, people have said. Only my older sister has a complexion as dark as mine, though her facial features are much less harshly defined than my own. To many people meeting her, she seems (they say) Polynesian. I am the only one in the family whose face is severely cut to the line of ancient Indian ancestors. My face is mournfully long, in the classical Indian manner; my profile suggests one of those beak-nosed Mayan sculptures—the eaglelike face upturned, open-mouthed, against the deserted, primitive sky.

'We are Mexicans,' my mother and father would say, and taught   2
their four children to say whenever we (often) were asked about our ancestry. My mother and father scorned those 'white' Mexican-Americans who tried to pass themselves off as Spanish. My parents would never have thought of denying their ancestry. I never denied it: My ancestry is Mexican, I told strangers mechanically. But I never forgot that only my older sister's complexion was as dark as mine.

My older sister never spoke to me about her complexion when   3
she was a girl. But I guessed that she found her dark skin a burden. I knew that she suffered for being a 'nigger.' As she came home from grammar school, little boys came up behind her and pushed her down to the sidewalk. In high school, she struggled in the adolescent competition for boyfriends in a world of football games and proms, a world where her looks were plainly uncommon. In college, she was afraid and scornful when dark-skinned foreign students from countries like Turkey and India found her attractive. She revealed her fear of dark skin to me only in adulthood when, regarding her own three children, she quietly admitted relief that they were all light.

That is the kind of remark women in my family have often made   4
before. As a boy, I'd stay in the kitchen (never seeming to attract any notice), listening while my aunts spoke of their pleasure at having light children. (The men, some of whom were dark-skinned from years of working out of doors, would be in another part of the house.)

It was the woman's spoken concern: the fear of having a dark-skinned son or daughter. Remedies were exchanged. One aunt prescribed to her sisters the elixir of large doses of castor oil during the last weeks of pregnancy. (The remedy risked an abortion.) Children born dark grew up to have their faces treated regularly with a mixture of egg white and lemon juice concentrate. (In my case, the solution never would take.) One Mexican-American friend of my mother's, who regarded it a special blessing that she had a measure of English blood, spoke disparagingly of her husband, a construction worker, for being so dark. 'He doesn't take care of himself,' she complained. But the remark, I noticed, annoyed my mother, who sat tracing an invisible design with her finger on the tablecloth.

There was affection too and a kind of humor about these matters. With daring tenderness, one of my uncles would refer to his wife as *mi negra*. An aunt regularly called her dark child *mi feito* (my little ugly one), her smile only partially hidden as she bent down to dig her mouth under his ticklish chin. And at times relatives spoke scornfully of pale, white skin. A *gringo's* skin resembled *masa*—baker's dough—someone remarked. Everyone laughed. Voices chuckled over the fact that the *gringos* spent so many hours in summer sunning themselves. ('They need to get sun because they look like *los muertos*.')   5

I heard the laughing but remembered what the women had said, with unsmiling voices, concerning dark skin. Nothing I heard outside the house, regarding my skin, was so impressive to me.   6

In public I occasionally heard racial slurs. Complete strangers would yell out at me. A teenager drove past, shouting, 'Hey, Greaser! Hey, Pancho!' Over his shoulder I saw the giggling face of his girl friend. A boy pedaled by and announced matter-of-factly, 'I pee on dirty Mexicans.' Such remarks would be said so casually that I wouldn't quickly realize that they were being addressed to me. When I did, I would be paralyzed with embarrassment, unable to return the insult. (Those times I happened to be with white grammar school friends, *they* shouted back. Imbued with the mysterious kindness of children, my friends would never ask later why I hadn't yelled out in my own defense.)   7

In all, there could not have been more than a dozen incidents of name-calling. That there were so few suggests that I was not a primary victim of racial abuse. But that, even today, I can clearly remember particular incidents is proof of their impact. Because of such   8 incidents, I listened when my parents remarked that Mexicans were often mistreated in California border towns. And in Texas. I listened carefully when I heard that two of my cousins had been refused admittance to an 'all-white' swimming pool. And that an uncle had been told by some man to go back to Africa. I followed the progress of the southern black civil rights movement, which was gaining prominent notice in Sacramento's afternoon newspaper. But what most intrigued me was the connection between dark skin and poverty. Because I heard my mother speak so often about the relegation of dark people to menial labor, I considered the great victims of racism to be those who were poor and forced to do menial work. People like the farmworkers whose skin was dark from the sun.

After meeting a black grammar school friend of my sister's, I   9
remember thinking that she wasn't really 'black.' What interested me was the fact that she wasn't poor. (Her well-dressed parents would come by after work to pick her up in a shiny green Oldsmobile.) By contrast, the garbage men who appeared every Friday morning seemed to me unmistakably black. (I didn't bother to ask my parents why Sacramento garbage men always were black. I thought I knew.) One morning I was in the backyard when a man opened the gate. He was an ugly, square-faced black man with popping red eyes, a pail slung over his shoulder. As he approached, I stood up. And in a voice that seemed to me very weak, I piped, 'Hi.' But the man paid me no heed. He strode past to the can by the garage. In a single broad movement, he overturned its contents into his larger pail. Our can came crashing down as he turned and left me watching, in awe.

'*Pobres negros*,' my mother remarked when she'd notice a head-   10
line in the paper about a civil rights demonstration in the South. 'How the *gringos* mistreat them.' In the same tone of voice she'd tell me about the mistreatment her brother endured years before. (After my grandfather's death, my grandmother had come to America with her son and five daughters.) 'My sisters, we were still all just teenagers. And since *mi pápa* was dead, my brother had to be the head of the family. He had to support us, to find work. But what skills did he have! Twenty years old. *Pobre*. He was tall, like your grandfather. And strong. He did construction work. "Construction!" The *gringos* kept him digging all day, doing the dirtiest jobs. And they would pay him next to nothing. Sometimes they promised him one salary and paid him less when he finished. But what could he do? Report them? We

weren't citizens then. He didn't even know English. And he was dark. What chances could he have? As soon as we sisters got older, he went right back to Mexico. He hated this country. He looked so tired when he left. Already with a hunchback. Still in his twenties. But old-looking. No life for him here. *Pobre.'*

Dark skin was for my mother the most important symbol of a life 11 of oppressive labor and poverty. But both my parents recognized other symbols as well.

My father noticed the feel of every hand he shook. (He'd smile 12 sometimes—marvel more than scorn—remembering a man he'd met who had soft, uncalloused hands.)

My mother would grab a towel in the kitchen and rub my oily 13 face sore when I came in from playing outside. 'Clean the *graza* off your face!' (*Greaser!*)

Symbols: When my older sister, then in high school, asked my 14 mother if she could do light housework in the afternoons for a rich lady we knew, my mother was frightened by the idea. For several weeks she troubled over it before granting conditional permission: 'Just remember, you're not a maid. I don't want you wearing a uniform.' My father echoed the same warning. Walking with him past a hotel, I watched as he stared at a doorman dressed like a Beefeater. 'How can anyone let himself be dressed up like that? Like a clown. Don't you ever get a job where you have to put on a uniform.' In summertime neighbors would ask me if I wanted to earn extra money by mowing their lawns. Again and again my mother worried: 'Why did they ask *you*? Can't you find anything better?' Inevitably, she'd relent. She knew I needed the money. But I was instructed to work after dinner. ('When the sun's not so hot.') Even then, I'd have to wear a hat. *Un sombrero de* baseball.

(*Sombrero.* Watching gray cowboy movies, I'd brood over the 15 meaning of the broad-rimmed hat—that troubling symbol—which comically distinguished a Mexican cowboy from real cowboys.)

From my father came no warnings concerning the sun. His fear 16 was of dark factory jobs. He remembered too well his first jobs when he came to this country, not intending to stay, just to earn money enough to sail on to Australia. (In Mexico he had heard too many stories of discrimination in *los Estado Unidos.* So it was Australia, that distant island-continent, that loomed in his imagination as his

'America.') The work my father found in San Francisco was work for the unskilled. A factory job. Then a cannery job. (He'd remember the noise and the heat.) Then a job at a warehouse. (He'd remember the dark stench of old urine.) At one place there were fistfights; at another a supervisor who hated Chinese and Mexicans. Nowhere a union.

His memory of himself in those years is held by those jobs.   17
Never making money enough for passage to Australia; slowly giving up the plan of returning to school to resume his third-grade education—to become an engineer. My memory of him in those years, however, is lifted from photographs in the family album which show him on his honeymoon with my mother—the woman who had convinced him to stay in America. I have studied their photographs often, seeking to find in those figures some clear resemblance to the man and the woman I've known as my parents. But the youthful faces in the photos remain, behind dark glasses, shadowy figures anticipating my mother and father.

◆ WORKING WITH WORDS

With a Spanish-English dictionary, look up the following Spanish words and phrases used in the text. Why do you think Rodriguez uses Spanish to express these concepts?

1. *como los ricos*
2. *propria*
3. *sombrero*
4. *los estados unidos*
5. *pobres negros*
6. *gringos*
7. *los muertos*

◆ EXAMINING CONTENT

1. What does Rodriguez see when he examines his face?
2. Where did he grow up?
3. How did women in the author's family regard the skin color of their children?

4. Why didn't his parents ever get to Australia? Why did they want to go there in the first place?
5. What intrigued Rodriguez the most about the southern civil rights movement?
6. What other symbols designated class to Rodriguez's parents?

◆ RESPONDING TO IDEAS

1. What connection do you think exists between poverty and skin color?
2. Why did Rodriguez's parents "scorn those 'white' Mexican Americans who tried to pass themselves off as Spanish"? (para. 2)
3. Explain the significance given to the texture of a man's hands.
4. Do you think that the significance of skin color is the same in Mexico as it is in the United States? Why or why not?
5. What other characteristics are considered indicative of class in the United States?
6. How do you think the various responses to Rodriguez's looks influenced his self-esteem?

◆ MORE WRITING TOPICS

Using one of the following as a title and theme, write an essay expressing your views:

1. The Significance of Skin Color and Class in the United States (or another country)
2. A Comparison between Attitudes toward Skin Color in the United States and (another country)
3. How Would You Explain the Differences between Races to a Visitor from Another Planet?

◆ **PREREADING**

1. "Children who grow up in a single parent home are more likely to have certain types of problems." Do you agree or disagree with this statement? Explain.
2. How is the difficulty of having a single parent compounded by poverty?
3. Some sociologists believe that young boys in general are "at risk" in our society. Do you think this is true?

◆ **VOCABULARY**

stickball (para. 5)—a street game resembling baseball
asphyxiation (para. 5)—suffocation
expectorating (para. 11)—spitting

⇒ *NOTE:* The excerpt from the short story that you are about to read contains many words considered vulgar or obscene. Consider why an author chooses to include these words. What effect do they have upon the reader? What do they tell us about the characters using them? Also, think about why some English words are considered taboo. If you have some familiarity with other languages, is this the case in those languages as well? When is it appropriate to use these words? Who makes the rules?

Drown
Junot Diaz

The following is an excerpt from "Drown," which is the title story in a critically acclaimed collection by Junot Diaz, a brash young writer who was born in the Dominican Republic and lives in the United States. In it, the narrator describes growing up as a poor Dominican in New Jersey. In this particular passage, he tells about going shopping with his mother in the suburban mall.

My mother tells me Beto's home, waits for me to say something,   1
but I keep watching the TV. Only when she's in bed do I put on my
jacket and swing through the neighborhood to see. He's a pato* now

---

*slang expression for homosexual

but two years ago we were friends and he would walk into the apartment without knocking, his heavy voice rousing my mother from the Spanish of her room and drawing me up from the basement, a voice that crackled and made you think of uncles or grandfathers.

We were raging then, crazy the way we stole, broke windows, the way we pissed on people's steps and then challenged them to come out and stop us. Beto was leaving for college at the end of the summer and was delirious from the thought of it—he hated everything about the neighborhood, the break-apart buildings, the little strips of grass, the piles of garbage around the cans, and the dump, especially the dump.   2

I don't know how you can do it, he said to me. I would just find a job anywhere and go.   3

Yeah, I said. I wasn't like him. I had another year to go in high school, no promises elsewhere.   4

Days we spent in the mall or out in the parking lot playing stickball, but nights were what we waited for. The heat in the apartments was like something heavy that had come inside to die. Families arranged on their porches, the glow from their TV washing blue against the brick. From my family apartment you could smell the pear trees that had been planted years ago, four to a court, probably to save us all from asphyxiation. Nothing moved fast, even the daylight was slow to fade, but as soon as night settled Beto and I headed down to the community center and sprang the fence into the pool. We were never alone, every kid with legs was there. We lunged from the boards and swam out of the deep end, wrestling and farting around. At around midnight abuelas, with their night hair swirled around spiky rollers, shouted at us from their apartment windows. ¡Sinvergüenzas!* Go home!   5

I pass his apartment but the windows are dark; I put my ear to the busted-up door and hear only the familiar hum of the air conditioner. I haven't decided yet if I'll talk to him. I can go back to my dinner and two years will become three.   6

Even from four blocks off I can hear the racket from the pool—radios too—and wonder if we were ever that loud. Little has changed, not the stink of chlorine, not the bottles exploding against the lifeguard station. I hook my fingers through the plastic-coated hurricane fence. Something tells me that he will be here; I hop the fence, feeling stupid when I sprawl on the dandelions and the grass.   7

---

*shameless ones

Nice one, somebody calls out.   8

Fuck me, I say. I'm not the oldest motherfucker in the place, but   9
it's close. I take off my shirt and my shoes and then knife in. Many of
the kids here are younger brothers of the people I used to go to school
with. Two of them swim past, black and Latino, and they pause when
they see me, recognizing the guy who sells them their shitty dope.
The crackheads have their own man, Lucero, and some other guy
who drives in from Paterson, the only full-time commuter in the area.

The water feels good. Starting at the deep end I glide over the   10
slick-tiled bottom without kicking up a spume or making a splash.
Sometimes another swimmer churns past me, more a disturbance of
water than a body. I can still go far without coming up. While everything above is loud and bright, everything below is whispers. And
always the risk of coming up to find the cops stabbing their search-
lights out across the water. And then everyone running, wet feet slapping against the concrete, yelling, Fuck you, officers, you puto sucios,*
fuck you.

When I'm tired I wade through to the shallow end, past some   11
kid who's kissing his girlfriend, watching me as though I'm going to
try to cut in, and I sit near the sign that runs the pool during the day.
*No Horseplay, No Running, No Defecating, No Urinating, No Expectorat-
ing.* At the bottom someone has scrawled in *No Whites, No Fat Chiks*
and someone else has provided the missing *c*. I laugh. Beto hadn't
known what expectorating meant though he was the one leaving for
college. I told him, spitting a greener by the side of the pool.

Shit, he said. Where did you learn that?   12

I shrugged.   13

Tell me. He hated when I knew something he didn't. He put his   14
hands on my shoulders and pushed me under. He was wearing a
cross and cutoff jeans. He was stronger than me and held me down
until water flooded my nose and throat. Even then I didn't tell him;
he thought I didn't read, not even dictionaries.

We live alone. My mother has enough for the rent and groceries   15
and I cover the phone bill, sometimes the cable. She's so quiet that
most of the time I'm startled to find her in the apartment. I'll enter a
room and she'll stir, detaching herself from the cracking plaster walls,

---

*dirty whores

from the stained cabinets, and fright will pass through me like a wire. She has discovered the secret to silence: pouring café without a splash, walking between rooms as if gliding on a cushion of felt, crying without a sound. You have traveled to the East and learned many secret things, I've told her. You're like a shadow warrior.

And you're like a crazy, she says. Like a big crazy.   16

When I come in she's still awake, her hands picking clots of lint   17
from her skirt. I put a towel down on the sofa and we watch television together. We settle on the Spanish-language news: drama for her, violence for me. Today a child has survived a seven-story fall, busting nothing but his diaper. The hysterical baby-sitter, about three hundred pounds of her, is head-butting the microphone.

It's a goddamn miraclevilla,* she cries.   18

My mother asks me if I found Beto. I tell her that I didn't look.   19

That's too bad. He was telling me that he might be starting at a   20
school for business.

So what?   21

She's never understood why we don't speak anymore. I've tried   22
to explain, all wise-like, that everything changes, but she thinks that sort of saying is only around so you can prove it wrong.

He asked me what you were doing.   23

What did you say?   24

I told him you were fine.   25

You should have told him I moved.   26

And what if he ran into you?   27

I'm not allowed to visit my mother?   28

She notices the tightening of my arms. You should be more like   29
me and your father.

Can't you see I'm watching television?   30

I was angry at him, wasn't I? But now we can talk to each other.   31

Am I watching television here or what?   32

Saturdays she asks me to take her to the mall. As a son I feel I   33
owe her that much, even though neither of us has a car and we have to walk two miles through redneck territory to catch the M15.

Before we head out she drags us through the apartment to make   34
sure the windows are locked. She can't reach the latches so she has me

---

*like a miracle

test them. With the air conditioner on we never open windows but I go through the routine anyway. Putting my hand on the latch is not enough—she wants to hear it rattle. This place just isn't safe, she tells me. Lorena got lazy and look what they did to her. They punched her and kept her locked up in her place. Those morenos ate all her food and even made phone calls. Phone calls!

That's why we don't have long-distance, I tell her but she shakes 35 her head. That's not funny, she says.

She doesn't go out much, so when she does it's a big deal. She 36 dresses up, even puts on makeup. Which is why I don't give her lip about taking her to the mall even though I usually make a fortune on Saturdays, selling to those kids going down to Belmar or out to Spruce Run.

I recognize like half the kids on the bus. I keep my head buried 37 in my cap, praying that nobody tries to score. She watches the traffic, her hands somewhere inside her purse, doesn't say a word.

When we arrive at the mall I give her fifty dollars. Buy some- 38 thing, I say, hating the image I have of her, picking through the sale bins, wrinkling everything. Back in the day, my father would give her a hundred dollars at the end of each summer for my new clothes and she would take nearly a week to spend it, even though it never amounted to more than a couple of t-shirts and two pairs of jeans. She folds the bills into a square. I'll see you at three, she says.

I wander through the stores, staying in sight of the cashiers so 39 they won't have reason to follow me. The circuit I make has not changed since my looting days. Bookstore, record store, comic-book shop, Macy's. Me and Beto used to steal like mad from these places, two, three hundred dollars of shit in an outing. Our system was sim- ple—we walked into a store with a shopping bag and came out loaded. Back then security wasn't tight. The only trick was in the exit. We stopped right at the entrance of the store and checked out some worthless piece of junk to stop people from getting suspicious. What do you think? we asked each other. Would she like it? Both of us had seen bad shoplifters at work. All grab and run, nothing smooth about them. Not us. We idled out of the stores slow, like a fat seventies car. At this, Beto was the best. He even talked to mall security, asked them for directions, his bag all loaded up, and me, standing ten feet away, shitting my pants. When he finished he smiled, swinging his shopping bag up to hit me.

You got to stop that messing around, I told him. I'm not going   40
to jail for bullshit like that.

You don't go to jail for shoplifting. They just turn you over to   41
your old man.

I don't know about you, but my pops hits like a motherfucker.   42

He laughed. You know my dad. He flexed his hands. The nig-   43
ger's got arthritis.

My mother never suspected, even when my clothes couldn't all   44
fit in my closet, but my father wasn't that easy. He knew what things
cost and knew that I didn't have a regular job.

You're going to get caught, he told me one day. Just you wait.   45
When you do I'll show them everything you've taken and then they'll
throw your stupid ass away like a bad piece of meat.

He was a charmer, my pop, a real asshole, but he was right. No-   46
body can stay smooth forever, especially kids like us. One day at the
bookstore, we didn't even hide the drops. Four issues of the same
Playboy for kicks, enough audio books to start our own library. No
last minute juke either. The lady who stepped in front of us didn't
look old, even with her white hair. Her silk shirt was half unbuttoned
and a silver horn necklace sat on the freckled top of her chest. I'm
sorry fellows, but I have to check your bag, she said. I kept moving,
and looked back all annoyed, like she was asking us for a quarter or
something. Beto got polite and stopped. No problem, he said, slam-
ming the heavy bag into her face. She hit the cold tile with a squawk,
her palms slapping the ground. There you go, Beto said.

Security found us across from the bus stop, under a Jeep Chero-   47
kee. A bus had come and gone, both of us too scared to take it, imag-
ining a plainclothes waiting to clap the cuffs on. I remember that when
the rent-a-cop tapped his nightstick against the fender and said, You
little shits better come out here real slow, I started to cry. Beto didn't
say a word, his face stretched out and gray, his hand squeezing mine,
the bones in our fingers pressing together.

Nights I drink with Alex and Danny. The Malibou Bar is no   48
good, just washouts and the sucias we can con into joining us. We
drink too much, roar at each other and make the skinny bartender
move closer to the phone. On the wall hangs a cork dartboard and a
Brunswick Gold Crown blocks the bathroom, its bumpers squashed,
the felt pulled like old skin.

When the bar begins to shake back and forth like a rumba, I call   49
it a night and go home, through the fields that surround the apartments. In the distance you can see the Raritan, as shiny as an earth-
worm, the same river my homeboy goes to school on. The dump has
long since shut down, and grass has spread over it like a sickly fuzz,
and from where I stand, my right hand directing a colorless stream of
piss downward, the landfill might be the top of a blond head, square
and old.

In the mornings I run. My mother is already up, dressing for   50
her housecleaning job. She says nothing to me, would rather point to
the mangú* she has prepared than speak.

◆ WORKING WITH WORDS

The narrator of "Drown" is a drug dealer, and the language of the story is
that of the street. Yet we recognize these words; they are familiar, despite their
characterization as so-called street language. We have heard and even used
them before. Refer back to the note on page 150 about the use of vulgar language. Write a paragraph answering one of the questions raised in that note.

◆ EXAMINING CONTENT

1. Describe the narrator's neighborhood.
2. Where does the narrator go with his mother? Why?
3. What does he do for a living?
4. Why does he hang up the phone in the middle of his mother's
   conversation?
5. What is the red-haired man with the southern accent promoting?
6. What illegal activities does the narrator do with his friend Beto?

◆ RESPONDING TO IDEAS

1. From what we learn about them from the reading, what is the difference
   between the narrator's personality and that of his friend Beto?
2. Describe the narrator's relationship with his mother.

————————

*a typical dish eaten for breakfast containing plantains

3. The narrator seems to describe his shoplifting career with a mixture of pride and regret. How is he different now than he was then?
4. How do you think his life would have been different had his father been a responsible role model?
5. Why do you think the narrator doesn't seek out his old friend directly?

◆ MORE WRITING TOPICS

Agree or disagree with one of the following:

1. Teenage boys are at greater risk for failure than anyone else in today's society.
2. If a teenager commits a crime, he or she should be treated like an adult.
3. Poverty is no excuse for uncivilized behavior.

◆ **PREREADING**

1. When you were a child, did you ever feel different from everyone around you? If so, why?
2. Do you know anyone who was alive during the Great Depression? How does that person describe that time?
3. Do children or adults handle poverty better? Why?

◆ **VOCABULARY**

shenanigans (para. 3)—goings on
epithet (para. 4)—characterization
irreverent (para. 6)—lacking respect
decipher (para. 12)—decode, translate
ingenious (para. 22)—clever

That Was Living
Kathleen Ann Gonzalez

Kathleen Ann Gonzalez teaches English in the San Jose, California, area. She is the recipient of a 1994 Summer Seminar Grant from the National Endowment for the Humanities. She also won a San Jose State University Phelan Award in 1989 for the following story.

My father used to tell stories of his childhood that absolutely   1
fascinated me. He grew up in the Depression, and kids back then had to think of free ways to have fun, things that didn't require toys or special equipment or admission costs. Modern kids like me didn't know how to have real fun because we needed money to have it. We needed other things to entertain us. No so my Dad.

Picture San Jose when Stevens Creek Boulevard was still a black-   2
topped road. Orchards didn't just dot the landscape, they dominated it. The miles of rich, black Santa Clara Valley soil outnumbered the few miles of concrete and asphalt, and everyone's backyard gardens flourished gloriously under the clear, unblemished sky. Little Santa Clara was still a sleepy town—unless you were little Gilbert and his brother and cousins striving to wake up the streets.

The kids all called Gilbert Four Eyes. Because he wore glasses?   3
No. Because Gilbert's pants had holes in the knees that looked like
eyes looking back. Or if you counted the holes in his seat, you would
have to call him Six Eyes. Everyone had a nickname in those days.
Cousin Joaquin was *Chapolín*—the grasshopper—because he couldn't
walk anywhere, he had to skip. And Angelo was known as Ninnybottle because by age five you could still see him playing in the streets
with the big rubber nipple of his baby bottle between his lips. They
all called cousin Arthur Ol' Batatabloomers like a sweet potato because he had the baggiest drawers of the bunch. Nor were the girls exempt from such verbal shenanigans. Cousin Teresa went by Pinocchio
since she had the bad habit of pulling on the end of her nose. Poor
Maria Louisa caught the derision of her cousins by gossiping too
often. *Moscamuerta*—the Dead Fly—was her curse.

Yet the saddest fate must have belonged to little moon-faced   4
Carlos. He had the darkest complexion of the cousins and the sweet-
est disposition of all. One day Angelo, equipped with ninnybottle,
was playing in the yard when the Devil jumped on his shoulder and
tickled his ear. Looking over at Carlos, Angelo couldn't help shouting,
"Chocolate bar! Chocolate bar!" For Carlos, this was devastation. He
froze, and huge, glistening tears wept from his black eyes as he looked
at his cousin. The other kids gathered round to join in the chant.
"Chocolate bar!" "Carlos is a chocolate bar!" How heartless kids can
be. But it was later, after World War II when Carlos was dying of cancer, that Angelo stood steadfastly by his side and would not leave
him. Carlos would not utter a single epithet throughout his painful
dying; Angelo always said, "That's the mark of a true gentleman."

Of course, adults were not exempt from this nickname game.   5
Tio Pepe, better known as *Pies de Tablas* or Flatfoot, had worked for
years in the boiler room of the Pratt-Low Cannery to earn his name.
Even Gilbert's papa had a nickname—*Pintaíscho* or the Painted One,
because his run-in with smallpox left scars like paint marks all over
his face. We've come so far since then. Nowadays, kids only have to
worry about acne. Gilbert knew better than to call his papa anything
but "Sir." Some of the cousins, however, were not so respectful (or
maybe they just ran faster). Uncle Frank, or tio Paco, who smoked
that bitter Tuxedo-brand tobacco, was taunted with the epithet *Paco
Retaco*. Maybe he wasn't really "shaped like a taco," but his broken leg
from his Pratt-Low days kept him from catching up with his abusers.

But is it abuse or fun? In fun, the kids could be so irreverent,   6
too. My dad tells of a humid summer evening when he and Joaquin
were wandering around downtown Santa Clara and got themselves
into mischief. Santa Clara evenings are so beautiful—the earth keeps
its warmth from soaking up the daylight sunshine, and it is a delight
to feel the toasty dirt under one's feet. A little breeze wafts down off
the Almaden foothills and ruffles the leaves on the big walnut trees.
This is how I recall summer as a child, when it's so tempting to stroll
along the streets of the neighborhood, so I can picture Gilbert and
Joaquin wandering down Franklin Street by Santa Clara University
just looking for something to do.

That night there happened to be a congregation of evangelists   7
meeting to hear the stump speaker. They had gathered in a dusty
brown tent in the dirt lot downtown by the post office on the corner
of Monroe and Franklin. The piano clanged and the preacher bellowed. The followers rolled on the swept dirt floor in the ecstasy of
their faith. As Gilbert and he shuffled along kicking their shoes in the
earth, Joaquin spotted a shininess in the weeds of the empty lot and
stooped to pick up the broken knife. Mischief gleamed in his childish
eye. He and Gilbert stealthily crept closer to the Holy Rollers' tent,
keeping their footsteps to a silent patter, until they reached its side.
Fwack, Fwack. The ropes snapped apart, the tent collapsing in a heap
over its inhabitants. "Praises be!" cried the folks from the floor. The
piano continued to bang as two guilty cousins ran all the way home
to Lewis Street.

Gilbert and Joaquin could always forget their misdeeds by com-   8
mitting more the next day. They might play at "the Pit." They might
make rubber guns. Or they might have weed wars with the Portuguese kids on the next street.

"Mama, Fred and I are going to play at the Pit," Gilbert would   9
cry as the two of them slid out the back door hiding the mischievous
grins on their faces.

"All right, boys. Alfredo, you watch after your little brother."   10

Out at the Pit, the boys would have a field day scurrying   11
through the wreckage looking for broken wheels and skates, ball
bearings, inner tubes, bottle tops, and anything else fanciful or useful for their wild imaginations. The rats scurried through the wreckage, too, but with the different plan of hiding from young boys with
good aim.

The Pit. Needless to say, Mama didn't know that the Pit was the   12
secret code name for the city dump. When Papa came home from
work and asked where the boys were, he didn't expect to hear the Pit
either, but he could decipher the inexpert code name and know Fred
and Gilbert's secret. Off he marched to drag the boys home.

Papa made another famous march one time at the old swim-   13
ming hole. Little Gilbert and Fred wheeled out their one rickety bike,
Fred pumping Gilbert on the handlebars. It was much harder to pedal
on those dirt lanes and blacktops, but I suppose there was less traffic
for the bikers to fear. They traveled down Trimble Road. Back then,
Trimble was one lonely lane that led to the next sleepy town called
Milpitas. You wouldn't recognize Trimble now as Montague Ex-
pressway. The boys had wheeled a package of weenies from
Mama—it was their turn to bring them—and the Portuguese boys
brought summer squash and horse beans from their backyard gardens. Once at the creek bed, they made a bonfire, wet the food, and
buried it in the ashes to fix themselves a true tramp-style meal while
they swam in the water hole.

Now, as I've said, this was the Depression. Only rich kids had   14
money for swimming trunks, and Mama better not catch her kids
cutting the legs off their trousers, even if there were holes in the
knees. What else could Gilbert and Fred do but join the others
skinny-dipping?

Just picture the bright sun sifting cozily down through the trees,   15
creating shadow patterns on the creek bed. The boys recline around
the burning logs, accidentally dropping weenies in the fire from time
to time, digging squash from the ashes to then toss from palm to palm
while it cooked. A near pastoral perfection.

Suddenly, silence broken by a piercing whistle. I can even hear   16
that whistle in my head because my father used it to call my brothers
and me when we were children. Gilbert and Fred froze because they
knew it meant only one thing: Papa.

There stood Papa on the bridge above them. There stood Papa   17
viewing them in the buff. There stood Papa giving them the Look.
Papa disappeared. The boys dressed as fast as they could, pulled the
clothes over their still-wet bodies, and hopped on their one bike to
pedal at breakneck speed down Trimble Road to home.

"Don't ever swim there again," said Papa in that even, calm   18
voice that struck worse fear than a bellowing threat.

Gilbert always wondered why Papa never said any more to   19
them about the water hole that day, why they never got a thrashing.
But they knew they had done wrong.

The days spent with the Portuguese kids weren't always so pas-   20
toral and peaceful, though. At other times a bitter rivalry caused war,
battlefront, and artillery. Then there were rubber guns.

My dad made these simple wooden toys for me when I was a   21
kid, and I thought them better than any of the fancy plastic popguns
or space ray guns. With a rubber gun, I could be on even par with my
bigger, older brothers because I was the feline, stealthy little sister
who could use guerrilla tactics. But back in Dad's childhood memory,
those rubber guns meant serious playing and a means of survival.

A rubber gun consisted of a chunk of wood cut in the shape of   22
a gun—usually a handgun or rifle, a clothespin snitched from
Mama's line, and cut strips of inner tubes from the Pit or the one bi-
cycle. The inner-tube bands were stretched from the nose of the gun
to the clothespin at the back, which acted as the trigger. Joaquin, one
of the more ingenious cousins, had fashioned a machine gun by
adding a wooden wheel to his rifle with a volley of twenty-five
clothespins. He had the further advantage of confounding his enemy
should his gun fall into their hands because they wouldn't know the
sequence to shoot the bands in and would instead shoot themselves.
Another of the boys had discovered that knotting the inner tube in
the middle made his shot go further and harder, leaving a swollen
scarlet welt on its target's arm.

The kids would hide behind the cars, garbage cans, or white-   23
washed fences and aim at their rivals. All of the families on Monroe
Street were Spanish or Mexican, but if the cousins crept one block
over out of their territory onto Lewis, they entered the street of the
Portuguese. Gilbert's family was the only Spanish one on the block.
Perhaps without understanding their own feelings, the cousins saw
this one difference as reason enough for battle.

If rubber guns didn't work or if the kids couldn't find discarded   24
inner tubes that week, they could always resort to using weed bombs.
Weeds were plentiful and free and fast and easy to fashion into potent
weapons. Just pull up a handful of weeds with a good-sized hunk of
dirt on the bottom, soak the dirt in some gutter water to make it extra
sticky and wet, add a hefty rock to be particularly nasty, pack the dirt
bomb into a solid sphere, and chuck it at full speed at *el loco* across the

street. The weeds make a wonderful comet tail at the back to direct your aim and accelerate the bomb.

Little Four Eyes squatted behind the walnut tree on the corner. 25 From the corner of his eye he spied a movement across the street on Lewis Street. Four Eyes turned his head and motioned over his shoulder to Ninnybottle, "There's the enemy!" The two of them gathered forces, pulled together their stockpile of rocks and weeds, and conferred on how best to attack. The enemy hadn't realized he'd been spotted. Ninnybottle fired first, getting gutter water all over his hand-me-down shirt and down his arm in the process. "Rats," he muttered. But the shot had struck its mark. The enemy was hit! Up he stood, spattered mud and grass dripping down the side of his face. "Papa's gonna get you!" yelled Fred across the street to Gilbert as he wiped his cheek with his sleeve. Ninnybottle and Four Eyes just giggled as they slunk off to gloat over their victory.

Angelo and Gilbert often paired together—or were paired to- 26 gether by the others—because they were the two littlest of the cousins. But they were happy to stick together, even when victimized, because it was better than being a single victim. In fact, whenever the cousins played "Tarzan, King of the Jungle," Gilbert and Angelo were always duped.

In the empty lot behind the Trinity Church on Monroe and Lib- 27 erty stood two ancient fig trees. Their limbs were gnarled and tangled in muscular contortions, their leaves and branches twined in and about each other to form an endless, answerless labyrinth. Most of the kids knew just how to crawl among the puzzle to find their way in and out. But there were penalties for those who were not so smart.

This was the war between the Warriors and the Peasants in the 28 great Tarzan trees. Of course, it was also the war between the Big and the Little. Angelo and Gilbert were the Little, the Peasants. All the others were the Big. If the Big decided the Little were being mean to them—and this was a totally arbitrary decision based on whether or not they felt mean—they could sentence the Little to stay in the hoosegow where the leaves and branches and limbs wove so tightly together as to form an inescapable deep cell from which the Little could not escape, being too short.

"That Arthur, he's so mean," grumbled Gilbert from inside their 29 tree prison. "We've gotta go see the new Tarzan movie next Saturday and find out how he gets even."

"I just wish I could call the animals to help us," said Angelo. 30
"Where's Cheeta when you need him?"

The only way they could escape the dungeon was to give their 31
captors the secret password: "A gotcha boom ba oh beedy um." But
do you think Gilbert could remember this?

"A gotcha." "A bootcha." "A botcha goom." 32

"Rats." 33

I wonder if that's why Angelo developed a photographic mem- 34
ory later in life.

So Gilbert and Angelo and Fred and all the cousins would find 35
a way to get to the movies on Saturday so they could cheer their
heroes Tarzan or the Lone Ranger. The movies were only ten cents
then, but in those poor days that was a nearly impossible amount to
gather. The cousins couldn't let down their heroes by not going to the
movies. Where there's a will, there's a way.

The "way" was through Pepsi-Cola, an upstart company at that 36
time. Five Pepsi bottle tops and a penny would get Gilbert into the
show where he could cheer Tom Mix or Buck Rogers, laugh with
Spanky or Groucho, or yell along with Tarzan. Gilbert and Fred
arranged with all the local gas stations and Ma and Pa groceries to
clean out their pop machines and collect all the bottle tops.

Of course, since Pepsi-Cola was just a baby, not many people 37
bought that soda at that time. This left the boys with bags of extra
bottle tops after they had collected all the Pepsi ones. What to do?
Well, why not pave the backyard walkway! Just what I would have
thought of. The walkway became a steady chore for the boys. From
the back stoop, past the walnut tree, by the toolshed, to the vegetable
garden, Gilbert and Fred would smack the bottle tops into the soft
soil. Turn one over, heft the wooden mallet, and tap, tap. Take another, tap, tap. The job never ended because once the first layer settled deeper in the dirt, another layer had to be added. Wooden mallet,
tap, tap.

Even with all the hard work and poverty, I envy the children of 38
my dad's generation because they had opportunities I will never have.
That's a switch—people usually think that my generation has more
opportunities since we have computers and TV and pavement. But
I disagree. I look back at little Gilbert and Fred and wish I could
have swum in the creeks when they still consisted of water instead of
rocks. I wish I could have looked forward for months to the traveling

Ringling Brothers instead of being bored by having too many enter-
tainments to choose from. And, most of all, I wish I could have pulled
mounds of dripping vermillion watermelon in my little red wagon
back from the pickling plant to my Santa Clara home. That's why I
envy Gilbert most.

Watermelon quenches that summer thirst in the dry heat of   39
Santa Clara. The Santa Clara Pickling and Preserve Factory stood
downtown beside the Santa Clara Mortuary and behind the Casa
Grande Theater. On Washington between Franklin and Liberty, it was
only a few blocks from Gilbert's home. Those few blocks were a long
journey for Four Eyes's little legs, but it would be worth every mouth-
watering bite. The pickling factory only wanted the rinds, so they
threw their unwanted red hearts in the bin out back. What a field day
for *los niños!* Fred used to say that someday when he was rich he
would buy himself a whole watermelon. But with the melon hearts
practically in his backyard, Fred could live like a king in the middle
of the Depression. The king of hearts!

The kids would often tramp down as a group to the pickling   40
factory and then load up their wagons and tubs and sacks with all
the watermelon they could carry. They would play the child Saint
Nick and deliver the fruit to the relatives that lived all along Monroe
Street. Gilbert's tia Rosario, Nino Martin, and Nina Lola, Piez de
Tablas, and Paco Retaco. It was important that the cousins be nice to
Nino Martin because his was the home where the recalcitrant cousins
were sent for "reeducation."

Despite the bottle-top hunts or the watermelon trips, Gilbert   41
and the others never knew they were poor. The Depression raged,
work was scarce, and they often had to do without; yet their basic
needs were always met. Somehow Mama found a way to make the
beans stretch a little further, and Papa was a wizard at finding a use
for every last nail, scrap of wood, or ounce of human energy. Wasting
was simply not considered.

It wasn't until the cousins went to Fremont Elementary that they   42
realized they were different from the other kids. Many of the little girls
had starched new frocks and Shirley Temple curls. Or the boys would
not be wearing hand-me-downs from previous generations of cousins.
Gilbert realized his own poverty one day when it was time for milk
and graham crackers during recess. Gilbert had no nickel but he still
got his snack. Someone (his teacher?) was watching out for him.

It's funny for me to think of all the cousins as children running 43 around the streets of Santa Clara. To me, Monroe was the old part of town where my great Aunt Rose and Uncle Dort lived. It was the area of my rival high school, first called Santa Clara High and then Buchser Junior High. I can hardly picture that the house where I grew up in Mariposa Gardens was a prune orchard on the outskirts of town when my father was growing up.

I know the cousins as middle-aged people with children my 44 own age and older. I picture them gathered together at the funeral of Maria Louisa or at the wedding of Joaquin's son, where I have seen them laughing and reliving the days of their youth, the stories I have just recounted. I imagine them with their nicknames. I wonder if I will ever have the chance to relive my own childhood with my youthful friends in this city of Santa Clara that so swiftly grows and changes and dissipates out to the hills.

◆ WORKING WITH WORDS

In the following sentences, look the italicized words up in the dictionary and write synonyms for them. Then explain why you think the author used the particular words she did.

1. My father used to tell stories of his childhood that absolutely *fascinated* me.
2. Orchards didn't just dot the landscape; they *dominated* it.
3. Nor were girls exempt from verbal *shenanigans*.
4. For Carlos, this was *devastation*.
5. The piano *clanged* and the preacher *bellowed*.
6. The rats *scurried* through the wreckage too.
7. Another of the boys had discovered that knotting the inner tube in the middle made his shot go further and harder, leaving a *swollen scarlet welt* on his arm.
8. In fact, whenever the cousins played "Tarzan, King of the Jungle," Gilbert and Angelo were always *duped*.

◆ EXAMINING CONTENT

1. What are some of the nicknames the children make up for one another?
2. What were the adults called? Why weren't they exempt from this game?

3. Describe some of the favorite destinations of the children.
4. Describe some of the toys that were homemade.
5. How were Gilbert, Angelo, and Fred able to afford to go to the movies?
6. How did the children quench their thirst in the hot dry summers?
7. What happened to the children that Gonzalez writes about?

◆ RESPONDING TO IDEAS

1. What are the most distinctive characteristics of these children growing up in a poor California neighborhood?
2. Even though the children were poor, they had a lot of fun. How can you account for this?
3. Do you think that the children were safer than the average child in a similar neighborhood today? Why or why not?
4. Do you believe the children felt they were deprived and poor? Why?
5. Today's children are committing an unprecedented number of violent acts. How do you account for this? What makes them different from the children of the depression era who were mischievous but not dangerous, as described by Gonzalez's father?

◆ MORE WRITING TOPICS

Write a three- to five-paragraph letter to the editor of your local newspaper on one of the following topics:

1. Our Community Needs More Recreational Facilities for Teens
2. Children Today Have More Stressful Lives Than We Did in the Past
3. The Support of An Extended Family Is More Important Today than Ever Before

◆ **PREREADING**

1. Which is harder to write about: yourself or something outside yourself? Which kind of writing do you prefer to read? Why? Which kind do you prefer to write? Why?
2. How important is it to tell the truth when you write? Should you do so even if it offends the reader?
3. What is a stereotype? Can you think of negative ones? Positive ones?

Theme for English B
Langston Hughes

A major figure in the literary movement known as the Harlem Renaissance, James Langston Hughes wrote novels, stories, plays, songs, essays, memoirs, and poetry, of which the following is an example. He is thought to be the first African American to have made a living from writing.

Theme for English B

The instructor said,

Go home and write
a page tonight.
And let that page come out of you—
5   *Then, it will be true.*

I wonder if it's that simple?
I am twenty-two, colored, born in Winston-Salem.
I went to school there, then Durham, then here
to this college on the hill above Harlem.
10   I am the only colored student in my class.
The steps from the hill lead down into Harlem,
through a park, then I cross St. Nicholas,
Eighth Avenue, Seventh, and I come to the Y,
the Harlem Branch Y, where I take the elevator
15   up to my room, sit down, and write this page:

It's not easy to know what is true for you or me
at twenty-two, my age. But I guess I'm what
I feel and see and hear, Harlem, I hear you:

hear you, hear me—we two—you, me, talk on this page.
20   (I hear New York, too.) Me—who?

Well, I like to eat, sleep, drink, and be in love.
I like to work, read, learn, and understand life.
I like a pipe for a Christmas present,
or records—Bessie, bop, or Bach.
25   I guess being colored doesn't make me *not* like
the same things other folks like who are other races.
So will my page be colored that I write?

Being me, it will not be white.
But it will be
30   a part of you, instructor.
You are white—
Yet a part of me, as I am a part of you.
That's American.
Sometimes perhaps you don't want to be part of me.
35   Nor do I often want to be a part of you.
But we are, that's true!
As I learn from you,
I guess you learn from me—

although you're older—and white—
40   and somewhat more free.

This is my page for English B.

◆ WORKING WITH WORDS

Following are lists of words that have at one time or another been *socially acceptable designations* for different ethnic groups.

Colored	white	Hispanic	Indian
Negro	Caucasian	Latino/Latina	Native American
Black	European-American	Spanish	
Afro-American		Spanish-speaking	
African American		Latino American	

Give your reaction to or your feelings about some or all of these words.

◆ EXAMINING CONTENT

1. What are the places of this poem? What significance do they have?
2. What does the line "I feel and see and hear, Harlem, I hear you" mean?
3. Why is it significant that he is "the only colored student in my class"?
4. Who or what are "Bessie, bop, and Bach" (line 24)? What is the significance of the three being together?
5. Why is it "not easy to know what is true"?

◆ RESPONDING TO IDEAS

1. Do you think this is a good assignment? Explain.
2. From what you can tell from the poem, what kind of person is the student?
3. How is he struggling with identity? What lines of the poem show this struggle?
4. Does the poet's voice sound like a twenty-two-year-old college student? Consider the fact that Langston Hughes was forty-nine when he wrote "Theme for English B." How does this change the way you think about the poem, and the voice of its student?
5. According to the poem, the teacher instructed the class to write a page, a theme. Do you think writing a *poem* was an appropriate response? Why or why not? How do you think it would have been different if it were written in prose instead of poetry?
6. How does this poem compare to the one in Chapter One by Aurora Levin Morales?

◆ MORE WRITING TOPICS

1. Have you ever been alone in a crowd, the only one of your kind, when everyone else was something else? If you have had that experience, describe it. If you have not, imagine what it must be like. In either case, write an essay about being the only one who is different.
2. Is it a teacher's job to help a student learn about himself or herself, to learn to cope with society? Or is the teacher's responsibility to the class as a whole? Or should a teacher just teach, no matter who, or how many, or what kind of students are in the class? In a short essay, describe what you think a teacher's responsibility is (if any) to each individual student in a class.

◆ **PREREADING**

1. Think about the single-parent issues that were raised when you read the excerpt from Junot Diaz's "Drown" (pp. 150–56). Has your thinking changed at all?
2. Is it easier to raise boys or girls? Why?
3. Is it sometimes appropriate for parents to rely on older children to help raise younger children?

◆ **VOCABULARY**

rigidity (para. 6)—stiffness, inflexibility
pantomimes (para. 18)—acting out, without words
delirious (para. 23)—feeling crazy, light-headed
overconscientious (para. 37)—overly careful

I Stand Here Ironing
Tillie Olsen

Tillie Olsen (1912–   ) grew up in a working class family in Omaha. Poverty drew her to social activism, which led to her arrest more than once when she was young. Much of her writing was not published until late in her life. She won the O. Henry Award for best short story in 1961. "I Stand Here Ironing" was published in the same collection.

I stand here ironing, and what you asked me moves tormented   1
back and forth with the iron.

"I wish you would manage the time to come in and talk with   2
me about your daughter. I'm sure you can help me understand her. She's a youngster who needs help and whom I'm deeply interested in helping."

"Who needs help." . . . Even if I came, what good would it do?   3
You think because I am her mother I have a key, or that in some way you could use me as a key? She has lived for nineteen years. There is all that life that has happened outside of me, beyond me.

And when is there time to remember, to sift, to weigh, to esti-   4
mate, to total? I will start and there will be an interruption and I will
have to gather it all together again. Or I will become engulfed with
all I did or did not do, with what should have been and what cannot
be helped.

She was a beautiful baby. The first and only one of our five that   5
was beautiful at birth. You do not guess how new and uneasy her
tenancy in her now-loveliness. You did not know her all those years
she was thought homely, or see her poring over her baby pictures,
making me tell her over and over how beautiful she had been—and
would be, I would tell her—and was now, to the seeing eye. But the
seeing eyes were few or nonexistent. Including mine.

I nursed her. They feel that's important nowadays. I nursed all   6
the children, but with her, with all the fierce rigidity of first motherhood, I did like the books then said. Though her cries battered me to
trembling and my breasts ached with swollenness, I waited till the
clock decreed.

Why do I put that first? I do not even know if it matters, or if it   7
explains anything.

She was a beautiful baby. She blew shining bubbles of sound.   8
She loved motion, loved light, loved color and music and textures. She
would lie on the floor in her blue overalls patting the surface so hard
in ecstasy her hands and feet would blur. She was a miracle to me, but
when she was eight months old I had to leave her daytimes with the
woman downstairs to whom she was no miracle at all, for I worked or
looked for work and for Emily's father, who "could no longer endure"
(he wrote in his good-bye note) "sharing want with us."

I was nineteen. It was the pre-relief, pre-WPA* world of the de-   9
pression. I would start running as soon as I got off the streetcar, running up the stairs, the place smelling sour, and awake or asleep to
startle awake, when she saw me she would break into a clogged weeping that could not be comforted, a weeping I can hear yet.

After a while I found a job hashing at night so I could be with   10
her days, and it was better. But it came to where I had to bring her to
his family and leave her.

---

*WPA—Works Progress Administration: a federal program to hire the
unemployed

It took a long time to raise the money for her fare back. Then   11
she got chicken pox and I had to wait longer. When she finally came,
I hardly knew her, walking quick and nervous like her father, looking
like her father, thin, and dressed in a shoddy red that yellowed her
skin and glared at the pockmarks. All the baby loveliness gone.

She was two. Old enough for nursery school they said, and I   12
did not know then what I know now—the fatigue of the long day,
and the lacerations of group life in the kinds of nurseries that are only
parking places for children.

Except that it would have made no difference if I had known. It   13
was the only place there was. It was the only way we could be together, the only way I could hold a job.

And even without knowing, I knew. I knew the teacher that was   14
evil because all these years it has curdled into my memory, the little
boy hunched in the corner, her rasp, "why aren't you outside, because
Alvin hits you? that's no reason, go out, scaredy." I knew Emily hated
it even if she did not clutch and implore "don't go Mommy" like the
other children, mornings.

She always had a reason why we should stay home. Momma,   15
you look sick. Momma, I feel sick. Momma, the teachers aren't there
today, they're sick. Momma, we can't go, there was a fire there last
night. Momma, it's a holiday today, no school, they told me.

But never a direct protest, never rebellion. I think of our others   16
in their three-, four-year-oldness—the explosions, the tempers, the
denunciations, the demands—and I feel suddenly ill. I put the iron
down. What in me demanded that goodness in her? And what was the
cost, the cost to her of such goodness?

The old man living in the back once said in his gentle way: 17
"You should smile at Emily more when you look at her." What *was*
in my face when I looked at her? I loved her. There were all the acts
of love.

It was only with the others I remembered what he said, and it   18
was the face of joy, and not of care or tightness or worry I turned to
them—too late for Emily. She does not smile easily, let alone almost
always as her brothers and sisters do. Her face is closed and sombre,
but when she wants, how fluid. You must have seen it in her pantomimes, you spoke of her rare gift for comedy on the stage that
rouses laughter out of the audience so dear they applaud and applaud and do not want to let her go.

Where does it come from, that comedy? There was none of it in   19
her when she came back to me that second time, after I had had to
send her away again. She had a new daddy now to learn to love, and
I think perhaps it was a better time.

Except when we left her alone nights, telling ourselves she was   20
old enough.

"Can't you go some other time, Mommy, like tomorrow?" she   21
would ask. "Will it be just a little while you'll be gone? Do you
promise?"

The time we came back, the front door open, the clock on the   22
floor in the hall. She rigid awake. "It wasn't just a little while. I didn't
cry. Three times I called you, just three times, and then I ran downstairs to open the door so you could come faster. The clock talked
loud. I threw it away, it scared me what it talked."

She said the clock talked loud again that night I went to the hos-   23
pital to have Susan. She was delirious with the fever that comes before red measles, but she was fully conscious all the week I was gone
and the week after we were home when she could not come near the
new baby or me.

She did not get well. She stayed skeleton thin, not wanting to eat,   24
and night after night she had nightmares. She would call for me, and I
would rouse from exhaustion to sleepily call back: "You're all right,
darling, go to sleep, it's just a dream," and if she still called, in a sterner
voice, "now go to sleep, Emily, there's nothing to hurt you." Twice, only
twice, when I had to get up for Susan anyhow, I went in to sit with her.

Now when it is too late (as if she would let me hold and com-   25
fort her like I do the others) I get up and go to her at once at her moan
or restless stirring. "Are you awake, Emily? Can I get you something?"
And the answer is always the same: "No, I'm all right, go back to
sleep, Mother."

They persuaded me at the clinic to send her away to a conva-   26
lescent home in the country where "she can have the kind of food
and care you can't manage for her, and you'll be free to concentrate
on the new baby." They still send children to that place. I see pictures
on the society page of sleek young women planning affairs to raise
money for it, or dancing at the affairs, or decorating Easter eggs or filling Christmas stockings for the children.

They never have a picture of the children so I do not know if   27
the girls still wear those gigantic red bows and the ravaged looks on

the every other Sunday when parents can come to visit "unless otherwise notified"—as we were notified the first six weeks.

Oh it is a handsome place, green lawns and tall trees and fluted   28
flower beds. High up on the balconies of each cottage the children
stand, the girls in their red bows and white dresses, the boys in white
suits and giant red ties. The parents stand below shrieking up to be
heard and the children shriek down to be heard, and between them
the invisible wall: "Not to Be Contaminated by Parental Germs or
Physical Affection."

There was a tiny girl who always stood hand in hand with   29
Emily. Her parents never came. One visit she was gone. "They moved
her to Rose Cottage." Emily shouted in explanation. "They don't like
you to love anybody here."

She wrote once a week, the labored writing of a seven-year-old.   30
"I am fine. How is the baby. If I write my leter nicly I will have a star.
Love." There never was a star. We wrote every other day, letters she
could never hold or keep but only hear read—once. "We simply do
not have room for children to keep any personal possessions," they
patiently explained when we pieced one Sunday's shrieking together
to plead how much it would mean to Emily, who loved so to keep
things, to be allowed to keep her letters and cards.

Each visit she looked frailer. "She isn't eating," they told us.   31

(They had runny eggs for breakfast or mush with lumps, Emily   32
said later, I'd hold it in my mouth and not swallow. Nothing ever
tasted good, just when they had chicken.)

It took us eight months to get her released home, and only the   33
fact that she gained back so little of her seven lost pounds convinced
the social worker.

I used to try to hold and love her after she came back, but her   34
body would stay stiff, and after a while she'd push away. She ate little. Food sickened her, and I think too much of life too. Oh she had
physical lightness and brightness, twinkling by on skates, bouncing
like a ball up and down up and down over the jump rope, skimming
over the hill; but these were momentary.

She fretted about her appearance, thin and dark and foreign-   35
looking at a time when every little girl was supposed to look or
thought she should look a chubby blonde replica of Shirley Temple.*

---

*Shirley Temple—child actress

The doorbell sometimes rang for her, but no one seemed to come and play in the house or be a best friend. Maybe because we moved so much.

There was a boy she loved painfully through two school se- 36 mesters. Months later she told me how she had taken pennies from my purse to buy him candy. "Licorice was his favorite and I brought him some every day, but he still liked Jennifer better'n me. Why, Mommy?" The kind of question for which there is no answer.

School was a worry to her. She was not glib or quick in a world 37 where glibness and quickness were easily confused with ability to learn. To her overworked and exasperated teachers she was an over-conscientious "slow learner" who kept trying to catch up and was absent entirely too often.

I let her be absent, though sometimes the illness was imaginary. 38 How different from my now-strictness about attendance with the others. I wasn't working. We had a new baby, I was home anyhow. Sometimes, after Susan grew old enough, I would keep her home from school, too, to have them all together.

Mostly Emily had asthma, and her breathing, harsh and labored, 39 would fill the house with a curiously tranquil sound. I would bring the two old dresser mirrors and her boxes of collections to her bed. She would select beads and single earrings, bottle tops and shells, dried flowers and pebbles, old postcards and scraps, all sorts of oddments; then she and Susan would play Kingdom, setting up landscapes and furniture, peopling them with action.

Those were the only times of peaceful companionship between 40 her and Susan. I have edged away from it, that poisonous feeling between them, that terrible balancing of hurts and needs I had to do between the two, and did so badly, those earlier years.

Oh there are conflicts between the others too, each one human, 41 needing, demanding, hurting, taking—but only between Emily and Susan, no, Emily toward Susan that corroding resentment. It seems so obvious on the surface, yet it is not obvious. Susan, the second child, Susan, golden- and curly-haired and chubby, quick and artic-ulate and assured, everything in appearance and manner Emily was not; Susan, not able to resist Emily's precious things, losing or some-times clumsily breaking them; Susan telling jokes and riddles to company for applause while Emily sat silent (to say to me later: that was *my* riddle, Mother, I told it to Susan); Susan, who for all the five years' difference in age was just a year behind Emily in developing physically.

I am glad for that slow physical development that widened the   42
difference between her and her contemporaries, though she suffered over it. She was too vulnerable for that terrible world of youthful competition, of preening and parading, of constant measuring of yourself against every other, of envy, "If I had that copper hair," "If I had that skin. . . ." She tormented herself enough about not looking like the others, there was enough of the unsureness, the having to be conscious of words before you speak, the constant caring—what are they thinking of me? without having it all magnified by the merciless physical drives.

Ronnie is calling. He is wet and I change him. It is rare there is   43
such a cry now. That time of motherhood is almost behind me when the ear is not one's own but must always be racked and listening for the child cry, the child call. We sit for a while and I hold him, looking out over the city spread in charcoal with its soft aisles of light. "*Shoogily*," he breathes and curls closer. I carry him back to bed, asleep. *Shoogily*. A funny word, a family word, inherited from Emily, invented by her to say: *comfort*.

In this and other ways she leaves her seal, I say aloud. And   44
startle at my saying it. What do I mean? What did I start to gather together, to try and make coherent? I was at the terrible, growing years. War years. I do not remember them well. I was working, there were four smaller ones now, there was not time for her. She had to help be a mother, and housekeeper, and shopper. She had to set her seal. Mornings of crisis and near hysteria trying to get lunches packed, hair combed, coats and shoes found, everyone to school or Child Care on time, the baby ready for transportation. And always the paper scribbled on by a smaller one, the book looked at by Susan then mislaid, the homework not done. Running out to that huge school where she was one, she was lost, she was a drop; suffering over the unpreparedness, stammering and unsure in her classes.

There was so little time left at night after the kids were bedded   45
down. She would struggle over books, always eating (it was in those years she developed her enormous appetite that is legendary in our family) and I would be ironing, or preparing food for the next day, or writing V-mail to Bill, or tending the baby. Sometimes, to make me laugh, or out of her despair, she would imitate happenings or types at school.

I think I said once: "Why don't you do something like this in the   46
school amateur show?" One morning she phoned me at work, hardly
understandable through the weeping: "Mother, I did it. I won, I won;
they gave me first prize; they clapped and clapped and wouldn't let
me go."

Now suddenly she was Somebody, and as imprisoned in her   47
difference as she had been in anonymity.

She began to be asked to perform at other high schools, even in   48
colleges, then at city and statewide affairs. The first one we went to,
I only recognized her that first moment when thin, shy, she almost
drowned herself into the curtains. Then: Was this Emily? The control,
the command, the convulsing and deadly clowning, the spell, then
the roaring, stamping audience, unwilling to let this rare and precious laughter out of their lives.

Afterwards: You ought to do something about her with a gift   49
like that—but without money or knowing how, what does one do? We
have left it all to her, and the gift has as often eddied inside, clogged
and clotted, as been used and growing.

She is coming. She runs up the stairs two at a time with her light   50
graceful step, and I know she is happy tonight. Whatever it was that
occasioned your call did not happen today.

"Aren't you ever going to finish the ironing, Mother? Whistler   51
painted his mother in a rocker. I'd have to paint mine standing over
an ironing board." This is one of her communicative nights and she
tells me everything and nothing as she fixes herself a plate of food
out of the icebox.

She is so lovely. Why did you want me to come in at all? Why   52
were you concerned? She will find her way.

She starts up the stairs to bed. "Don't get me up with the rest in   53
the morning." "But I thought you were having midterms." "Oh,
those," she comes back in, kisses me, and says quite lightly, "in a couple of years when we'll all be atom-dead they won't matter a bit."

She has said it before. She *believes* it. But because I have been   54
dredging the past, and all that compounds a human being is so heavy
and meaningful in me, I cannot endure it tonight.

I will never total it all. I will never come in to say: She was a   55
child seldom smiled at. Her father left me before she was a year old.
I had to work her first six years when there was work, or I sent her
home and to his relatives. There were years she had care she hated.

She was dark and thin and foreign-looking in a world where the pres-
tige went to blondeness and curly hair and dimples, she was slow
where glibness was prized. She was a child of anxious, not proud, love.
We were poor and could not afford for her the soil of easy growth. I was
a young mother, I was a distracted mother. There were other children
pushing up, demanding. Her younger sister seemed all that she was
not. There were years she did not want me to touch her. She kept too
much in herself, her life was such she had to keep too much in herself.
My wisdom came too late. She has much to her and probably little will
come of it. She is a child of her age, of depression, of war, of fear.

Let her be. So all that is in her will not bloom—but in how many   56
does it? There is still enough left to live by. Only help her to know—
help make it so there is cause for her to know—that she is more than
this dress on the ironing board, helpless before the iron.

◆ WORKING WITH WORDS

Look up the following words and using the context in which they appear
and the dictionary write their meanings. Then write the opposite meanings
of each word.

1. engulfed (para. 4)
2. decreed (para. 6)
3. clogged (para. 9)
4. shoddy (para. 11)
5. curdled (para. 14)
6. rouses (para. 18)

◆ EXAMINING CONTENT

1. At what point in her life did Emily's mother have her? What was going
   on in the world at that time?
2. Why did Emily's father leave?
3. Why did Emily have to be separated from her mother?
4. Make a list of the difficulties that Emily had to overcome.
5. What talent enabled Emily to be a success in school?
6. Does Emily's mother feel she failed her? Why or why not?
7. What expectations does Emily's mother have for her eldest daughter?

◆ RESPONDING TO IDEAS

1. Are Emily's circumstances similar to those of many children today? How?
2. In your opinion, does Emily's mother love her?
3. How do you think having so many siblings affected Emily?
4. Interpret the line in which Emily says about her mother, "I'd have to paint mine standing over an ironing board." (para. 51)
5. Were you surprised that Emily was a funny comedic actress? Why or why not?
6. Make a prediction of your own about Emily's future.
7. How—if at all—would Emily's life be different had she been born today?

◆ MORE WRITING TOPICS

Address one of the following statements in a short, organized, convincing essay:

1. People need to study, pass a test, and get a license in order to be allowed to drive a car, but anyone can have children whenever they want.
2. It doesn't make sense to require welfare mothers to work, unless child care is more readily available.

◆ MAKING THE FINAL COPY

◆ Go back to your journal and look at all the responses you have written to readings and answers you have given to questions in this chapter. Try to develop a thesis statement from ideas you have already written about and write a three or four paragraph essay.

◆ Write a letter to the editor of a newspaper on the topic of homelessness, welfare reform, tax-supported child care, or sex-based or race-based discrimination in society.

◆ Write a four-paragraph essay on one of the following topics:
   ◆ Is "workfare" welfare?
   ◆ Does skin color affect a person's chances of having a successful employment interview?
   ◆ Should the state support child care?
   ◆ What is the effect of prejudice against the working poor in our society?
   ◆ What are the causes of homelessness?
   ◆ How could the current administration help prevent poverty?

After you have completed your first draft, read it aloud to the class. Then, in groups, use the revising and editing checklists to improve your draft

◆ REVISING CHECKLIST

Read over the draft you have completed for the purpose of revising it—that is, improving the content. Use the questions below as a starting point for revision.

- ◆ Does the composition have an introduction? Does the introductory paragraph of the composition make the main idea of the composition clear? Remember, there is more than one way to respond and write an introduction. It must include the most important point, however.
- ◆ Is the development clear and specific? Remember to avoid generality. Be specific. For instance, if you are telling an anecdote remember to include the answers to *Where? When? Who? Why?* Be sure it is clear *how* the anecdote is related to the topic.
- ◆ Is the choice of language appropriate? Be aware of street language, slang and trendy expressions. Academic writing is usually more formal. (Of course, if you are writing dialogue, you have some flexibility in terms of writing in the way your characters would realistically speak.)
- ◆ Are any ideas repeated? Sometimes writers repeat and are not aware of it.
- ◆ Are any ideas not relevant and do these need to be deleted? Sometimes writers digress from the topic. Ask yourself after each sentence, "How does this relate to the ideas preceding and following it?"
- ◆ Is the conclusion appropriate? Does it reflect the main idea and let the reader know that the essay is ending?

◆ EDITING CHECKLIST

Now that you have written and revised your draft, it is time to edit it. Read it over once more, checking for mechanical errors. Use the following questions as a starting point for editing.

- ◆ Is each sentence complete? Avoid fragments. Does each sentence have a subject and a verb and make complete sense?
- ◆ How long are your sentences? Are they too long and contain too many commas? Remember, a comma may not connect two complete sentences. If necessary, refer to an English usage guide.
- ◆ Did you indent each paragraph? Are the paragraphs an appropriate length?

◆ Is your verb tense consistent? If you are telling an anecdote in the past, stay in the past. Do not switch to the present or another tense for no reason.

◆ Does subject and verb agreement exist, especially when the present tense is used? Remember, verbs may consist of more than one word. Make sure the auxiliary verbs are also correct.

◆ Are proper nouns capitalized? Does every sentence begin with a capital?

◆ EDITING EXERCISE

Pronouns

Be consistent with the use of pronouns. Do not change pronouns without a clear understanding of the antecedent (or word the pronoun represents).

Do not use the pronoun *you* for general reference. It should not be used to denote the idea of "people" in the general sense. It should be used only to address the reader specifically and directly.

The more specific your examples are when you are illustrating or supporting a point, the more effective your writing will be. Being specific will help you avoid problems with ambiguous or misleading pronouns.

We should be aware of class distinctions in society. You must never forget that prejudice exists in the form of classism, or elitism.

(Notice how *you* is out of place here.)

Everyone should be aware of class distinctions in society. We must never forget that prejudice exists in the form of classism, or elitism.

(To whom is the sentence directed? Every single person [everyone]? All of us [we]? The reader [you]? Be consistent.)

Also, avoid the loose use of pronouns that might indicate vagueness:

They say students should be checked for weapons in school.

(*Who* says it? Be more specific.)

You never know what innocent-looking child might be carrying a concealed gun.

(*At whom* is this information directed?)

Keeping this in mind, notice the inconsistencies in the following:

> I believe that one's experience helps shape who you are. In
> addition, we are influenced by society and our culture. Each
> person's identity is formed by your background and ethnicity.
>   For example, when Langston Hughes said "I am a part of
> you, instructor" ("Theme for English B") he was talking directly
> to his professor and to the relationship an instructor has with
> his student. For one thing, all teachers at one time were
> students, and he can remember when he received a similar
> assignment.
>   You have to realize that we are all interrelated in some way,
> and the context of your relationships is very important. When I
> stop and think about it, this is something that we can notice in all
> aspects of our social life.

Notice that Hughes's use of *you* in his poem is appropriate; unfortu-
nately, the pronoun usage in the earlier composition is inconsistent. Locate
all the inconsistencies, and correct them.

Be sure always to check your own drafts for pronoun consistency and
other pronoun errors.

◆ STUDENT DRAFT

Read the following draft, then check using the Revising Questions and the
Editing Questions. What are the draft's strengths and weaknesses? How
would you tell the writer to improve it?

> Some people think that the homeless are people who
> deserve the way they live because they are either on drugs or
> have an alcohol problem. Yet, if you ask them, they really don't
> have much experience with any individual homeless persons.
> If they did, they would see that many people who can't afford
> rent work and make an honest living; they don't make enough
> money to pay for rent for an apartment, especially if they have
> a family.
>   Take Maria, for example. Who left an abusive husband in
> Mexico. She became homeless because she was afraid he would
> start abusing her daughters. So she took her three daughters and
> tried to make a better life here in the United States. At first Maria
> had a difficult time. She took work as a maid until she could find
> better work to do. This was not earning her enough money to
> pay for an apartment, so she wound up in the Homeless Shelter.

She was such a model guest there, cleaning the place and asking for extra chores, that the Volunteer for Homeless agency let her have a subsidized apartment which they relegate for only those people they feel have potential to make it.

Soon there after, Maria met Jose, a fellow Mexican. Jose fell in love not only with Maria but with her three beautiful daughters. He asked her to marry him and now they live in a lovely little house in Piscataway, New Jersey where Jose has a job as a cook in an Italian restaurant.

Maria found work at K-Mart because her English has improved so much that she can now sell merchandise in a store.

I would love those people who stereotype the homeless and would stop all aid to this population to meet the Sanchez family, Maria, Jose, Isabel, Leticia and Sandra. They are lovely model citizens who needed help in their journey through life.

CHAPTER
6
Voices of Men and Women

PREREADING

1. Has anyone you know ever been abused because of stereotypical notions about gender roles?
2. How are gender stereotypes different in the late twentieth/early twenty-first century from those of the mid-twentieth century? Do you think these stereotypes will continue to change?
3. Do different cultures have different attitudes about gender roles? Can you cite any examples?

◆ VOCABULARY

turmeric (para. 5)—a yellow spice common in Indian food
auspicious (para. 5)—heralding good fortune
incandescent (para. 6)—glowing from within
nectar (para. 8)—a sweet liquid extracted from fruit
pomegranate (para. 28)—a bitter fruit common in the Mediterranean area

The Mistress of Spices
Chitra Banerjee Divakaruni

The following is an excerpt from The Mistress of Spices *by San Francisco writer-teacher Chitra Banerjee Divakaruni. Winner of many awards for her writing, including the PEN Oakland Josephine Miles Prize for Fiction, Divakaruni has also won acclaim for her work helping abused women. She is originally from India.*

When you open the bin that sits by the entrance to the store 1
you smell it right away, though it will take a little while for your
brain to register that subtle scent, faintly bitter like your skin and
almost as familiar.

Brush the surface with your hand, and the silky yellow powder 2
will cling to the pads of your palm, to your fingertips. Dust from a butterfly wing.

Bring it to your face. Rub it on cheek, forehead, chin. Don't be 3
hesitant. For a thousand years before history began, brides—and those
who long to be brides—have done the same. It will erase blemishes
and wrinkles, suck away age and fat. For days afterward, your skin
will give off a pale golden glow.

Each spice has a day special to it. For turmeric it is Sunday, when 4
light drips fat and butter-colored into the bins to be soaked up glowing, when you pray to the nine planets for love and luck.

Turmeric which is also named *halud,* meaning yellow, color of 5
daybreak and conch-shell sound. Turmeric the preserver, keeping
foods safe in a land of heat and hunger. Turmeric the auspicious spice,
placed on the heads of newborns for luck, sprinkled over coconuts at
pujas, rubbed into the borders of wedding saris.

But there is more. That is why I pick them only at the precise 6
moment when night slides into day, those bulbous roots like gnarly-
brown fingers, why I grind them only when Swati the faith-star shines
incandescent in the north.

When I hold it in my hands, the spice speaks to me. Its voice is 7
like evening, like the beginning of the world.

I am turmeric who rose out of the ocean of milk when the devas and 8
asuras churned for the treasures of the universe. I am turmeric who came after
the nectar and before the poison and thus lie in between.

Yes, I whisper, swaying to its rhythm. You are turmeric, shield 9
for heart's sorrow, anointment for death, hope for rebirth.

Together we sing this song, as we have many times.   10

And so I think at once of turmeric when Ahuja's wife comes into   11
my store this morning wearing dark glasses.

Ahuja's wife is young and seems even younger. Not a brash,   12
buoyant young but raw and flinching, like someone who's lately been
told and told she's not good enough.

She comes every week after payday and buys the barest staples: 13
cheap coarse rice, *dals* on sale, a small bottle of oil, maybe some atta
to make *chapatis*. Sometimes I see her hold up a jar of mango achar or
a packet of *papads* with hesitant wanting. But always she puts it back.

I offer her a *gulab-jamun* from the *mithai* case, but she blushes   14
fiercely and painfully and shakes her head.

Ahuja's wife has of course a name. Lalita. *La-li-ta*, three liquid   15
syllables perfect-suited to her soft beauty. I would like to call her by
it, but how can I while she thinks of herself only as a wife.

She has not told me this. She has said little to me, in all her times   16
of coming, except *"Namaste"* and "Is this on sale" and "Where can I
find." But I know it as I know other things.

Such as: Ahuja is a watchman at the docks and likes a drink or   17
two. Or three or four, recently.

Such as: She too has a gift, a power, though she does not think   18
of it so. Every cloth she touches with her needle blooms.

One time I found her leaning over the showcase where I keep   19
fabrics, looking at the palloo of a sari embroidered with *zari* thread.

I took it out. "Here," I said, draping it over her shoulder. "That   20
mango color looks so nice on you."

"No, no." She drew back quick and apologetic. "I was only see-   21
ing the stitching."

"Ah. You stitch."   22

"I used to a lot, once. I loved it. In Kanpur I was going to sewing   23
school, I had my own Singer machine, lot of ladies gave me stitching
to do."

She looked down. In the dejected curve of her neck I saw what   24
she did not say, the dream she had dared to: One day soon, maybe perhaps why not, her own shop, Lalita Tailor Works.

But four years back a well-meaning neighbor came to her   25
mother and said, Bahenji, there's a boy, most suitable, living in phoren,
earning American dollars, and her mother said Yes.

"Why don't you work in this country," I asked. "I'm sure many   26
ladies here too need stitching. Wouldn't you like—"

She gave me a longing look. "O yes." Then stopped.   27

Here is what she wants to tell me, only how can she, it is not   28
right that a woman should say such things about her man: All day at
home is so lonely, the silence like quicksand sucking at her wrists and
ankles. Tears she cannot stop, disobedient tears like spilled pomegranate seeds, and Ahuja shouting when he returns home to her
swollen eyes.

He refuses that his woman should work. *Aren't I man enough*   29
man enough man enough. The words shattering like dishes swept from
the dinner table.

Today I pack her purchases, meager as always: *masoor dal,* two   30
pounds of *atta,* a little *jeera.* Then I see her looking in the glass case at
a silver baby rattle, her eyes dark as a well to drown in.

For that is what Ahuja's wife wants most of all. A baby. Surely   31
a baby would make everything right, even the heaving, grunting,
never-ending nights, the weight pinning her down, the hot sour animal breath panted into her. His voice like the callused flat of a hand
arcing out of the dark.

A baby to negate it all, tugging at her with its sweetmilk   32
mouth.

Child-longing, deepest desire, deeper than for wealth or lover   33
or even death. It weighs down the air of the store, purple like before
a storm. It gives off the smell of thunder. Scorches.

O Lalita who is not yet Lalita, I have the balm to lay over your   34
burning. But how unless you ready yourself, hold yourself open to the
storm? How unless you ask?

Meanwhile I give you turmeric.   35

A handful of turmeric wrapped in old newspaper with the   36
words of healing whispered into it, slipped into your grocery sack
when you are not looking. The string tied into a triple flower knot, and
inside, satin-soft turmeric the same color as the bruise seeping onto
your cheek from under the dark edge of your glasses.

◆ WORKING WITH WORDS

Divikaruni uses imagery to stimulate the senses. For example, in the very first
sentence she talks about

. . . that subtle scent, faintly bitter like your skin and almost as familiar.

In the second, she compares a particular spice to

Dust from a butterfly wing.

This sort of description gives us both information as well as a more subtle message that stimulates our brains with sensory impressions. List at least five additional examples of this sort of imagery in the selection.

◆ EXAMINING CONTENT

1. According to the author, what are the characteristics of turmeric?
2. Describe Ahuja's wife, Lalita.
3. Why did Lalita stop stitching?
4. Why doesn't Lalita's husband Ahuja want her to work?
5. Why does she want a baby?

◆ RESPONDING TO IDEAS

1. How would turmeric help Lalita? How does the author use the spice as a metaphor?
2. Just from what you have read, why do you think Divakaruni called this book *The Mistress of Spices?*
3. What is your opinion about Ahuja's behavior toward his wife?
4. What do you think will happen in the future?
5. Is Lalita's situation typical of women in the United States? Is it typical of women in other parts of the world? Tell what you know about differing ways that some cultures deal with women.

◆ MORE WRITING TOPICS

Write about one of the following:

1. In a well-organized essay, describe how improving the treatment of women in a given culture is a benefit for everyone in that culture.
2. Is it possible that different groups—for example, men and women—can be substantially different, and yet equal in the eyes of the law and the society in which they live?

◆ **PREREADING**

1. Why is it so important today for teenagers to be "cool"?
2. How have teenagers in times past tried to gain acceptance with peers?
3. How does the media manipulate today's youth into buying products to be popular?

◆ **VOCABULARY**

amoebic (para. 1)—resembling an amoeba, a one-celled organism
gossamer (para. 1)—filmy, fine
omnivorous (para. 1)—feeding on both plants and animals
subsume (para. 2)—to make part of a whole
banalities (para. 3)—things devoid of freshness
obtusely (para. 3)—not quick or alert in perception
mien (para. 4)—face
patina (para. 4)—shiny surface
feigned (para. 7)—pretended
nonchalance (para. 7)—carefree manner
homogeneity (para. 7)—of the same kind
epiphany (para. 8)—sudden intuition or perception
iconoclast (para. 8)—one who attacks cherished beliefs
demographics (para. 10)—statistical data for a population
astute (para. 13)—keenly perceptive
oblivious (para. 13)—completely unaware

The Accidental Asian: Notes of a Native Speaker

Eric Liu

In his young life Eric Liu has been a successful television commentator, a print and on-line columnist, an editor, an anthologist, and a speechwriter for the president of the United States. He has studied at Yale and Harvard. Born in America, he has, in his 1998 memoir entitled The Accidental Asian: Notes of a Native Speaker *(from which the following piece is excerpted), examined issues of race in the United States with a careful, original, and highly articulate eye for detail.*

As a child, I lived in a state of "amoebic bliss," to borrow the 1
felicitous phrase of the author of *Nisei Daughter,* Monica Sone. The
world was a gossamer web of wonder that began with life at home,
extended to my friendships, and made the imaginary realm of day-
dream seem as immediate as the real. If something or someone was
in my personal web of meaning, then color or station was irrelevant.
I made no distinctions in fourth grade between my best friend, a black
boy named Kimathi, and my next-best friend, a white boy named
Charlie—other than the fact that one was number one, the other number two. I did not feel, or feel for, a seam that separated the textures
of my Chinese life from those of my American life. I was not "bicul-
tural" but omnicultural, and omnivorous, too. To my mind, I differed
from others in only two ways that counted: I was a faster runner than
most, and a better student. Thus did work blend happily with play,
school with home, Western culture with Eastern: it was all the same
to a self-confident boy who believed he'd always be at the center of
his own universe.

As I approached adolescence, though, things shifted. Suddenly, 2
I could no longer subsume the public world under my private concept
of self. Suddenly, the public world was more complicated than just a
parade of smiling teachers and a few affirming friends. Now I had to
contend with the unstated, inchoate, but inescapable standards of
cool. The essence of cool was the ability to conform. The essence of con-
formity was the ability to anticipate what was cool. And I wasn't so
good at that. For the first time, I had found something that did not
come effortlessly to me. No one had warned me about this transition
from happy amoeboid to social animal; no one had prepared me for
the great labors of fitting in.

And so in three adjoining arenas—my looks, my loves, my man- 3
ners—I suffered a bruising adolescent education. I don't mean to over-
dramatize: there was, in these teenage banalities, usually something
humorous and nothing particularly tragic. But in each of these realms,
I came to feel I was not normal. And obtusely, I ascribed the difficulties of that age not to my age but to my color. I came to suspect that
there was an order to things, an order that I, as someone Chinese,
could perceive but not quite crack. I responded not by exploding in
rebellion but by dedicating myself, quietly and sometimes angrily,
to learning the order as best I could. I was never ashamed of being
Chinese; I was, in fact, rather proud to be linked to a great civilization.

But I was mad that my difference should matter now. And if it had to matter, I did not want it to defeat me.

Consider, if you will, my hair. For the first eleven years of my   4
life, I sported what was essentially the same hairstyle: a tapered bowl cut, the handiwork of my mother. For those eleven joyful years, this low-maintenance do was entirely satisfactory. But in my twelfth year, as sixth grade got under way, I became aware—gradually at first, then urgently—that bangs were no longer the look for boys. This was the year when certain early bloomers first made the height-weight-physique distribution in our class seem startlingly wide—and when I first realized that I was lingering near the bottom. It was essential that I compensate for my childlike mien by cultivating at least a patina of teenage style.

This is where my hair betrayed me. For some readers the words   5
"Chinese hair" should suffice as explanation. For the rest, particularly those who have spent all your lives with the ability to comb back, style, and part your hair *at will*, what follows should make you count your blessings. As you may recall, 1980 was a vintage year for hair that was parted straight down the middle, then feathered on each side, feathered so immaculately that the ends would meet in the back like the closed wings of angels. I dreamed of such hair. I imagined tossing my head back casually, to ease into place the one or two strands that had drifted from their positions. I dreamed of wearing the fluffy, tailored locks of the blessed.

Instead, I was cursed. My hair was straight, rigid, and wiry. Not   6
only did it fail to feather back; it would not even bend. Worse still, it grew the wrong way. That is, it all emanated from a single swirl near the rear edge of my scalp. Parting my hair in any direction except back to front, the way certain balding men stage their final retreat, was a physical impossibility. It should go without saying that this was a disaster. For the next three years, I experimented with a variety of hairstyles that ranged from the ridiculous to the sublimely bad. There was the stringy pothead look. The mushroom do. Helmet head. Bangs folded back like curtains. I enlisted a blow-dryer, a Conair set on high heat, to force my hair into postures of submission. The results, though sometimes innovative, fell always far short of cool.

I feigned nonchalance, and no one ever said anything about it.   7
But make no mistake: this was one of the most consuming crises of my inner life as a young teen. Though neither of my parents had ever

had such troubles, I blamed this predicament squarely on my Chinese genes. And I could not abide my fate. At a time when homogeneity was the highest virtue, I felt I stood out like a pigtailed Manchu.

My salvation didn't come until the end of junior high, when one of my buddies, in an epiphany as we walked past the Palace of Hair Design, dared me to get my head shaved. Without hesitation, I did it— to the tearful laughter of my friends and, soon afterward, the tearful horror of my mother. Of course, I had moments of doubt the next few days as I rubbed my peach-fuzzed skull. But what I liked was this: I had managed, without losing face, to rid myself of my greatest social burden. What's more, in the eyes of some classmates, I was now a bold (if bald) iconoclast. I've worn a crew cut ever since.   8

Well-styled hair was only one part of a much larger preoccupation during the ensuring years: wooing girls. In this realm I experienced a most frustrating kind of success. I was the boy that girls always found "sweet" and "funny" and "smart" and "nice." Which, to my highly sensitive ear, sounded like "leprous." Time and again, I would charm a girl into deep friendship. Time and again, as the possibility of romance came within reach, I would smash into what I took to be a glass ceiling.   9

The girls were white, you see; such were the demographics of my school. I was Chinese. And I was convinced that this was the sole obstacle to my advancement. It made sense, did it not? I was, after all, sweet and funny and smart and nice. Hair notwithstanding, I was not unattractive, at least compared with some of the beasts who had started "going out" with girls. There was simply no other explanation. Yet I could never say this out loud: it would have been the whining of a loser. My response, then, was to secretly scorn the girls I coveted. It was *they* who were subpar, whose small-mindedness and veiled prejudice made them unworthy.   10

My response, too, was to take refuge in my talents. I made myself into a Renaissance boy, playing in the orchestra but also joining the wrestling team, winning science prizes but also editing the school paper. I thought I was defying the stereotype of the Asian American male as a one-dimensional nerd. But in the eyes of some, I suppose, I was simply another "Asian overachiever."   11

In hindsight, it's hard to know exactly how great a romantic penalty I paid for being Chinese. There may have been girls who would have had nothing to do with me on account of my race, but I   12 never knew them. There were probably girls who, race aside, simply didn't like me. And then there were girls who liked me well enough but who also shied from the prospect of being part of an interracial couple. With so many boys out there, they probably reasoned, why take the path of greater resistance? Why risk so many status points? Why not be "just friends" with this Chinese boy?

Maybe this stigma was more imagined than real. But being an   13 ABC ("American-born Chinese," as our parents called us) certainly affected me another way. It made me feel like something of a greenhorn, a social immigrant. I wanted so greatly to be liked. And my earnestness, though endearing, was not the sort of demeanor that won girls' hearts. Though I was observant enough to notice how people talked when flirting, astute enough to mimic the forms, I was oblivious to the subterranean levels of courtship, blind to the more subtle rituals of "getting chicks" by spurning them. I held the view that if you were manifestly a good person, eventually someone of the opposite sex would do the rational thing and be smitten with you. I was clueless. Many years would pass before I'd wise up.

It wasn't just dating rituals that befuddled me as a youth. It was   14 ritual of all kinds. Ceremony, protocol, etiquette—all these made me feel like an awkward stranger. Things that came as second nature to many white kids were utterly exotic to me. American-style manners, for instance. Chinese families often have their own elaborate etiquette, but "please" and "may I" weren't the sort of words ever heard around my house. That kind of formality seemed so beside the point. I was never taught by my parents to write thank-you notes. I didn't even have the breeding to *say* "Thank you" after sleeping over at a friend's house. I can recall the awful, sour feeling in my stomach when this friend told me his mother had been offended by my impoliteness. (At that point, I expressed my thanks.) . . .

◆ WORKING WITH WORDS

Give the meaning that each of the following prefixes provides to the word to which it is attached. Then, give several examples of words beginning with each of the prefixes.

1. Bi-	3. Demo-	5. Sub-
2. Omni-	4. Homo-	6. Epi-

◆ EXAMINING CONTENT

1. How did Liu describe his feelings when he was a child?
2. What personal strengths had he come to rely on while growing up?
3. What was the first major problem he encountered in his desire to be cool? What was his solution?
4. What does the phrase "feigned nonchalance" (para. 7) mean?
5. How did girls tend to think of Liu?

◆ RESPONDING TO IDEAS

1. Although Liu's English was fine, even superior, he couldn't master the subtleties of flirting. Why not?
2. What did he mean by a "glass ceiling"? (para. 9)
3. Liu tells his story with a wry sense of humor. Give examples from the text that make us smile.
4. Compare Liu's feelings about his looks with those of Richard Rodriguez on page 144 in the previous chapter.
5. Do standards for looks vary from culture to culture? Why do you think this is?

◆ MORE WRITING TOPICS

1. Can the looks of a particular ethnic group or race be considered more or less fashionable than those of another? Comment on this phenomenon in an essay that is clear and straight to the point.
2. Think of the different ways that people alter their appearances. Some are subtle, and some are radical. They can vary from combing one's hair a different way, or changing one clothing style, to doing permanent physical changes to the face or the body. Write an essay on this topic, telling how you feel about fashion, appearance, and people.

◆ **PREREADING**

1. In many cultures rituals demonstrate boys' coming of age. Can you think of any such ceremonies?
2. Do you think it is difficult for a boy to prove to his peers that he has courage? Is it the same or different for a girl?
3. Do you think that hunting is a moral or immoral activity? Explain.

◆ **VOCABULARY**

oppressive (para. 6)—a heavy quality
amulet (para. 7)—a necklace with a charm
reptilian (para. 11)—scaly; having the quality of a reptile
bile (para. 16)—a secretion from the liver

Tortuga
Rudolfo Anaya

Professor of languages and literature at the University of New Mexico, Rudolfo Anaya tells the following story about coming of age and the tribal nature of hunting. He is the winner of several writing prizes, including the PEN Center USA West Literary Award. "Salomon's Story" was included in his 1979 collection called Tortuga.

Before I came here I was a hunter, but that was long ago. Still, it was in the pursuit of the hunt that I came face to face with my destiny. This is my story.   1

We called ourselves a tribe and we spent our time hunting and fishing along the river. For young boys that was a great adventure. Each morning I stole away from my father's home to meet my fellow hunters by the river. My father was a farmer who planted corn on the hills bordering the river. He was a good man. He kept the ritual of the seasons, marked the path of the sun and the moon across the sky, and he prayed each day that the order of things not be disturbed.   2

He did his duty and tried to teach me about the rhythm in the weather and the seasons, but a wild urge in my blood drove me   3

from him. I went willingly to join the tribe along the river. The call of
the hunt was exciting, and daily the slaughter of the animals with the
small of blood drove us deeper and deeper into the dark river. I became a member of the tribe, and I forgot the fields of my father. We
hunted birds with our crude weapons and battered to death stray rac-
coons and rabbits. Then we skinned the animals and filled the air
with the smoke of roasting meat. The tribe was pleased with me and
welcomed me as a hunter. They prepared for my initiation.

I, Salomon, tell you this so that you may know the meaning of   4
life and death. How well I know it now, how clear are the events of the
day I killed the giant river turtle. Since that day I have been a storyteller, forced by the order of my destiny to reveal my story. I speak
to tell you how the killing became a horror.

The silence of the river was heavier than usual that day. The   5
heat stuck to our sweating skin like a sticky syrup and the insects
sucked our blood. Our half-naked bodies moved like shadows in the
brush. Those ahead and behind me whispered from time to time, com-
plaining that we were lost and suggesting that we turn back. I said
nothing, it was the day of my initiation, I could not speak. There had
been a fight at camp the night before and the bad feelings still lin-
gered. But we hunted anyway, there was nothing else to do. We were
compelled to hunt in the dark shadows of the river. Some days the
spirit for the hunt was not good, fellow hunters quarreled over small
things, and still we had to start early at daybreak to begin the long
day's journey which would not bring us out until sunset.

In the branches above us the bird cries were sharp and frightful.   6
More than once the leader lifted his arm and the line froze, ready for
action. The humid air was tense. Somewhere to my left I heard the
river murmur as it swept south, and for the first time the dissatisfac-
tion which had been building within me surfaced. I cursed the oppressive darkness and wished I was free of it. I thought of my father
walking in the sunlight of his green fields, and I wished I was with
him. But it was not so; I owed the tribe my allegiance. Today I would
become a full member. I would kill the first animal we encountered.

We moved farther than usual into unknown territory, hacking   7
away at the thick underbrush; behind me I heard murmurs of dis-
sension. Some wanted to turn back, others wanted to rest on the warm
sandbars of the river, still others wanted to finish the argument which
had started the night before. My father had given me an amulet to

wear and he had instructed me on the hunt, and this made the leader jealous. Some argued that I could wear the amulet, while others said no. In the end the jealous leader tore it from my neck and said that I would have to face my initiation alone.

I was thinking about how poorly prepared I was and how my 8 father had tried to help, when the leader raised his arm and sounded the alarm. A friend behind me whispered that if we were in luck there would be a deer drinking at the river. No one had ever killed a deer in the memory of our tribe. We held our breath and waited, then the leader motioned and I moved forward to see. There in the middle of the narrow path lay the biggest tortoise any of us had ever seen. It was a huge monster which had crawled out of the dark river to lay its eggs in the warm sand. I felt a shiver, and when I breathed the taste of copper drained in my mouth and settled in my queasy stomach.

The giant turtle lifted its huge head and looked at us with dull, 9 glintless eyes. The tribe drew back. Only I remained facing the monster from the water. Its slimy head dripped with bright green algae. It hissed a warning. It had come out of the water to lay its eggs, now it had to return to the river. Wet, leathery eggs, fresh from the laying, clung to its webbed feet, and as it moved forward it crushed them into the sand. Its gray shell was dry, dulled by the sun, encrusted with dead parasites and green growth; it needed the water.

"Kill it!" the leader cried, and at the same time the hunting horn 10 sounded its too-rou which echoed down the valley. Ah, its call was so sad and mournful I can hear it today as I tell my story. . . . Listen, Tortuga, it is now I know that at that time I could have forsaken my initiation and denounced the darkness and insanity that urged us to the never-ending hunt. I had not listened to my father's words. The time was not right.

"The knife," the leader called, and the knife of the tribe was 11 passed forward, then slipped into my hand. The huge turtle lumbered forward. I could not speak. In fear I raised the knife and brought it down with all my might. Oh, I prayed to no gods, but since then how often I have wished that I could undo what I did. One blow severed the giant turtle's head. One clean blow and the head rolled in the sand as the reptilian body reared back, gushing green slime. The tribe cheered and pressed forward. They were as surprised as I was that the kill had been so swift and clean. We had hunted smaller tortoises before and we knew that once they retreated into their shells it took hours to kill them. Then knives and spears had to be poked into the holes and the turtle had to be turned on its back so the tedious task of cutting the softer underside could begin. But now I had beheaded the giant turtle with one blow.

"There will be enough meat for the entire tribe," one of the boys   12
cried. He speared the head and held it aloft for everyone to see. I could only look at the dead turtle that lay quivering on the sand, its death urine and green blood staining the damp earth.

"He has passed his test," the leader shouted, "he did not need   13
the amulet of his father. We will clean the shell and it will be his shield! And he shall now be called the man who slew the turtle!"

The tribe cheered, and for a moment I bathed in my glory. The   14
fear left me, and so did the desire to be with my father on the harsh hills where he cultivated his fields of corn. He had been wrong; I could trust the tribe and its magic. Then someone shouted and we turned to see the turtle struggling toward us. It reared up, exposing the gaping hole where the head had been, then it charged, surprisingly swift for its huge size. Even without its head it crawled toward the river. The tribe fell back in panic.

"Kill it!" the leader shouted, "Kill it before it reaches the water!   15
If it escapes into the water it will grow two heads and return to haunt us!"

I understood what he meant. If the creature reached the safety   16
of the water it would live again, and it would become one more of the ghosts that lurked along our never-ending path. Now there was nothing I could do but stand my ground and finish the killing. I struck at it until the knife broke on its hard shell, and still the turtle rumbled toward the water, pushing me back. Terror and fear made me fall on the sand and grab it with my bare hands. Grunting and gasping for breath I dug my bare feet into the sand. I slipped one hand into the dark, bleeding hole where the head had been and with the other I grabbed its huge feet. I struggled to turn it on its back and rob it of its strength, but I couldn't. Its dark instinct for the water and the pull of death were stronger than my fear and desperation. I grunted and cursed as its claws cut into my arms and legs. The brush shook with our violent thrashing as we rolled down the bank towards the river. Even mortally wounded it was too strong for me. At the edge of the river, it broke free from me and plunged into the water, trailing frothy blood and bile as it disappeared into the gurgling waters.

Covered with turtle's blood, I stood numb and trembling. As I   17
watched it disappear into the dark waters of the river, I knew I had
done a wrong. Instead of conquering my fear, I had created another
shadow which would return to haunt us. I turned and looked at my
companions; they trembled with fright.

"You have failed us," the leader whispered. "You have angered   18
the river gods." He raised his talisman, a stick on which hung chicken
feathers, dried juniper berries and the rattler of a snake we had killed
in the spring, and he waved it in front of me to ward off the curse.
Then they withdrew in silence and vanished into the dark brush, leaving me alone on that stygian bank.

Oh, I wish I could tell you how lonely I felt. I cried for the tur-   19
tle to return so I could finish the kill, or return its life, but the force of
my destiny was already set and that was not to be. I understand that
now. That is why I tell you my story. I left the river, free of the tribe,
but unclean and smelling of death.

That night the bad dreams came, and then the paralysis. . . .   20

◆ WORKING WITH WORDS

Anaya uses rich and vivid imagery in his writing. He creates a dark mood or
ambience with his stories, which often use violence to create drama. Write
down five phrases or sentences from the story that are examples of such imagery, and tell why you selected these passages.

◆ EXAMINING CONTENT

1. What did the protagonist's father do for a living?
2. Why did he go away from his father?
3. What did hunting teach the young boy?
4. Why was the leader jealous?
5. Why did the protagonist believe he was poorly prepared for the
   hunt?
6. What happened to the turtle finally?
7. Why did the boy have bad dreams after the turtle returned to the
   water?

◆ RESPONDING TO IDEAS

The story you just read can be seen as a metaphor, or a comparison with something other than its literal meaning. Of the excerpt, Anaya says the following:

> The story reflects my growing up along the river and the fishing and hunting that we used to do as kids. Later on in life, reflecting on that aspect of our nature as hunters, I realized that we had done some things wrong. I also learned that the relationship between the hunter and the animal that is hunted is very special.

With this quote in mind, answer the following:

1. How did Salomon make a mistake with the animal that he hunted, and how did this mistake affect the rest of his life?
2. In many societies the turtle is symbolic. What symbol do you think the turtle in this story stands for?
3. What ambivalence did Salomon feel about hunting? Find the part in the story that explains this and read it aloud.
4. Do you think the author of the story has conflicting feelings about killing animals in a hunt for pleasure? What part of the story makes you think this?

◆ MORE WRITING TOPICS

Write an essay addressing one of the following questions:

1. Is there more than one way for a boy to be masculine?
2. What are the gender stereotypes attached to males in our culture? In other cultures?
3. Is it possible for men to be both sensitive and strong?

◆ **PREREADING**

1. In this chapter we have been reading about coming of age rituals in diverse cultures. Tell about an incident in your childhood in which you were struggling to gain peer acceptance.
2. Is peer acceptance more difficult to obtain, and peer pressure stronger, in an urban setting or a small town? Why?

◆ **VOCABULARY**

demeanor (para. 12)—one's manner

nascent (para. 12)—beginning

hysterical (para. 28)—out of control

embezzlement (para. 48)—a crime involving the nonviolent theft of money, through fraud

necromancer (para. 74)—one who practices "black magic"

delegation (para. 80)—a group of people sent to carry a message or carry out a specific task

karma (para. 82)—a concept from Hinduism and Buddhism about the spiritual impact and ethical consequences of a person's actions

China Boy
Gus Lee

Born in America to a family of immigrants from Shanghai, Gus Lee has been a West Point cadet, a lawyer, a U.S. Army captain, a deputy district attorney for the City of Sacramento, and Director of Attorney Education for the State Bar of California. The following excerpt is taken from China Boy, *his first novel.*

After about twenty hours of instruction, I showed signs of progress in the Handle. 1

Tyrone Sykes's ballistic missile bounced off my head. 2

"Hey, China Boy. Got hit upside de head wif my ball! Go get it, sucka!" 3

I looked toward him as I rubbed my head. 4

"China Boy, whatdafuck you lookin at?" 5

I was stuck for an answer. But Mr. Barraza and the Duke would   6
not want me to retrieve the ball. At least, not without having my
brains bashed in for the sake of the Rules.

I was, by not doing what Tyrone wanted, adding cod-liver oil   7
to sauerkraut—worsening a situation that at its best was not attractive. But I was neither retrieving nor running. Tyrone and I marveled
at that.

He pushed me, and I rocked back. I tightened my mouth, say-   8
ing nothing. Usually I whined. He swung at me and I brought my
guard up, too late, taking a hard sharp punch in my gut, but waving
my fists back at him.

Tyrone stopped. This was weird. Like watching a pigeon at-   9
tack Evil.

He threw some more punches and I glanced one of them away   10
from me with a parry, and as he cursed me I ran, then stopped, and
ducked, and parried. When he delivered his last blow, he avoided my
face, and looked worried. I had persevered, and I shed tears more in
relief than in pain.

The word was out. China Boy was showing hints of being   11
human. The effect was dramatic; little kids stayed away. The beatings
ceased to be daily events. Even my second-grade teacher, Mrs. Gwen-
dolyn Halloran, commented on my weight. "You're filling out, Kai,"
she said, and I smiled uncontrollably, having to turn my back and
bury my face in my hands.

Pride precedes the fall. My attitude showed, and Edna told me   12
to rid myself of that "disgusting demeanor of arrogant superior-
ity"—which, no doubt, was merely the timid appearance of nascent
self-belief.

I wanted that feeling too badly, and would not take it from my   13
face. She slapped me and I willed myself to endure it, blinking as if a
thousand strobes were exploding between my ears, behind my eyes. I
used to duck and cover my face, receiving ten blows instead of one. My
mouth turned into an inverted U, but I did not cry. I felt anger, rage,
then nothing as my face turned red. There was no triumph in this.

She looked at me carefully and then inspected me. It was not   14
the added weight; I think it was the change in effect. I was beginning
to have a place in the world, and it probably worried her.

Oh, God, she must have thought: another Jane. Next, this little   15
skinny pidgin-tongued etiquetteless Asian ragamuffin would be

saying to her, Don't Tread on Me, with all the conviction of her colonial Pennsylvanian antecedents.

"Do not do that again," she admonished. I was not sure what she 16 was prohibiting.

I had thought for an instant of boxing her. No. She was as dan- 17 gerous as Big Willie. Fighting either of them would have been a cultural impossibility, physically unthinkable.

I told Tío Hector Pueblo what I was doing and tried fitfully, with 18 wild pantomime, to describe the boxing faculty and my lessons. Hector had said that he was going to teach me "street," and I expected to learn a secret kick or power punch. I remembered his muscular arm pumping in our house.

"I ready, Tío," I said. I flexed my right arm, showing him my 19 new, developing bicep.

"Say, *soy listo*. Dat mean, 'I ready,' " he said. "Dat's a mighty fine 20 muscle, my fren'," he added, nodding his head and pursing his lips in stern approval.

"*Soy listo, Tío*," I said. "Teach me secret kick?" 21

Instead, he taught me how to walk. 22

"*Joven*," he said, "you *walkando como un armadillo* dat go from 23 four leg to two leg."

Through a quirk of nature, I, a reptile, had suddenly been ren- 24 dered a biped. I looked funny, awkward, bent as if bearing a heavy shell on my back and out of place. I guess that fit.

"*Joven*, you gotta show some *prestigio*. You gotta roll yo' shoulder 25 *back*. Now, put up yo' head, *tu cabeza*. Lif up high. Keep yo' back mo' straight. Don't' forget yo' shoulder. . . . Jesus Cristo, wha's wrong wif yo' body, chico? Now, you try, take step same time—"

Hector gave that up and went to my facial expression, which 26 was bland in the extreme. It was that way to hide the fear.

"Cho' *anger*, niño! *Enojado!* You pissed! All dese kids poun you, 27 you angry! Even if yo' li'l body all shrivel' up an bent, no matta! Mean mug, dat's good. Now, you practice yo' *anger* face."

I tried, but I really didn't hate the kids on my block. My effort 28 made Hector roar. Hector's laugh was infectious—one of those free, melodically hysterical things that sweeps up innocent bystanders in the wake of the sound, the victim uncaring about the origin of the humor.

"I wan rearn secret kick," I said, still giggling.   29

"Niño, firs' you need a face. *Tu cara bonita,* it look so empty. Dat   30
piss kids off, dey tink dey got no effec' on you.

"Yo' *cara,* she start more fight den no secret kick can finish, you   31
get my meaning," he said.

I thought he was talking about cars in his shop.   32

"*Cara bonita.* Han'some face. Yo' han'some face, *niño. Hombre!*   33
You so much work! I gotta teach walkando, yo' face, gotta teach yo'
secret kick, gotta teach you *Español, también!*

"*Escucheme, joven.* You get big, someday, you 'member Hector   34
Pueblo, hokay?" He smiled and rubbed my hair.

When I started taking formal Spanish language classes in junior   35
high, I persisted in the belief that *walkando* was the correct idiomatic
gerund for the infinitive *andar,* to walk.

"Señor Losada," I said. "*Yo aprendí Español cuando era un joven,*   36
y la palabra correcta es 'walkando.' "

My lessons in Y.M.C.A. sports, Panhandle *walkando,* street face,   37
and Spanish were wiping out my afternoons and Saturdays at home.
I was not missed. Janie had found a cluster of friends near Anza and
Encanto, where people had lawns, cars, and televisions. Edna en-
couraged her to spend as much time away from home as possible.
Overnights were encouraged.

Mrs. Halloran was at my desk. "You're wanted in the princi-   38
pal's office," she said.

My father was there, carrying a suitcase. He smiled at me. I   39
grinned back; I had not seen him for two weeks. We got into the Ford
and drove through the hills of the City to the bank on Jackson Street
in Chinatown.

In the dark and high-ceilinged back offices, Father handed   40
the suitcase to Curzon Fong, the executive vice-president. While
Fong Syensheng spun the series of multiple combination locks on the
case, I stood against the wall and gazed upward at the golden
framed portrait of Madame Amethyst Jade Cheng. Click-click, click-
click, sounded the tumblers. Inside the locked case were stacks
of English currency, bound in yellow wrappers imprinted with un-
cut red Chinese chops, signature stamps. The money smelled stale,
and humid.

I could feel my father reaching out to me, trying desperately to   41
make a connection, to impart knowledge and wisdom. This was not
playing catch; this was important. I looked up at him as suddenly as
if he had spoken to me, and he glanced down and nodded. He was
telling me something about money, about himself and Mr. Fong, that
was somehow connected to me.

When we were outside of the bank, he said, "Never steal." While   42
driving me back to school, he added, "Always work hard. Then you
can name your ticket. You understand?"

I shook my head, worried. I did not know why I would   43
want to name a ticket something else. A Muni bus ticket? To change
its name?

"What new name for 'ticket,' Baba?" I asked.   44

"Agh!" he said, "Uh," his hand gesturing, making small rotat-   45
ing circles, "work hard."

He did not know how to decode children, for he had never seen   46
the process in his own house. I wanted to help him, but I felt con-
stricted, struggling against the limitations of understanding and language. I was looking for a way of saying, "Just talk. Say anything.
Don't ask if I understand. Tell why Mah-mee died, what I did to invite the Cancer God into our home. How I can live with Edna. If we'll
have Chinese food at home again," but the way was not clear.

"Okay, Father. I work hard," I said, not believing that this pro-   47
vided the answer. He nodded, and I breathed again.

The continuing struggles of the China Lights Bank required my   48
father to travel. He went to Hong Kong, Singapore, Jakarta, and
Taipei. He usually returned with money for the bank, but none of it
filtered to our home. Later, when the embezzlement scandal of the
bank became common knowledge, I realized how impeccably honest
Father had been.

To see Toussaint during school hours, I had to play with him   49
during recess and lunch. That meant leaving the protective circle of
the yard teacher. My lack of athletic abilities made that difficult.

Periodically, one of Big Willie's cohorts would punch me a   50
few times for grins or my lunch money, driven by greed or the im-
prints of indelible practice. I tried parries, but they were tight, tense,
and ineffective. The Bashers tightened lips, hunched shoulders, and
let fly.

The beatings were not as frequent as in the beginning of my   51
street education, but I still had headaches and a bad stomach after
any encounter with Willis Mack.

"China Boy, you'se jus a stupid fool ofa chink. You'se standin   52
here in my schoo' yard, like ratfacedogshit. I'se gonna teach ya'll some
Fist City, China Boy." He laughed. "Gimme yo' face. . . ." Willie Mack
was a talker. He had a promising future as a charismatic political or-
ator, and I always wished that he had moved on to politics, at the cost
of junior terrorism, sooner.

But my Y.M.C.A. dodgeball practice, with dive-and-rolls, and   53
tumbling, which taught shoulder rolls, were paying off. In dodgeball.

Robert Chill was the Y.M.C.A. fix-it man, and one of the reasons   54
why I was improving in sports. He sounded like a junkyard dog
jangling through refuse when he walked, his tools, wires, hammers,
clamps, and plumb lines jangling like uncoordinated pogo sticks. He
wore long dirty hair. In the fifties, that was as cool as saying you
sought sexual congress with ostriches.

We loved his tool bag as much as we did watching our boxing   55
faculty give demonstrations of its storied, professional past.

Mr. Chill liked to offer himself as a dodgeball target, yelping   56
and giggling as we tossed the ball his way. He was special to me, because he was worse in dodgeball than I. Even I could hit him.

"Kai," said he. "Athletics is just *trying.* All you gotta do is put   57
out, and you can play *sports* anywhere." I didn't believe him. But of
course, he was right.

"China," said Toussaint, "ya'll lookin less like a gimp in dodge.   58
Got less spaz in ya."

"Rearn dodgeball an roun' ball at Y. Rearn swimmin."   59

Toussaint's eyes opened wide. No one in the 'hood knew how   60
to swim.

"Dat's cool," he said, not meaning it.   61

"Rearn box, too, Toussaint," I said. I had kept it a secret from   62
kids. It was the kind of disclosure that could only lead to more trouble. Someone would say, Oh yeah? So show yo' stuff, ratface! I must
have thought that I was learning something, to have told him.

"Ya'll fought back 'gainst Tyrone Sykes cuz a da Y.M.C.A.? Not   63
cuz *I* teaches ya'll how ta fist?"

"Toos. Ya teach me good. Y help, too. Big man. Name, Misser   64
Baza. Misser Baza rike Sippy, Toos. He be fighta," I said.

"China—ya mean a *pro,* wif *gloves,* an a *ring?*"   65

I nodded. I imagined Toussaint having Mr. Barraza and Mr.   66
Lewis as his teachers. Toussaint could be another Rufus Monk. He
had such courage—what Mr. Barraza called Heart. What the Y called
Spirit. What I called Wishful Thinking.

Toos's wild punches, if coached, could flatten houses.   67

"Toussaint—ask Momma sen you Y, wif me!"   68

His eyes lit up with the thought. Then he said, "Nah, not fo' me.   69
Don't dig fightin, jes' fo' fightin. Ain't cool." He didn't say: China,
whatever the Y costs, whatever the bus costs, we don't have it.

J.T. Cooper came up to Toos.   70

"China Boy be bad luck, Toos," he said.   71

"Howzat," said Toos.   72

"No way our charms gonna work wif him," he said. "China Boy   73
ain't black. Ain't fey, ain't white. He a voodoo ghost!"

"J.T., you'se a crazy dude wif dat charm an voodoo."   74

J.T.'s mother was an unlicensed necromancer. She had left Sta-   75
mina Jones's Holy Christian Church of Almighty God, our only congregation, to rattle stones, shuffle chicken feathers, and speak to
roaches on the kitchen floor. Reverend Jones had asked Mrs. Cooper
to return to the flock, to no avail.

She had done the necromancy with a modicum of debonair de-   76
tachment until the Army called out her husband for the second time.
He had served already in World War II.

His departure for Oakland Army Base was preceded by wild   77
parties and loud music, which I remembered watching, and hearing,
from our window before Edna came into our home.

"Lucian, he went to Ko-rea. But his spirit? It here, in my   78
kitchen."

She began to cast horoscopes for her friends. Initially, her pre-   79
dictions were so wildly entertaining that many of the women who
scoffed at her rejection of Jesus for the love of poultry bones cast aside
their disbelief and hiked up her stairs.

"My momma know *everythin,*" said J.T. "Ain't *nut'in* da wom-   80
anfolk on dis block don tell her."

Mrs. Cooper missed her husband and told others that he was   81
sending her messages through the radio and through the copper
plumbing in the upstairs apartment bathroom. My mother would
have liked her a lot. A delegation led by Mrs. Timms and backed up

by Mrs. LaRue went to the Cooper house, straggling up the steep wooden, slivered stairs, to petition her to return to the church.

Mrs. Cooper, besides having the corner on the neighborhood gossip, supported an outlandish sense of humor and possessed the superior alto in the choir. In her absence, the less qualified voices in the congregation were obtaining entirely too much purchase, and her laughter was missed on bingo night.   82

The delegation left looking somber, with a great shaking of heads. Mrs. Cooper would not kill any of the cockroaches that infested her house. I understood that completely; Mrs. Cooper's karma was *excellent*.   83

"Oughta fix these here stairs," said Mrs. Timms.   84

One day the whole neighborhood came out when J.T.'s mother flew screaming from their door in her nightclothes. She stood at the top of the stoop and bent from the waist, her hands between her knees, gathering her nightie.   85

"My husban's bin kilt in Ko-rea!" she wailed in a voice broken with wild grief. "Da roaches tole me dat!"   86

But the Army people didn't come to pay a visit, and she got no star on her window. Her status as a prophet went the way of the 1929 stock market.   87

Her coin was down, and J.T. stopped calling me a ghost.   88

"Cool, Toos, cool. China Boy ain't no ghost. But, he still be the China Boy, and it be the same fucken thing! He ain't got no color in 'em, wif all dat voodoo in dere."   89

"J.T., sometimes yo mouf gimme a headache in mah neck!" said Toussaint.   90

"China. Someday ya'll gotta start talkin like me. Save some skin on da hans. And yo' face. Now, China, lissen. Say dis, 'I ain't fo' yo pushin on, no mo'!' Go 'head—say it!"   91

"Uh. I no, uh, I ain't fo' no push me, uh—pushin, uh, on you? Me?" I tried.   92

"Lordy. Momma save us bof," said Toos.   93

◆ WORKING WITH WORDS

There is much dialect dialogue in the preceding excerpt that exemplifies urban or "street" language. If it seems difficult to understand, once it is read aloud the meaning becomes clear. Write eight examples of dialect dialogue, then write a "translation" of it in regular English.

> Example: "Got hit upside de head wif my ball" (para. 3)
> *Was hit in the head with my ball.*

◆ EXAMINING CONTENT

1. How was China Boy ill suited for life in the streets?
2. Why was China Boy in trouble with Tyrone?
3. What defensive attitude was China Boy taking with his peers that made him unpopular?
4. How did he learn Spanish? Was it different from what he learned in school? How?
5. Describe J.T.'s mother.
6. Why does Toussaint want China Boy to talk differently?

◆ RESPONDING TO IDEAS

1. Explain how fighting can be thought of as a metaphor in this story.
2. How is China Boy being stereotyped by the other students in his school? How could he have improved the situation?
3. Why do you think China Boy's mother would have liked Mrs. Timms?
4. Why is it not considered cool to swim and box?
5. Why do you think the author used so much dialect in telling the story?

◆ MORE WRITING TOPICS

1. Kids fighting to survive in the jungle of adolescence develop many different strengths. Some are fighters, and others must learn to use their wits. Write a descriptive essay about yourself or someone you know who had to use ingenious means to be accepted among peers.
2. What can adults do to make adolescence less difficult for children?

◆ **PREREADING**

1. What is a child worth to a family? What is a boy worth? What is a girl worth?

2. In some cultures, girls are worth less than boys. Why do you think this is so? What could be done to change that culture?

◆ **VOCABULARY**

cowbird (para. 5)—a blackbird that is known to lay its eggs in the nests of other birds

gloat (para. 21)—indulge in ridiculous satisfaction

deigned (para. 30)—to condescend; to agree with or agree to do something reluctantly

opulent (para. 34)—luxurious; indicative of wealth

gutted (para. 35)—disemboweled

The Woman Warrior: Memoirs of a Girlhood among Ghosts
Maxine Hong Kingston

Maxine Hong Kingston was born and raised in California. She has taught high school English there and in Hawaii. In her memoir, The Woman Warrior: Memoirs of a Girlhood among Ghosts, *from which the following excerpt is taken, she tells what it was like to be part of an American generation living among a Chinese immigrant older generation.*

My American life has been such a disappointment.   1

"I got straight A's, Mama."   2

"Let me tell you a true story about a girl who saved her village."   3

I could not figure out what was my village. And it was impor-   4
tant that I do something big and fine, or else my parents would sell
me when we made our way back to China. In China there were so-
lutions for what to do with little girls who ate up food and threw
tantrums. You can't eat straight A's.

When one of my parents or the emigrant villagers said, "Feed-   5
ing girls is feeding cowbirds," I would thrash on the floor and scream
so hard I couldn't talk. I couldn't stop.

"What's the matter with her?"   6

"I don't know. Bad, I guess. You know how girls are. 'There's   7
no profit in raising girls. Better to raise geese than girls.' "

"I would hit her if she were mine. But then there's no use wast-   8
ing all that discipline on a girl. 'When you raise girls, you're raising
children for strangers.' "

"Stop that crying!" my mother would yell. "I'm going to hit you   9
if you don't stop. Bad girl! Stop!" I'm going to remember never to hit
or to scold my children for crying, I thought, because then they will
only cry more.

"I'm not a bad girl," I would scream. "I'm not a bad girl. I'm   10
not a bad girl." I might as well have said, "I'm not a girl."

"When you were little, all you had to say was 'I'm not a bad   11
girl,' and you could make yourself cry," my mother says, talking-story
about my childhood.

I minded that the emigrant villagers shook their heads at my sis-   12
ter and me. "One girl—and another girl," they said, and made our
parents ashamed to take us out together. The good part about my
brothers being born was that people stopped saying, "All girls," but I
learned new grievances. "Did you roll an egg on *my* face like that when
I was born?" "Did you have a full-month party for *me*?" "Did you turn
on all the lights?" "Did you send *my* picture to Grandmother?" "Why
not? Because I'm a girl? Is that why not?" "Why didn't you teach me
English?" "You like having me beaten up at school, don't you?"

"She is very mean, isn't she?" the emigrant villagers would say.   13

"Come, children. Hurry. Hurry. Who wants to go out with Great-   14
Uncle?" On Saturday mornings my great-uncle, the ex-river pirate,
did the shopping. "Get your coats, whoever's coming."

"I'm coming. I'm coming. Wait for me."   15

When he heard girls' voices, he turned on us and roared, "No   16
girls!" and left my sisters and me hanging our coats back up, not looking at one another. The boys came back with candy and new toys.
When they walked through Chinatown, the people must have said,
"A boy—and another boy—and another boy!" At my great-uncle's
funeral I secretly tested out feeling glad that he was dead—the six-foot
bearish masculinity of him.

I went away to college—Berkeley in the sixties—and I studied, 17
and I marched to change the world, but I did not turn into a boy. I
would have liked to bring myself back as a boy for my parents to welcome with chickens and pigs. That was for my brother, who returned
alive from Vietnam.

If I went to Vietnam, I would not come back; females desert fam- 18
ilies. It was said, "There is an outward tendency in females," which
meant that I was getting straight A's for the good of my future husband's family, not my own. I did not plan ever to have a husband. I
would show my mother and father and the nosey emigrant villagers
that girls have no outward tendency. I stopped getting straight A's.

And all the time I was having to turn myself American-feminine, 19
or no dates.

There is a Chinese word for the female I—which is "slave." 20
Break the women with their own tongues!

I refused to cook. When I had to wash dishes, I would crack one 21
or two. "Bad girl," my mother yelled, and sometimes that made me
gloat rather than cry. Isn't a bad girl almost a boy?

"What do you want to be when you grow up, little girl?" 22

"A lumberjack in Oregon." 23

Even now, unless I'm happy, I burn the food when I cook. I do 24
not feed people. I let the dirty dishes rot. I eat at other people's tables
but won't invite them to mine, where the dishes are rotting.

If I could not-eat, perhaps I could make myself a warrior like 25
the swordswoman who drives me. I will—I must—rise and plow the
fields as soon as the baby comes out.

Once I get outside the house, what bird might call me; on what 26
horse could I ride away? Marriage and childbirth strengthen the
swordswoman, who is not a maid like Joan of Arc. Do the women's
work; then do more work, which will become ours too. No husband
of mine will say, "I could have been a drummer, but I had to think
about the wife and kids. You know how it is." Nobody supports me at
the expense of his own adventure. Then I get bitter: no one supports
me; I am not loved enough to be supported. That I am not a burden has
to compensate for the sad envy when I look at women loved enough
to be supported. Even now China wraps double binds around my feet.

When urban renewal tore down my parents' laundry and paved 27
over our slum for a parking lot, I only made up gun and knife fan-
tasies and did nothing useful.

From the fairy tales, I've learned exactly who the enemy are. I 28
easily recognize them—business-suited in their modern American executive guise, each boss two feet taller than I am and impossible to
meet eye to eye.

I once worked at an art supply house that sold paints to artists. 29
"Order more of that nigger yellow, willya?" the boss told me. "Bright,
isn't it? Nigger yellow."

"I don't like that word," I had to say in my bad, small-person's 30
voice that makes no impact. The boss never deigned to answer.

I also worked at a land developers' association. The building 31
industry was planning a banquet for contractors, real estate dealers,
and real estate editors. "Did you know the restaurant you chose for
the banquet is being picketed by CORE and the NAACP?" I squeaked.

"Of course I know." The boss laughed. "That's why I chose it." 32

"I refuse to type these invitations," I whispered, voice unreliable. 33

He leaned back in his leather chair, his bossy stomach opulent. 34
He picked up his calendar and slowly circled a date. "You will be
paid up to here," he said. "We'll mail you the check."

If I took the sword, which my hate must surely have forged 35
out of the air, and gutted him, I would put color and wrinkles into
his shirt.

It's not just the stupid racists that I have to do something about, 36
but the tyrants who for whatever reason can deny my family food
and work. My job is my own only land.

To avenge my family, I'd have to storm across China to take 37
back our farm from the Communists; I'd have to rage across the
United States to take back the laundry in New York and the one in
California. Nobody in history has conquered and united both North
America and Asia. A descendant of eighty pole fighters, I ought to be
able to set out confidently, march straight down our street, get going
right now. There's work to do, ground to cover. Surely, the eighty
pole fighters, though unseen, would follow me and lead me and pro-
tect me, as is the wont of ancestors.

Or it may well be that they're resting happily in China, their 38
spirits dispersed among the real Chinese, and not nudging me at all
with their poles. I mustn't feel bad that I haven't done as well as the
swordswoman did; after all, no bird called me, no wise old people
tutored me. I have no magic beads, no water gourd sight, no rabbit
that will jump in the fire when I'm hungry. I dislike armies.

I've looked for the bird. I've seen clouds make pointed angel   39
wings that stream past the sunset, but they shred into clouds. Once at
a beach after a long hike I saw a seagull, tiny as an insect. But when
I jumped up to tell what miracle I saw, before I could get the words
out I understood that the bird was insect-size because it was far away.
My brain had momentarily lost its depth perception. I was that eager
to find an unusual bird.

The news from China had been confusing. It also had something   40
to do with birds. I was nine years old when the letters made my parents, who are rocks, cry. My father screamed in his sleep. My mother
wept and crumpled up the letters. She set fire to them page by page
in the ashtray, but new letters came almost every day. The only letters
they opened without fear were the ones with red borders, the holiday
letters that mustn't carry bad news. The other letters said that my
uncles were made to kneel on broken glass during their trials and
had confessed to being landowners. They were all executed, and the
aunt whose thumbs were twisted off drowned herself. Other aunts,
mothers-in-law, and cousins disappeared; some suddenly began writing to us again from communes or from Hong Kong. They kept asking for money. The ones in communes got four ounces of fat and one
cup of oil a week, they said, and had to work from 4 A.M. to 9 P.M.
They had to learn to do dances waving red kerchiefs; they had to sing
nonsense syllables. The Communists gave axes to the old ladies and
said, "Go kill yourself. You're useless." If we overseas Chinese would
just send money to the Communist bank, our relatives said, they
might get a percentage of it for themselves. The aunts in Hong Kong
said to send money quickly; their children were begging on the side-
walks and mean people put dirt in their bowls.

When I dream that I am wire without flesh, there is a letter on   41
blue airmail paper that floats above the night ocean between here and
China. It must arrive safely or else my grandmother and I will lose
each other.

My parents felt bad whether or not they sent money. Sometimes   42
they got angry at their brothers and sisters for asking. And they would
not simply ask but have to talkstory too. The revolutionaries had
taken Fourth Aunt and Uncle's store, house, and lands. They attacked
the house and killed the grandfather and oldest daughter. The grandmother escaped with the loose cash and did not return to help. Fourth
Aunt picked up her sons, one under each arm, and hid in the pig

house, where they slept that night in cotton clothes. The next day she found her husband, who had also miraculously escaped. The two of them collected twigs and yams to sell while their children begged. Each morning they tied the faggots on each other's back. Nobody bought from them. They ate the yams and some of the children's rice. Finally Fourth Aunt saw what was wrong. "We have to shout 'Fuel for sale' and 'Yams for sale,' " she said. "We can't just walk unobtrusively up and down the street." "You're right," said my uncle, but he was shy and walked in back of her. "Shout," my aunt ordered, but he could not. "They think we're carrying these sticks home for our own fire," she said. "Shout." They walked about miserably, silently, until sun-down, neither of them able to advertise themselves. Fourth Aunt, an orphan since the age of ten, mean as my mother, threw her bundle down at his feet and scolded Fourth Uncle, "Starving to death, his wife and children starving to death, and he's too damned shy to raise his voice." She left him standing by himself and afraid to return empty-handed to her. He sat under a tree to think, when he spotted a pair of nesting doves. Dumping his bag of yams, he climbed up and caught the birds. That was where the Communists trapped him, in the tree. They criticized him for selfishly taking food for his own family and killed him, leaving his body in the tree as an example. They took the birds to a commune kitchen to be shared.

It is confusing that my family was not the poor to be cham-   43
pioned. They were executed like the barons in the stories, when they were not barons. It is confusing that birds tricked us.

What fighting and killing I have seen have not been glorious   44
but slum grubby. I fought the most during junior high school and al-ways cried. Fights are confusing as to who has won. The corpses I've seen had been rolled and dumped, sad little dirty bodies covered with a police khaki blanket. My mother locked her children in the house so we couldn't look at dead slum people. But at news of a body, I would find a way to get out; I had to learn about dying if I wanted to be-come a swordswoman. Once there was an Asian man stabbed next door, words on cloth pinned to his corpse. When the police came around asking questions, my father said, "No read Japanese. Japa-nese words. Me Chinese."

I've also looked for old people who could be my gurus. A   45
medium with red hair told me that a girl who died in a far country fol-lows me wherever I go. This spirit can help me if I acknowledge her,

she said. Between the head line and heart line in my right palm, she said, I have the mystic cross. I could become a medium myself. I don't want to be a medium. I don't want to be a crank taking "offerings" in a wicker plate from the frightened audience, who, one after another, asked the spirits how to raise rent money, how to cure their coughs and skin diseases, how to find a job. And martial arts are for unsure little boys kicking away under fluorescent lights.

I live now where there are Chinese and Japanese, but no emi-   46
grants from my own village looking at me as if I had failed them. Living among one's own emigrant villagers can give a good Chinese far from China glory and a place. "That old busboy is really a swordsman," we whisper when he goes by, "He's a swordsman who's killed fifty. He has a tong ax in his closet." But I am useless, one more girl who couldn't be sold. When I visit the family now, I wrap my American successes around me like a private shawl; I *am* worthy of eating the food. From afar I believe my family loves me fundamentally. They only say, "When fishing for treasures in the flood, be careful not to pull in girls," because that is what one says about daughters. But I watched such words come out of my own mother's and father's mouths; I looked at their ink drawing of poor people snagging their neighbors' flotage with long flood hooks and pushing the girl babies on down the river. And I had to get out of hating range. I read in an anthropology book that Chinese say, "Girls are necessary too"; I have never heard the Chinese I know make this concession. Perhaps it was a saying in another village. I refuse to shy my way anymore through our Chinatown, which tasks me with the old sayings and the stories.

The swordswoman and I are not so dissimilar. May my people   47
understand the resemblance soon so that I can return to them. What we have in common are the words at our backs. The ideographs for revenge are "report a crime" and "report to five families." The reporting is the vengeance—not the beheading, not the gutting, but the words. And I have so many words—"chink" words and "gook" words too—that they do not fit on my skin.

◆ WORKING WITH WORDS

Kingston's Swordswoman confronts emperors and barons and other rulers. Each of the following words refers to a type of ruler. What is the word for what each ruler rules over? (Example: A *king* rules over a *kingdom*.) Some of the answers are obvious, and some are more obscure and will probably require a dictionary.

emperor   monarch   dictator

baron   czar   duke

sheik   sultan   shah

◆ EXAMINING CONTENT

1. How did the narrator react when she was called a "bad girl"?
2. What were some of the ways in which she acted out the "bad girl" role—in her childhood, and later on?
3. What did Chinese emigrants say when they saw the narrator and her sister out with her parents?
4. What terrifying news did they receive from relatives in China?
5. Why was she fascinated with looking at corpses in her youth?
6. Why did Fourth Aunt scold Fourth Uncle?

◆ RESPONDING TO IDEAS

1. Consider this passage, from para. 43:

   It is confusing that my family was not the poor to be championed. They were executed like the barons in the stories, when they were not the barons.

   Who was executing them? Why was it confusing? How would it have been less confusing if they had been barons?
2. Reread para. 20. How can language be used to control people? Think of some other examples of language conventions that affect people.
3. What is meant by the "outward tendency" in girls?
4. What does the symbol of the swordswoman mean to the narrator?

◆ MORE WRITING TOPICS

1. Write an essay in which you give examples of cultural traditions that tend to work against the development of self-esteem, particularly in young girls.

2. Of what beneficial purpose is the powerful heroic figure in children's literature, children's movies, and myths?

◆ MAKING THE FINAL COPY

Choose one of the following and write a composition, revising and editing it until you have a final copy.

1. Reread any of your journal entries and write a draft responding to ideas in the readings you have done in this chapter. Refer to ideas in at least two chapter readings to support your point of view.
2. Write an essay on one of the following topics:
   - ◆ Today's children are at risk from conditions of crime, poverty, and neglect more than ever before. What are some of the ways the average citizen could improve the future for these children? Be specific and use examples from the stories we have just read.
   - ◆ Girls are now at greater risk of sexual abuse both from adults and their peers than in the past. Write a letter to the editor of your newspaper about ways that schools and social agencies can help prevent more abuse.
   - ◆ Today's boys are being sent to prison for violent crimes more than ever before. How can these crimes be avoided? What do you think is missing from our modern lifestyle that causes conditions leading to violence?

◆ REVISING CHECKLIST

Read over the draft you have completed for the purpose of revising it—that is, improving the content. Use the questions below as a starting point for revision.

- ◆ Does the composition have an introduction? Does the introductory paragraph of the composition make the main idea of the composition clear? Remember, there is more than one way to respond and write an introduction. However, it must include the most important point.
- ◆ Is the development clear and specific? Remember to avoid generality. Be specific. For instance, if you are telling an anecdote, remember to include the answers to *Where? When? Who? Why?* Be sure it is clear *how* the anecdote is related to the topic.
- ◆ Is the choice of language appropriate? Be aware of street language, slang, and trendy expressions. Academic writing is usually more formal.

(Of course, if you are writing dialogue, you have some flexibility in terms of writing in the way your characters would realistically speak.)

◆ Are any ideas repeated? Sometimes writers repeat and are not aware of it.

◆ Are any ideas not relevant and do these need to be deleted? Sometimes writers digress from the topic. Ask yourself after each sentence, "How does this relate to the ideas preceding and following it?"

◆ Is the conclusion appropriate? Does it reflect the main idea and let the reader know that the essay is ending?

◆ EDITING CHECKLIST

Now that you have written and revised your draft, it is time to edit it. Read it over once more, checking for mechanical errors. Use the following questions as a starting point for editing.

◆ Is each sentence complete? Avoid fragments. Does each sentence have a subject and a verb and make complete sense?

◆ How long are your sentences? Are they too lines long and do they contain too many commas? Remember, a comma may not connect two complete sentences. If necessary, refer to an English usage guide.

◆ Did you indent each paragraph? Are the paragraphs an appropriate length?

◆ Is your verb tense consistent? If you are telling an anecdote in the past, stay in the past. Do not switch to the present or another tense for no reason.

◆ Does subject and verb agreement exist, especially when the present tense is used? Remember, verbs may consist of more than one word. Make sure the auxiliary verbs are also correct.

◆ Are proper nouns capitalized? Does every sentence begin with a capital?

◆ EDITING EXERCISE

Tense Consistency

When you write, it is important to be aware of the tenses you are using. You must remember that tense in verbs signals the concept of time in which an action (or feeling or state of being) occurred. You cannot just arbitrarily change the tense form of a verb unless you are sure of the time frame being used in the meaning of the sentence you are writing.

Look at the following example:

> There was a time when the world was much safer for children. I remember leaving my children alone in a large store or market for a few seconds without feeling afraid. A few years ago, I leave them alone in the toy section in Macy's for a few minutes while I went to look for a pot to use in the kitchen. I come back and they were fine for the few minutes it took to buy the pot. Furthermore, they enjoy the sense of freedom and the grown-up feeling of being left alone for a few minutes.
>
> Now, I would never leave my child alone for even a second. There were too many dangers present in our society today. We cannot trust the innocent-looking stranger in a store; he or she could be a child-abuse criminal just waiting to pounce on a vulnerable child waiting for mother to return. In fact, teenagers are even abducted from shopping malls on a regular basis. Just the other day, I read in the *New York Times* how two fourteen-year olds are missing after a shopping spree at a New Jersey mall.
>
> We must support legislation to stop this kind of criminal from destroying our children. They were the citizens of the future and need to be protected from abuse by sick adults. If we don't, they will grow up and abuse other children and the endless cycle continued as tomorrow's abusers.

Look at the preceding draft. Where are the inconsistencies in verb tenses? Change the verbs to the correct tense for the time being expressed in the context of the writing.

Glossary of Writing and Cultural Terms

Anecdote—a brief story about an event told to explain or illustrate a point (chap. 1)

Borrowed words—words used in English borrowed from another language (chap. 4)

Clustering—a method of getting ideas on paper before writing by using circular diagram (chap. 1)

Dependent clause (sometimes called a subordinate clause) also has a subject and a verb but begins with a subordinating word (e.g., because, if, when, while, who, etc.) and can *not* stand alone as a sentence (chap. 2)

Example:

When Esmeralda enrolled in the new school, her mother was very concerned.
The single underlined portion is a dependent clause.
The double underlined portion is the independent clause.

Diaspora—a scattering of a group of people, usually caused by persecution (chap. 1)

Draft—the first rough copy of an essay (chap. 1)

Expository essay—an essay in which the reader explains, develops, and argues for a main idea or thesis (chap. 1)

Independent clause—a sentence, or a part of a sentence, that can stand alone, with its own subject and predicate (chap. 2)

Interactive reading—a process in which the reader interacts with the writer and asks questions (chap. 1)

Kalahari—a desert region in southwest Africa

Ladakhi—a people living in the Himalayas who practice Buddhism and have a self-contained culture

Maori—indigenous people of New Zealand and Australia (chap. 2)

Narrator—person telling the story

Nisei—second-generation Japanese living in the United States (chap. 3)

Pronoun consistency—pronouns in a sentence must have a clear referent.

Protagonist—a hero, the person who drives the action of a story

Reader-response essay—an essay in which the reader asks a question, makes a point, or connects with ideas in the text (chap. 1)

Revising—the process of writing a better version of the original essay (chap. 1)

Stereotype—an exaggerated description of a category based on an opinion

Subject-verb agreement—When using the present tense, when the subject is plural, the verb should not end in an –*s*; when the subject is singular, the verb ends in an –*s*.

Children run. The child runs.

The *children* ran outside to play; *they were* happy to find the weather perfect for a baseball game.

not

The *children* ran outside to play; they *was* happy to find the weather perfect for a baseball game. (chap. 5)

Taina/o—the original inhabitants of the Caribbean area; indigenous people of Puerto Rico (chap. 1)

Transition words—words that lead the reader from one idea to the next. Examples are for example, finally, at the same time (chap. 4)

Acknowledgments

All selections are reprinted with permission of the copyright holder.

Anaya, Rudolf. "Salomon's Story," from *Tortuga*. In *Growing Up Chicana/o*, Tiffany Ana Lopez, ed. 1994. New York: Avon Books, pp. 212–216.

Ashton-Warner, Sylvia. Excerpt from *Teacher*. 1963. New York: Simon and Schuster, pp. 32–38.

Chang, Pang-Mei Natasha. Excerpt from *Bound Feet & Western Dress*. 1996. New York: Bantam Doubleday, pp. 18–24.

Cisneros, Sandra. "Only Daughter." In *Latina: Women's Voices from the Borderlands*, Lillian Castillo-Speed, ed. 1995. New York: Simon and Schuster, pp. 156–160.

Danticat, Edwidge. Excerpt from *Breath, Eyes, Memory*. 1994. New York: Random House (Vintage Books), pp. 40–49.

Díaz, Junot. Excerpt from "Drown." In *Drown*. 1996. New York: Riverhead Books, pp. 91–99.

Divakaruni, Chitra Banerjee. Excerpt from *The Mistress of Spices*. 1997. New York: Anchor Books, pp. 13–16.

González, Kathleen Ann. "That Was Living." In *Latina: Women's Voices from the Borderlands*. Lillian Castillo-Speed, ed. 1995. New York: Simon and Schuster, pp. 97–106.

González, Louie. "The Foot", "Doña Toña of Nineteenth Street." In *Growing Up Chicana/o*, Tiffany Ana López, ed. 1993. New York: Avon Books, pp. 60–66.

Hoffman, Eva. Excerpt from *Lost In Translation*. 1989. New York: E.P. Dutton Inc., pp. 104–106.

Hughes, Langston. "Theme for English B." In *Literature*, Joel Wingard, ed. 1996. New York: HarperCollins, pp. 709–710.

Hurston, Zora Neale. Excerpt from *Dust Tracks on a Road*. 1995 (original 1942). New York: HarperCollins, pp. 19–23.

Kingsolver, Barbara. Excerpt from *Homeland*. 1993. New York: HarperCollins, pp. 4–14.

Kingston, Maxine. Excerpt from *The Woman Warrior: Memoirs of a Girlhood among Ghosts*. 1976. New York: Random House, pp. 45–53.

Lee, Chang-Rae. Excerpt from *Native Speaker*. 1995. New York: Riverhead Books, pp. 73–77.

Lee, Gus. Excerpt from *China Boy*. 1994. New York: Penguin Books, pp. 1–5, 179–186.

Lee, Richard Borshay. "Eating Christmas in the Kalahari." In *Anthropology* 98/99. 1998. New York: MacGraw-Hill Publishers, pp. 27–30.

Liu, Eric. Excerpt from *The Accidental Asian: Notes of a Native Speaker*. 1998. New York: Random House, Inc., pp. 38–44.

Mora, Pat. "Remembering Lobo." In *Latina: Women's Voices from the Borderlands*, Lillian Castillo-Speed, ed. 1995. New York: Simon and Schuster, pp. 74–77.

Morales, Aurora Levins. "Child of the Americas." In *Literature*, Joel Wingard, ed. 1996. New York: HarperCollins, p. 261.

Mura, David. Excerpt from *Turning Japanese*. 1991. New York: Bantam Doubleday, Inc., pp. 49–50, 140–148.

Norberg-Hodge, Helen. Excerpt from *Ancient Futures*. 1991. San Francisco: Sierra Club Publishers, pp. 22–26.

Olsen, Tillie, "I Stand Here Ironing." In *Literature*, Joel Wingard, ed. 1996. New York: HarperCollins, pp. 222–227.

Rodriguez, Richard. Excerpt from *Hunger of Memory*. 1983. New York: Bantam Books, pp. 114–123.

Rose, Mike. Excerpt from *Lives on the Boundary*. 1989. New York: Penguin Books, pp. 26–31.

Santiago, Esmeralda. Excerpt from *When I Was Puerto Rican*. 1993. New York: Addison Wesley, pp. 225–228.

Trice, Dawn Turner. Excerpt from *Only Twice I've Wished for Heaven*. 1996. New York: Doubleday, Inc., pp. 10–21.

Index